Law and Authors

Law and Authors

A Legal Handbook for Writers

JACQUELINE D. LIPTON

UNIVERSITY OF CALIFORNIA PRESS

University of California Press
Oakland, California

© 2020 by Jacqueline D. Lipton

Cataloging-in-Publication Data is on file at the
Library of Congress.

ISBN 978-0-520-30180-1 (cloth : alk. paper)
ISBN 978-0-520-30181-8 (pbk. : alk. paper)
ISBN 978-0-520-97224-7 (ebook)

Manufactured in the United States of America

28 27 26 25 24 23 22 21 20
10 9 8 7 6 5 4 3 2 1

CONTENTS

Writing a book is always a significant undertaking, involving not only a time commitment but a real passion for the subject matter. This book, for me, was born out of a passion to bring some (hopefully) accessible legal information to those who need it, in an area where accurate and user-friendly legal information can be hard to come by. This is no fault of anyone working in the area. It's just that the laws related to publishing, and to writing more generally, can be complex and can change significantly over time. The rise of digital technology is both a blessing and a curse here; it provides more information than ever before, but much of the information is inaccurate, out of date, or based on particular situations and not applicable to other contexts.

Attempting to explain "the law" to authors is no easy task and there's no one right way to do it. It was a challenging decision for me to even try, and I'm grateful to those who supported me on the way by discussing initial ideas for the book, helping me draft and redraft, and helping get the proposal and the final manuscript into the hands of those who could bring it to its intended audience. Thanking particular people is always a risk because I'm sure to leave someone out, but, at the risk of offending others, I'd particularly like to thank Cynthia Leitich Smith, Nova Ren Suma, and Bethany

Hegedus for early discussions about this concept (and to Bethany for giving me the perfect place to draft the initial proposal—shout out to The Writing Barn!). Kendra Levin provided wise counsel and encouragement, generously sharing many of her own experiences of writing a nonfiction book for authors. Chuck Sambuchino helped me get the proposal into shape to take it out into the world. And Jane Dystel, my agent, found the book the perfect home with editor Naomi Schneider and the University of California Press. I couldn't be in better hands than with Jane and Naomi, who understood, from the get-go, the importance of the project and the way to move it into the hands of readers who need it. (And an extra-special thanks to Miriam Goderich, who found me in the slush pile and connected me with Jane.) There are too many writing buddies to name, including the folks at VCFA and Highlights and the Djerassi Resident Artists Program, but all of you have provided support as well as space to write. In particular, thanks to Amelinda Bérubé, Bree Barton, Shellie Faught, and the rest of the Sassy Djerassis for commenting on multiple draft chapters. And a big thank you to my Youngstown critique group: Nikki Ericksen, Anthony Manna, and especially Rebecca Barnhouse, our fearless leader and my agency sister at DGBLM, for helping me find my voice for this book.

As always, the biggest thanks go to my family—Pat, Sean, Brianne, and Megan—for putting up with my absences and distractions while writing. You're the best family a law professor/writer could have.

Introduction

Setting the Stage: A Primer on the Law for Writers

In the early 2010s, paranormal romance writer J. A. Saare[1] was hitting her stride with two separate series of fantasy titles, alongside a number of popular romances published under the pen name Aline Hunter. The romance titles, published by the independent press Ellora's Cave, comprised the bulk of her sales, while her self-published work was achieving a growing fandom—notably, a vampire romance series, *Rhiannon's Law*. When she initially published the third book in that series, she included an author's note explaining to her readers that, due to the increase in digital piracy, she was considering ending the series prematurely. It didn't make financial sense for her to keep writing the books when she couldn't control the piracy.

Subsequently, Ellora's Cave hit some money problems of its own and eventually closed down, removing one of Saare's more reliable income streams. Ultimately, she got her rights back from Ellora's Cave, and she later found new publishers for most of her work. However, her challenges in the publishing world were not unusual, particularly when it comes to self-publishing, or publishing with a smaller or less established press. And Saare had an advantage over many other authors because she understood her legal rights and knew how to get her rights back from her publisher.

Not all authors, agents, or even editors have a thorough grasp of the legal landscape of the modern publishing world with its increased digitization and globalization. This is not surprising. The laws related to the creative arts have always been complex, often providing little clear guidance in any given situation. The sudden rise of digital technology in the early twenty-first century only added to the confusion. Even lawyers have a hard time with the finer points of digital copyright law, fair use, digital contracts, and rights related to free speech and defamation, so it's no surprise that authors get confused.

The book you're holding in your hands (or reading on your device) is a simple resource for writers and other publishing professionals who want to know more about their legal rights and responsibilities. As a regular speaker on these issues, I've realized that writers, in particular, have surprisingly few places to go for answers to basic legal questions. Some of the most common questions include the following:

Can I quote song lyrics in my novel?

(How much) am I allowed to write about real people?

Can I protect an idea for a story I haven't written yet?

Can I trademark my book title?

When and how should I register copyright in my book?

Do I have to include a © notice on my work?

Is fanfiction fair use? What about parody? How about educational use?

If you find yourself embroiled in a serious legal battle—and I hope you never do—you may need formal legal advice or representation. However, if you're simply going about your writing business, and concerned about how the law impacts you on a day-to-day basis, this book will give you information, and hopefully also some comfort, about the kinds of things you should and shouldn't have to worry about.

A BRIEF NOTE ON LEGAL JARGON

It's virtually impossible to write a book about legal issues without occasionally using some technical legal language. I'll do my best to avoid jargon, but whenever I do introduce a new legal term, I'll put it in italics and include a user-friendly explanation.

Law should never be an excuse for not writing, or an impediment to writing what you want to write. Legal issues can usually be dealt with somehow, at some point in the publishing process, so don't let fear of the law be one more excuse for not getting your butt into the chair and the words onto the page. There are so many distractions that keep us from getting the writing done: housework, socializing, day jobs, family obligations. Don't let the law be one more distraction for you!

For many writers, particularly those who self-publish, the law seems like a minefield blanketed with fog in the dead of night, an area where you should abandon all hope upon entering. It's true that the laws that may impact writers can be complex and confusing, even to lawyers. Sometimes legal representation (or at least legal advice) is necessary to avoid or resolve a sticky situation. In other cases—like copyright registration, basic rights reversions, or learning how to avoid a defamation lawsuit—the law is pretty straightforward, and you can typically handle the matter on your own. Throughout this book, I'll flag the situations where you might want to consult a lawyer, and suggest ways to find effective, knowledgeable, and affordable legal assistance in those cases.

It's important to understand up front that not all lawyers specialize in the kind of law you might need help with. Lawyers are a bit like doctors in that sense. A general practitioner usually can't help you with a rare condition; likewise, your local lawyer who drafted your will may not be the best

LITERARY AGENTS AND LAWYERS

Literary agents can be a great help with commercial, contract, and legal issues if you're publishing via the more traditional route—securing representation by a reputable agent and then having that agent submit your work to publishers. While most literary agents are not legal experts or lawyers (some are), they are generally experts in the terms you would expect to see in a standard publishing contract, and also in how to negotiate a publishing deal that will be of the greatest benefit to you.

Your agent's commission is based on your success, so they can be worth their weight in gold in negotiating, handling the money side of things, and generally protecting your interests. Sometimes matters will arise outside the expertise of your agent and, at that point, she—or you—may want to call in a legal expert. Many agencies retain contracts experts who vet their clients' publishing contracts. Not all of those experts are lawyers, but they all typically have significant experience with publishing contracts: for example, they may have previously worked for a contracts department at a publishing house.

person to help with a tricky copyright problem. However, they may be able to give you a referral to someone who can help. Your local lawyer may be of use in other ways, too—for example, by helping you incorporate an LLC (limited liability company), the most popular form of company for a writer to set up. An LLC can simply be a single-person company that you use for your writing business. Of course, you may not need to operate your writing business through a company. If you choose to do so, setting up an LLC is something most people can do relatively cheaply and easily on their own by following the guidelines on their state government's company registration website. Accountants can also help with this, as well as with organizing your company books. There may be tax benefits in your particular state to operating your writing as a business, through an LLC, and your accountant can certainly advise you there.

FINDING YOUR WAY AROUND THIS BOOK

I've organized this book so that you can dip in and out of different chapters without having to read the whole thing from cover to cover. If you're interested in whether parody is fair use, for example, you can dive right into chapter 5. If you have questions about social media marketing and copyright issues, you can turn straight to chapter 11. If you're considering using someone else's photograph in your book, but have concerns about permissions, take a look at chapter 12.

Because this book is intended as a basic handbook, rather than a comprehensive guide to all the law that could ever conceivably affect your writing career, there are some things that are covered either not at all or not in any detail. For example, I've taken the view that tax and accounting issues are best left to accountants and to books on accounting. Also, questions of corporate law and company formation are pretty simple issues that your local small-business development office or accountant can help with—or your state government website, as noted above. These are issues generally applicable to anyone who wants to start a company. If you're a beginning author, and wondering whether to start a company to limit your legal liability, yes, it's a good idea. But for most tax and accounting purposes, you likely won't be treated any differently than if you were writing and running your business as a private individual. By the time you're a best-selling author and you seriously have to worry about these issues, you should be able to afford a good accountant and attorney! (And you'll probably have an agent as well.) In any event, chapter 13 includes a list of further resources to help you with issues beyond the scope of this book.

My purpose in this book is to provide simple explanations for the most common questions people have about the laws related to publishing, including questions about copyright, fair use, permissions, trademarks, defamation, privacy, and the most common publishing contract clauses. While concepts introduced in later chapters will build on those of earlier chapters, I've also cross-referenced everything important, so you don't have to read from the beginning to understand it.

The early chapters explain the basics of copyright law and the fair use defense in cases of copyright infringement. The reason for starting with the difficult copyright stuff is that it's what most of your legal rights as an author are based on. Once you understand what a copyright is, and importantly what it isn't, you'll have an easier time understanding later chapters about contracting with agents and editors around your rights—the rights you're giving them and the rights you may be withholding to sell at a later time. For example, you might give a publisher North American rights to your book but reserve rights in other countries to sell to another publisher, if you (or your agent) think you'll get a better deal that way. Chapters 1 to 5 cover the following questions and more:

What is a copyright?

What works does it cover?

Do I have to register my copyright to protect my work?

Will copyright protect an idea for a book I haven't written yet?

What is a work for hire, and who owns its copyright?

What is copyright infringement?

Can I use snippets of other people's work in my book, like song lyrics or lines from a poem?

How is copyright infringement different from, and similar to, plagiarism?

What's the difference between the public domain and Creative Commons?

What is fair use, really, and what does it cover?

Once we understand the copyright basics, we'll turn to questions about how you can deal with your copyrights, including contracting with agents, editors, and self-publishing platforms like Amazon's Kindle Direct. Chapter 6 is focused on traditional publishing contracts (whereby you submit your work to agents and editors) and chapter 7 looks at self-publishing contracts (whereby you publish directly to your audience, using a platform like Kindle Direct). These chapters cover ways in which you might divide up your rights (e.g., book rights vs. television/movie rights vs. merchandising rights; North American vs. foreign rights) with publishers and others, as well as potential liability issues related to published work, including defamation, copyright infringement, and trademark infringement.

The rest of the book covers other legal issues that may affect writers, including trademarks and branding of your work (chapter 8); privacy and defamation, which may be of particular relevance to those writing memoir, biography, or historical fiction (chapters 9 and 10); laws that might affect marketing and publicity (chapter 11); photographic permissions (chapter 12); and suggestions for finding effective and affordable legal assistance when you need it (chapter 13).

Throughout the book, I make comparative comments about laws in other countries so that you'll be aware of those that differ significantly from American law. For example, privacy and defamation laws tend to have a lot more bite in European countries than in the United States. Memoir author Edmund White noted that for one of his books he had to make seventy-four changes requested by an American lawyer to avoid concerns about defamation law in the United States, while, for the British edition, he had to make 134 changes to avoid concerns about defamation.[2] The fair use defense to copyright infringement in the United States is also quite different from the corresponding laws in many other countries. If you're publishing in foreign markets, it's a good idea to understand such legal differences, and hopefully you'll be able to get the specific advice you need from an agent, editor, or lawyer for any particular foreign market you may want to explore. If you have an agent in the United States, she'll usually have colleagues in other markets who can help with this—another benefit of working with an agent.

If you're still reading this, I'm guessing that I haven't scared you out of the legal minefield but rather offered my hand as a guide to lead you through it, or at least the bits of it that are relevant to you. A little knowledge of the law can go a long way for writers, and that includes knowledge about when you actually do need to hire a lawyer. In many cases, you can easily anticipate a legal issue in plenty of time to deal with it yourself, or alternatively to recognize what kind of help (and how much) you might need, and know where to find it. Recall the earlier example of J. A. Saare. She knew enough about how copyrights work to get her rights back from a defunct publisher, which freed her to make deals with a new publisher and get her writing career back on track.

You don't have to be a lawyer to deal with legal issues. You don't even have to *have* a lawyer. This book will help you understand when a lawyer (or agent, or accountant, or other professional) may be useful or even necessary. I'll also give you lots of tips about dealing with many issues on your own, so that you don't have to worry about finding a lawyer.

And now, into copyright law . . .

CHAPTER ONE

Copyright Basics

Ownership, Registration, the Public Domain,
and Creative Commons

If you like science fiction, Sandra Bullock, or George Clooney, there's a good chance you've seen the award-winning movie *Gravity*. Have you also read the book of the same name, written by best-selling author Tess Gerritsen? The movie wasn't based on the book . . . or was it? Gerritsen argued that it was, in a court case that ran from 2014 to 2015. Gerritsen had sold the rights to make movie adaptations of the book to Katja Motion Picture Corporation and its parent company, New Line Productions, in 1999. Under her contract, she was entitled to a portion of the profits of any adaptation they produced. In 2008, New Line Productions was purchased by Warner Bros., which then produced the movie and released it in 2013. Gerritsen sued Warner Bros. for breach of the contract she had with Katja Motion Pictures.

Breach of contract, you ask? Why not sue for copyright infringement? Here's where it's important to understand what copyright is (and isn't) and who owns copyright in a given work (and who doesn't).

Gerritsen couldn't sue Warner Bros. for copyright infringement, or at least she didn't have a realistic chance of success, because, for one thing, she'd sold the film rights to Katja outright. The only copyrights she had left were the copyrights in the book (yes, you can split up your copyright into film rights, publication rights, television rights, audiobook rights, merchandising rights, etc.). While the film used some plot and character ideas similar to those in Gerritsen's book, they weren't sufficiently specific to support a copyright action. That's because copyright is really about, or is supposed to be about, copying literal expressions of ideas, and not the ideas themselves. Sometimes elements of a character or plot can be copyrighted, but they have to be quite distinctive for this to be the case. The idea of a female doctor stuck in a beleaguered space station in the wake of a series of unpredicted disasters likely doesn't rise to that level of uniqueness.

That's why Gerritsen resorted to a breach of contract claim. She argued that Warner Bros. owed her a share of the profits based on the film rights she'd assigned, under contract, to New Line. She was unsuccessful because she couldn't prove, as a matter of contract law, that Warner Bros. had assumed any of New Line's obligations to her under the original agreement.

If this all sounds like fancy legal footwork, you're right, and if you find it hard to follow you're not alone. The interplay between contract and copyright law can be very confusing to authors, agents, and even lawyers. Copyright, in particular, is one of the more challenging areas of *intellectual property law*.[1] Of all the laws that apply to publishing, copyright causes the most angst for authors. The most pressing copyright questions include these: What rights does copyright give me? What doesn't it protect? Is there any way to protect ideas and concepts that I haven't fully developed yet? How do I draft a contract that protects my copyrights and ensures that I get paid when other people use my work?

The reason these questions keep getting asked (and are often not answered, or not answered well) is that copyright law is complicated. I know "It's complicated" sounds like a bad breakup line, but unfortunately authors can't break up with copyright law. For better or worse, we need it, which means we need to understand at least the basics.

THE ANATOMY OF COPYRIGHT LAW

US copyright law is made up largely of two separate bodies of law that work together: *statutory law* and *common law*. Statutory law (or *legislation*) is the body of laws enacted by Congress, while common law is the law made by judges. Because the United States has a common law system, we use a combination of statutes and judge-made laws as the basis of copyright. The main copyright statute is the federal Copyright Act of 1976, the finer points of which are regularly interpreted by judges to clarify their application over time to new situations. The statute leaves enough flexibility for judges to adapt the law to new social, economic, and technological developments—for example, the rise of digital libraries and peer-to-peer file sharing technologies.

I've broken down all the copyright information into a number of chapters. This one focuses on what copyright is, and what kinds of creative works it covers. Later, we'll talk about how to protect your copyrights, how to avoid infringing other people's rights, and how to use contracts to license your rights to publishers and others. When you look at the copyright and contract chapters together, you will more clearly understand the situation Tess Gerritsen was in.

While there's no surefire way to ensure that you never face a copyright problem, some basic knowledge about how copyright works, and how you can use contracts to make deals involving your copyrights, should at least give you some comfort. Bear in mind that many high-profile authors who make their living through copyrights and contracts don't often understand the intricacies of the law until a problem arises. Gerritsen herself has said, "Before [the lawsuit] happened to me, I didn't know the difference between [breach of contract and copyright infringement]. I've never been involved in a lawsuit before, and did not expect I ever would be. So to be suddenly stuck in the middle of one feels like being trapped on an alien planet. But I've learned how vital this concept is."[2]

Let's start our journey into copyright territory by learning a little about what copyright is (and isn't). That's what this chapter is all about: simply the basics, like what and who does copyright protect, and for how long?

Why start out with the hardest part of publishing law in the first chapter? As I noted in the Introduction, we really need to start out here because copyrights are the cornerstone of everything publishing law is about. Copyright law gives us property rights in our work, which we then license to others to make money.

Just for fun, let's start with a pop quiz.

Which of the following do you think are true?

You must register your work at the Copyright Office for it to be legally protected.

Anything on the Internet can be copied freely because it's in the public domain.

You must include a © notice on your work for it to be protected.

Copyright can protect your idea for a book or story.

The public domain is the same thing as Creative Commons.

Would it surprise you to learn that not a single one of these statements is true? If so, you're in good company. Many non-copyright lawyers would likely be surprised too. This stuff is difficult, and it's a good sign that you've paid enough attention to even think about these questions in the first place. Don't worry—the answers are coming up if you read on.

WHAT COPYRIGHT IS (AND ISN'T)

The US Copyright Act of 1976 says that copyright applies to "original works of authorship fixed in a tangible medium of expression." While that sounds

Copyright Basics

CREATIVE COMMONS LICENSES

The idea for Creative Commons licenses came, unsurprisingly, from the Creative Commons organization. Their website usefully explains the terms of the main kinds of licenses they have developed and includes shorthand terms for each type of license (go to https://creativecommons.org/licenses).

One of the most popular Creative Commons licenses in open-source publishing is often called the "CC BY" license. This license allows anyone to do pretty much whatever they want with your work (copying, remixing, sharing), provided that they give you attribution—that is, they credit you as the creator of the work.

The most restrictive Creative Commons license is the "CC BY-NC-ND" license. It allows others to download and share your work without charge if they give you credit as the creator of the work, but it does not allow them to change the work in any way or make any commercial use of the work.

like legalspeak (because it is), all it basically means is that copyright applies to works you created yourself (i.e., works that are *original* to you as the author) and that you have *recorded* somewhere—for example in your computer, with pen and paper, or on your smartphone or other device. The recording can be in any format: text, images, sound recording, video recording, or other. The law only requires you to have recorded it somewhere in a relatively permanent form. (Tattoos have caused problems in this context.)

Now think for a moment about a question I posed above, about whether stuff you find on the Internet is free for you to copy (i.e., the common misconception that anything on the Internet is in the public domain). According to modern interpretations of copyright law, computer code is a tangible medium of expression—effectively, a digital recording. This means that any words, pictures, videos, music (etc.) on the Internet that are original to a particular author and still within their *copyright term,* or duration of copyright, are copyrighted (we'll talk about copyright term in a bit). Those things are not free for you to use without permission, and in some cases will require payment of a royalty.

THE PUBLIC DOMAIN AND CREATIVE COMMONS

Of course, there's a lot of *public domain* and *Creative Commons* work available on the Internet too—stuff that you can use for free. The difference between the public domain and the public copyright licenses offered by the nonprofit Creative Commons and other organizations is that material in the public domain is free to use without permission or payment because it is not copyrighted at all. Creative Commons works, on the other hand, are copyrighted, but the creators have released them with a license that allows you to use the work as long as the use complies with the terms of the license. Such licenses typically require things like *attribution* (i.e., giving credit) and often that any new work based on the original work is also made available under a similar license. In other words, you don't have to pay to use the work, but you may have to give credit to the creator and/or allow others to freely use the work you've created that was based on Creative Commons work.

One way to think about the difference between the public domain and Creative Commons—and here I have to admit I'm misusing a phrase commonly used in the software context—is to compare "free as the air" with "free beer." Like the public domain, the air belongs to everyone—no one has to pay to breathe it because no one owns it. It's free in the sense of free for the public to use, rather than simply free from costs that could be charged by the owner. By contrast, like the works licensed by Creative Commons, beer usually belongs to someone: a brewery, a bar, a retail outlet. The bar's owner can choose the terms on which to give you free beer. For example, she could say, "We'll give you a free beer if you agree to come back tomorrow and buy another one," or she could simply give the beer away with no strings attached. Either way, she owns

A BRIEF NOTE ON COPYRIGHT NOTICE

Most people are familiar with the © symbol typically found on copyrighted works. A *copyright notice* usually follows the © symbol with the name of the copyright holder and the year the work was created/copyrighted—for example, © Jacqueline Lipton, 2020. Copyright notices are not required by law and give you no particular legal rights. People typically include the notices simply to let the world know that they claim copyright in the work—which you can do effectively by registering your work with the US Copyright Office.

If you're self-publishing, it's probably a good idea to include a copyright notice on your work. If, on the other hand, you are submitting your work to agents and publishing houses, it's often a good idea to leave out the notice when you first submit, and let the publisher include it later. This is not a legal issue, but rather a matter of general practice in the publishing field. Some people feel that if you include a copyright notice when you first submit your work to agents, it will create a negative impression because (a) the agent may think you don't trust them to protect your interests; (b) you may create the impression that the work has already been published; or (c) you may create the impression that you think the work is ready to go "as is" and you won't be amenable to making edits suggested by an agent or editor.

Since the copyright notice doesn't give you any additional legal rights over simply registering your work at the Copyright Office, it's often a good idea not to include the notice until the work is ready for publication, whether you're self-publishing or working with a commercial press. Think back to the question in the pop quiz about whether a copyright notice is necessary to protect your work. Now you should see why it's not, strictly speaking, necessary, but it can be a good idea in the right circumstances.

Remember that *notice* and *registration* are two separate things. You can register a work without putting a © notice on it, and you can put a © notice on a work even if you haven't registered the copyright in it.

the beer and can decide the terms on which you can drink it, just as the owner of a copyrighted work can choose to make the work available free of charge, on any terms she likes or with no terms at all, through Creative Commons.

CATEGORIES OF COPYRIGHTED WORKS

In addition to requiring that an original work must be "fixed in a tangible medium of expression" to obtain copyright protection, the Copyright Act sets out the specific kinds of works the law protects. The most relevant category for authors is *literary works*—that is, the books we write. Copyright also covers *musical works*, including lyrics we may want to quote in our work; *dramatic works* (e.g., plays); *pictorial, graphic, and sculptural works*, which include art and illustrations; *motion pictures and other audiovisual works;* and other kinds of works—like sound recordings, pantomimes, choreographic works, and architectural works—that may be less immediately relevant to writers.

A special provision of the Act also extends copyright to *compilations* and *derivative works*. We'll examine these in more detail in later chapters, especially in chapter 5, where we'll look at fair use and fanfiction, an obvious example of a derivative work in the digital publishing world. For now, think of compilations as including, say, anthologies of short stories or poetry. Even an edited collection of essays can be a compilation. As I'm writing this, I happen to have a compilation on my desk: Meredith Maran's *Why We Write About Ourselves*, a collection of essays by well-known memoirists about why they have chosen to write a memoir. An encyclopedia is also a compilation of entries, usually written by different people. Wikipedia is an example of a *crowdsourced* compilation in which each entry is written by different people and edited by a team of editors. (Crowdsourcing invites the public to contribute to a project, like crowdsourced funding projects on GoFundMe or Kickstarter.)

Derivative works, on the other hand, are generally adaptations, dramatizations, and retellings of existing works (including prequels and sequels). They may be authorized, like Donald McCaig's *Rhett Butler's People*, a derivative work based on Margaret Mitchell's iconic *Gone with the Wind* that comprehensively tells the story of Rhett Butler and his family. This work was authorized by Mitchell's estate. An example of an unauthorized derivative work is Alice Randall's *The Wind Done Gone*, a retelling of *Gone with the Wind* from the perspective of the slaves. While, as retellings of the original story, both Randall's and McCaig's books are clearly derivative works, the estate had not given Randall permission to write her story, and the unauthorized book led to litigation for copyright infringement. This is because the right to create a derivative work is held by the author, or their estate, for the term of the copyright. We'll look at the litigation surrounding *The Wind Done Gone* in the next chapter.

CREATIVE WORK THAT ISN'T PROTECTED BY COPYRIGHT

It's not only necessary for authors to have a basic understanding of what is covered by copyright law. It can be equally important to appreciate what *isn't* covered. Because copyright protects works that are "fixed in a tangible medium of expression" (written down, recorded, etc.), it *does not* protect anything that isn't fixed in this way. For example, an idea for a book you haven't written or developed isn't copyrightable. You can't copyright a recipe, although you can copyright the precise written expression/format of the recipe in a cookbook. The actual method for making, say, a devil's food cake is not copyrightable, although a particular written expression of the recipe might be. However, the copyright protection would only extend to the words as written, not the idea for making the cake.

If you come up with an idea for a novel about a corrupt law firm that hires a naive and starry-eyed young lawyer who ultimately turns the tables on the firm and brings them to justice with the aid of the Feds, and you jot down the *logline* for it, you may have copyright in the logline, but not in the idea itself. If John Grisham comes along and writes *The Firm* before you start developing your idea, you can't sue him for copyright infringement. A logline is basically a

COPYRIGHTS IN LOGLINES AND OTHER SIMPLE WORDS OR PHRASES

A lot of people wonder about whether you can copyright simple words or phrases like a logline (such as "Jaws with Paws"—I just love saying that!) or even a term you've coined for your particular book. Think "muggles" from *Harry Potter* or "hobbit" from *Lord of the Rings*. If copyright protects original expression, shouldn't it protect these words and phrases?

It may surprise you to learn that usually it doesn't. This is because copyright law has a concept called "de minimis," which is a short form of "de minimis non curat lex." (It's Latin, of course. We law folks love our Latin!) The phrase literally means "The law does not concern itself with trifles." In copyright law, it basically means that copyright won't protect trivial things. Individual words and phrases usually fall within this notion.

A court in a well-known British copyright case in 1982 considered whether the word *Exxon* could be copyrighted by the Exxon Corporation. It was clearly an original word created by the corporation: however, the court said it couldn't be copyrighted. Instead, it was covered by trademark protection. In fact, the word *muggle* is trademarked—the US trademark registration is held by Warner Bros., which produced the *Harry Potter* movies. We'll talk more about trademark protection for words and phrases in chapter 8.

If you're a poet, you may be concerned that a single poem could be regarded as "de minimis" and so may not be copyrightable. That's not usually a problem in practice, because de minimis creations have to be "trivial" to be denied copyright protection. Even a haiku is generally sufficiently original and creative to be granted copyright protection. In other words, it's not merely "trivial." Certainly, a compilation or anthology of poetry will be copyrightable.

simple pitch or "elevator speech" explaining what your book is about, usually used for marketing purposes. One of my favorite loglines from the movies is "Jaws with Paws." (Can you guess which movie this was a logline for? *Cujo*, of course!)

By the same token, if someone else later writes a book with a similar plot but without copying Grisham's actual story, he can't sue them for copyright infringement unless the book is such a close approximation of his work that he can establish it as being a copy under the law. This usually requires a showing of "substantial similarity," a concept we'll look at in more detail in later chapters. A big part of Tess Gerritsen's problem with *Gravity* was that the film wasn't a close enough approximation of her original story to establish copyright infringement. Think again about the pop quiz at the beginning of this chapter. Can you see why copyright won't protect an underlying idea for a story, but only the actual expression of the work?

It's also worth noting that if two people write substantially similar books, songs, or movies without previously coming into contact with each other's work, each can hold copyright in his or her individual work independently of the other.

Copyright also does not protect works whose copyright has expired. These works are regarded as having entered the public domain. American copyrights in literary works now generally expire seventy years after the death of the original author, with some exceptions (see sidebar). The public domain consists of works and information that are not protected by any intellectual property rights, including patent, copyright, and trademark law. Authors are, of course, most concerned with copyright law. Works may be in the public domain because

+ they predate copyright law (e.g., the works of William Shakespeare),

+ their copyright term has expired (e.g., the works of Charles Dickens), or

+ they're uncopyrightable ideas (e.g., recipes).

Once a work's copyright has expired and it falls into the public domain, others may copy the work freely or create retellings of the story without fear of copyright infringement. For example, the original *Wizard of Oz* by Frank L. Baum is out of copyright now, although the iconic movie starring Judy Garland is still currently protected by copyright.

With book series it can be especially difficult to figure out when particular aspects of the works fall into the public domain. For example, most of the Sherlock Holmes books by Sir Arthur Conan Doyle have entered the public domain due to the expiration of their copyright terms. However, some later-written short stories about Sherlock Holmes and Dr. Watson will remain copyrighted until almost 2030. Doyle's estate has relied on the copyrights in these stories to seek royalties from many writers, television producers, and movie producers in relation to new books, TV shows, and movies, including the recent novel *A Slight Trick of the Mind* by Mitch Cullin and the movie *Mr. Holmes* starring Sir Ian McKellen.

Interestingly, Brittany Cavallaro's recent young adult series about teen sleuths Charlotte Holmes and Jamie Watson—distant descendants of the original Holmes and Watson—probably does not raise copyright issues. At least, no copyright infringement actions have apparently been threatened at the time of this writing. That may be because the young adult series doesn't actually use any characters or plots from the original Conan Doyle stories, but simply references them. The stories read more as an homage to the original books than as a reproduction of them.

Outside the series context, questions can arise as to whether a particular work has entered the public domain. This is because the American law on the duration of copyright has changed so much over the years. What started out as a renewable twenty-eight-year term now comprises the author's life plus seventy years. Moreover, some foreign works that had previously entered the public domain under US law had copyright restored to them in the late 1980s when the United States signed the Berne Convention, an international treaty that harmonizes certain aspects of copyright law globally.

A Google search can often provide useful information about whether a particular work is in the public domain, but sometimes you may need the assistance of an agent or attorney in working out whether someone still holds copyright. Photographs have caused difficulties in this respect, and I've included an entire chapter later in the book (chapter 12) on photographic permissions. One helpful rule of thumb: as of January 1, 2019, pretty much all works published before 1924 entered the public domain when the copyright term extension granted by Congress for those works expired.

A BRIEF NOTE ON COPYRIGHT DURATION

While the basic rule on copyright duration is that a copyright lasts for the author's life plus seventy years, there are some specific rules that apply to particular types of works and categories of authors—for example, authors writing under a pen name, writing anonymously, or writing under a *work made for hire* contract. Works made for hire (covered in more detail in chapter 3) are a special situation where the author never holds the initial copyright because she wrote the work under contract for someone else, with the understanding that the person commissioning the work would own the copyright.

The bottom line for most authors writing after January 1, 1978, in the United States is that the copyright term will commence at the date of the work's creation, and will last for the author's life plus seventy years. The rights will pass to the author's estate on his or her death. The estate will hold the rights until the expiration of seventy years from the author's death, at which point the work enters the public domain.

For a work that was written jointly by two or more authors, the copyright will last until seventy years after the last surviving author's death. For anonymous authors and those writing under a pen name, where the author's identity is unknown, the copyright will last for ninety-five years from the date of first publication or 120 years from the date of the work's creation, whichever expires first. However, if the author's identity is or becomes known, the basic rule applies: author's life plus seventy years.

An interesting factoid about copyright duration is that the idea that the rights should continue for a significant period after the author's death was originally supposed to cater to the author's family. The intent was that the author should be able to support his or her family (usually *his* family in the early years of copyright law) for a reasonable time after his death. In other words, his family could continue to live on the royalties after his death. This

(Continued)

(Continued)

idea was the premise of Nick Hornby's book *About a Boy,* adapted into a film starring Hugh Grant. The protagonist, Will Freeman, is a wealthy lay-about who lives off the royalties of a popular Christmas song written by his deceased father. He loathes the song but enjoys the lifestyle it provides him.

COPYRIGHT REGISTRATION

Copyright registration causes a lot of confusion because many people mistakenly believe that registration is the same thing as copyright ownership. In fact, they are two different, but related, issues. Saying that a work is "copyrighted" doesn't tell you anything about whether it's registered, even though many people use the terms synonymously. You don't need to register a copyright to own it, but registration is definitely desirable for a number of reasons, especially if disputes later arise about ownership or infringement.

To obtain a copyright, you simply have to affix your work in a tangible medium of expression—for example, write your book on paper or in digital form.

That's it.

Then you hold copyright in your book.

Simple enough?

Registration is a separate step that provides additional protections to copyright holders. Think back to that question at the beginning of the chapter about whether you have to register your copyright to own it. Can you see why the answer is no? Nevertheless, registration is a good idea because of the advantages it brings. Note that most countries don't have copyright registration systems at all. The United States is an outlier here.

Registration is an inexpensive and simple process that you can easily handle yourself online or through the post. The benefits of registration include creating a public record of copyright ownership and providing you what's called a *legal presumption* that the copyright is valid. If you register your copyright within five years of the first publication of your work, the law will presume that you own a valid copyright if someone else says that you don't. This could happen if, say, you sue or threaten to sue someone for infringement and they argue that you didn't hold a valid copyright in the first place. If you're registered, the court will presume your ownership is valid and will put the onus to prove otherwise on the other party (if the matter is ever brought to court).

Registration also gives you greater potential remedies for infringement. For example, if you have registered your copyright, you're entitled to ask for *statutory damages* in court. These are significant sums of money. The precise amounts are set out in the Copyright Act. You're also entitled to seek reimbursement for your attorney's fees, which can add up quickly, especially if you do end up in court. Statutory damages are typically much more than the actual loss suffered by a copyright holder as a result of infringement. The levels of statutory damages in the United States currently range from $750 to $30,000 per infringed work, at the court's discretion. If the copyright holder can establish "willful" infringement, the damages can be up to $150,000 per work. If the infringement is "innocent," the damages award may be dropped to $200 per work. While some of these amounts sound staggering, remember that most publishing cases don't end up in court. In order to claim statutory damages, a copyright holder must have registered the work either prior to the infringement or within three months of its publication.

When should you generally think about registering a copyright in your work? The answer may vary depending on your situation. If you are following the traditional publishing path, via submission of a work to an agent who then seeks a contract with a commercial press, the publisher will usually

A DIY GUIDE TO COPYRIGHT REGISTRATION

Copyright registration is a simple process that you can handle yourself through the Copyright Office's website (see the instructions at www.copyright.gov/help/faq/faq-register.html#register). Since May 2014, the basic registration fee has been thirty-five dollars for a single application (one author, one work). You have to include a copy of the work in your application. If you later substantially change or modify the work, you may want to re-register it to ensure protection for the new version. You can register a copyright under a pseudonym or under your legal name. Information entered on the register becomes part of the public record and is available to the public. A "work" can be as small as a poem or as large as a novel. You can ask a lawyer to handle your copyright registrations, but it's usually not worth the expense. Even a small law firm will likely charge a significant amount (often around $1,000) to register the copyright. Most lawyers will tell you that unless your registration is particularly complex (multiple works, joint authors, perhaps computer software programs that may raise issues of trade secrecy), you're better off mastering the copyright registration system yourself.

handle the copyright registration for you, after the contract has been finalized and prior to publication (often registering on your behalf as part of your publishing arrangement). However, if you're self-publishing, you should register your copyright before you publish. If you substantially revise the work later, you may want to register a new copyright. Is so, you don't have to amend the old registration. You can simply register the new version on the new date, under the same title and author name as the original registration.

You may have heard that you can establish copyright by sending a sealed copy of your work to yourself in the mail. This is often referred to as a "poor man's copyright." However, this approach doesn't give you any of the benefits of registration and it really doesn't create any better evidence of copyright ownership than a modern word-processing program, which will automatically create a record of the date the work was written and who created it.

MOVING ON . . .

Now that we've talked about what copyright is and isn't, we'll turn to the specific rights copyright law gives you, and how to protect those rights. These are the rights you'll eventually be licensing to publishers and distributors, so it's important to understand how they work.

CHAPTER TWO

Know Your (Copy)Rights

Understanding Your Rights and Protecting Your Work

In the wake of Hillary Clinton's failed presidential run in 2016, a number of books were written about her campaign. One of them, *Strong for a Moment Like This: The Daily Devotions of Hillary Rodham Clinton*, was penned by Clinton's longtime pastor, the Reverend Bill Shillady. The book was set to be released in August 2017, but in the lead-up to its publication, allegations were made that Shillady had copied content for the book from sermons by other pastors without attribution—that is, without giving them credit for their work. Abingdon Press, the publisher, undertook an extensive review of the allegations and ultimately withdrew the book from sale, citing its zero-tolerance policy for plagiarism.[1]

You may wonder why this was all about *plagiarism* rather than *copyright infringement*. In fact, there probably was copyright infringement here too, but the concern that caught the media's attention—and the publisher's—was plagiarism.

So, what's the difference between copyright infringement and plagiarism, and why does it matter? In many cases it doesn't. Lots of unauthorized copying situations also involve plagiarism. Copyright infringement is illegal, while plagiarism is, at best, a breach of an honor code or of professional norms or ethics, but both are taken seriously in the publishing business.

Copyright is about *copying* other people's work *regardless of whether you give credit or not*. Plagiarism is about *giving credit where credit is due*. Plagiarism is an ethical and moral wrong, as evidenced by the speedy action taken by Abingdon Press in the Shillady example. It can also be a breach of professional or academic codes of ethics, but it is generally not illegal in the United States, unlike the situation in many other countries, notably those in Europe.

Often the difference between copyright infringement and plagiarism doesn't matter much in practice. Many copyright infringements also involve plagiarism, but this is not always the case—for example, copyright piracy involves infringing a copyright *without* committing plagiarism. Think of all those pirated videos you watched in your basement when you were a teenager, or the video games your children downloaded for free from BitTorrent. Most of that material has been copied illegally (in breach of copyright) but it's not plagiarized, because no one other than the original creator is being credited for the work. The whole point of digital piracy is that you get the original work by the original creators without having to pay for it, or without having to pay the price the copyright holder wanted you to pay for it. The digital pirates don't want to take credit for the copyright holders' work. They don't want anyone to know who they are.

This chapter explains the different ways in which one might commit copyright infringement and/or plagiarism, and the consequences. The discussion will also help you understand your own rights in a situation where you think someone has copied your work either with or without attribution: when you might accuse them of plagiarism or copyright infringement (or both) and how you might address the problem.

Let's start out with some questions you should be able to answer by the end of this chapter:

What's the difference between copyright infringement and plagiarism?
    (You might be able to answer that one already . . .)

What rights does copyright give you?

Why doesn't the United States have a law against plagiarism?

What should you do if you suspect that someone has copied or plagiarized your work?

WHAT RIGHTS DOES COPYRIGHT GIVE YOU?

In chapter 1, we talked about the kinds of works that are protected by copyright: things like the text of your manuscript, the lyrics of your song, a photograph you took. Remember: copyright protects original literary and artistic works that are fixed in a tangible medium of expression.

Now, we need to understand exactly what *rights* the law of copyright gives you for such works. For the most part, these rights are set out in section 106 of the Copyright Act. I'm mentioning the section number because you will occasionally hear people (admittedly, mostly lawyers) talking about "section 106 rights" as a shorthand way of referring to what's protected by copyright. These rights revolve around unauthorized *copying* or *distribution* of someone's original work. In other words, if you copy someone else's work or distribute copies without permission, you will likely have infringed their copyright. You may also have committed plagiarism, but that would depend on whether you also *took credit* for their work. If you copy without authorization *and* take credit for the other person's work, you've both infringed the copyright and plagiarized the work. If you copy without taking credit (like quoting song lyrics in your novel and attributing the lyrics to the songwriter), then you won't have plagiarized, but you may have infringed the copyright.

The right to prevent other people from *copying* your work under copyright law is sometimes called the *reproduction right*, because it's a right to prevent unauthorized reproduction of your work. The *distribution right*, on the other hand, relates to actions such as selling, renting, or lending unauthorized copies or reproductions of someone else's work. If you hold copyright in a work, you have the sole (or exclusive) right under the Copyright Act to do, or authorize, all of these activities. You decide who can copy, sell, or license your work. Of course, if you later sell your copyright to someone else, they then hold the copyright and become the owner of all those rights. That's because copyright is like a property right: once you sell it to someone, they own it. That's effectively what happened to Tess Gerritsen with the sale of her movie adaptation rights (see chapter 1).

As we know from the previous chapter, the original author usually holds the initial copyright in the work. But that will not be the case if an author is writing under a *work-for-hire* agreement or other contractual arrangement that gives the initial copyright to the person or company that commissioned the work. We'll look at these kinds of arrangements in chapter 3.

The main section 106 rights relevant to authors are the copying and distribution rights. However, the Copyright Act also gives some other rights to copyright holders, many of which are more relevant to other kinds of copyrighted works like movies, music, or video games—for example, the right to control public performances or displays of a copyrighted work. That's why your children's school typically needs to get permission to mount this year's exciting production of *High School Musical*. It's a public performance of a copyrighted work.

THE DERIVATIVE WORKS RIGHT

There is one more right that can be particularly important to American authors and is specific to American copyright law: the *derivative works right*. The Copyright Act gives copyright owners the exclusive right to create, or authorize the making of, derivative works based on their work. Basically, this right has to do with the ability to control who makes new works based on preexisting works, like prequels, sequels, retellings, translations, and adaptations. The definition of *derivative work* in the Copyright Act is actually very broad. I've set out the legal definition below (avert your eyes if you want to avoid legalspeak):

> A "derivative work" is a work based upon one or more preexisting works, such as a translation, musical arrangement, dramatization, fictionalization, motion picture version, sound recording, art reproduction, abridgment, condensation, or any other form in which a work may be recast, transformed, or adapted. A work consisting of editorial revisions, annotations, elaborations, or other modifications which, as a whole, represent an original work of authorship, is a "derivative work".

If you actually read that passage, you probably got the sense of just how broad the idea of a derivative work is. However, for practical purposes, it's enough to think of it as anything based on your work. The derivative works right raises particular concerns for authors of *fanfiction* (also called "fanfic" or simply "fic"). These works retell existing stories in a variety of different ways and are typically written by fans of the original stories. One of the first fandoms, the one that developed around the original *Star Trek* television series in the 1960s, included fanfiction. Fans wrote stories that reimagined the characters and situations set up in the show. There were a lot of stories that cast Captain Kirk and Spock in a romantic relationship, as well as stories that interposed new female characters on the bridge in positions of authority, to highlight the show's lack of powerful female role models. We'll look more at fanfiction when we consider fair use in chapters 4 and 5. While most fanfiction is a derivative work by definition—a work that is a retelling of the original—much of it may also be fair use, depending on context.

The derivative works right has the potential to significantly limit what one can do with other people's work. For example, if you want to write a *Star Wars* book, you need Disney's permission. This is because the author and creator of the original movies, George Lucas, sold his work to Disney some

THE GENESIS OF THE DERIVATIVE WORKS RIGHT

The American derivative works right is actually an outgrowth of the basic "adaptation" and "translation" rights that appear in most countries' copyright laws. In the early days of copyright, way back in late eighteenth-century Europe, concerns were raised about the increasing cross-border trade in books. International treaties were signed to ensure that it would be a copyright infringement not only to *copy* the text of someone else's work, but also to *translate* it into another language for sale in another country. Unauthorized *adaptation* was also a concern because publishers worried that their competitors would make, say, unauthorized theatrical or musical versions of their books.

Even today, the two major international treaties on copyright law, the Berne Convention and the TRIPS Agreement, require all signatory countries to include, in their national laws, provisions to prevent the unauthorized adaptation or translation of a copyrighted work. Most individual countries have limited these rights simply to adaptation and translation, while the United States went much further in developing the derivative works right.

years ago. Of course, if the original work is in the public domain, you don't need permission. (If you need a reminder on what's in the public domain, look back at chapter 1.)

Disney itself has made a lot of money from taking fairy tales from the public domain—"Cinderella," "Snow White," "Rapunzel," and many others—and making its own movie-length cartoon retellings of the stories, which it then copyrights. There's nothing illegal about this. Disney only gets copyright in its own versions, not in the underlying fairy tales. Everyone else can still write their own versions, as long as they don't copy elements unique to the Disney film versions—like, say, Snow White's distinctive costume.

Many retellings of public-domain works are harder to spot than the Disney retellings of classic fairy tales. For example, think about the movie *10 Things I Hate About You*, a copyrighted popular movie from 1999 that retells Shakespeare's *The Taming of the Shrew* but sets the story in a contemporary high school with modern characters, language, and situations. *The Taming of the Shrew* is in the public domain, so anyone can retell it any way they like. What one can't do is copy the specific plot sequence, characters, or dialogue from *10 Things I Hate About You*, because copyright in that version is owned by Touchstone Pictures. Can you imagine if you had to pay for permission to retell any of Shakespeare's plays? How many more recent works might never have existed, like *West Side Story* or Baz Lurhmann's *Romeo + Juliet* with Leonardo DiCaprio and Claire Danes? Both are retellings of Shakespeare's *Romeo and Juliet*.

It's really not clear whether having a broad derivative works right, as we do in the United States, is a good or a bad thing. The right definitely gives a lot of protection to authors and other copyright owners who want to control reworkings of their original creations, but, by the same token, it limits what other people can do with those works.

Some creators of copyrighted works don't mind unauthorized derivative works, while others are highly protective of their original creations. Stephenie Meyer, the author of the popular young adult series *Twilight*, which features sparkly vampires, has stated she has no problem with *Fifty Shades of Grey* by E. L. James, which started out as *Twilight* fanfiction. Meyer has subsequently complained about James taking advantage of her work, but she has never actually threatened to sue James for copyright infringement. Other authors, however, have taken a strong stand against unauthorized derivative works. Still in the vampire realm, best-selling author Anne Rice has publicly stated that she does not allow fanfiction based on her work. In chapter 4, we'll consider whether some fanfiction may, in fact, be fair use, regardless of what the author "allows."

DERIVATIVE WORKS RIGHT VS.
COPYING/REPRODUCTION RIGHT

You may be interested to know that in practice, many court cases involving retellings of other works are argued as infringements of the *reproduction* right rather than the *derivative works* right, even though they clearly involve retellings of the original story. This is because the lawyers typically decide how to argue a case in court and, if they can manage to argue *substantial similarity* through copying, it's just as easy to go ahead with a reproduction-right claim. Substantial similarity is the test that courts have developed to figure out if a new work sufficiently copies an existing work to be regarded as a copyright infringement. Of course, lawyers often argue infringements of *both* the reproduction right and the derivative works right in the same case.

When Alice Randall retold Margaret Mitchell's iconic *Gone with the Wind* from the slaves' perspective in her own novel, *The Wind Done Gone,* the case was argued under the basic copying (reproduction) right, rather than the derivative works right. Even though Randall changed the names of the characters and told the story from a new perspective, the character descriptions and plotlines were found to be so similar to Mitchell's original novel that an argument about infringing the basic reproduction right was plausible, although ultimately the case was settled out of court. As a result of the settlement, the book continued to be sold with a disclaimer on the front cover saying it was "unauthorized." The publisher also made a donation to Morehouse College as part of the settlement.

The case involving an unauthorized Harry Potter lexicon was also argued mainly under the reproduction right rather than the derivative works right. The court found that the unauthorized lexicon had copied enough material—words, characters, ideas, and descriptions of magical spells and magical creatures—from J. K. Rowling's books to be an unauthorized copy, regardless of whether the lexicon was also a derivative work.

ENFORCING YOUR COPYRIGHT

Now that you know what copyright law gives you in terms of rights, you need to understand how those rights might impact you as an author. Copyright law might affect you (1) if you're concerned that someone is infringing your rights, (2) if someone accuses you of infringing their rights, or (3) if you're worried that something you want to write in the future might infringe someone's rights.

In this chapter, we'll focus on the first situation: how to enforce your own rights. We'll look at the possibility of infringing, and more importantly of *avoiding infringing*, other people's rights in chapters 4 and 5, where we consider the *fair use defense* to copyright infringement. (Defenses are basically legal arguments you can make to explain why you don't think your work actually infringed someone's rights.)

One issue that perennially confuses authors is what actually constitutes "copying" for the purposes of a copyright infringement claim. This is partly because the digital, cut-and-paste culture enables new kinds of copying on a much larger scope and scale than ever before possible. Consider the anecdote about J. A. Saare in the introduction to this book. Her problem was large-scale digital piracy: other people were simply copying her entire books and releasing them free of charge online, in competition with her commercially available digital copies. That's clearly a copyright infringement: it's a complete, word-for-word copy of a copyedited book or series of books. And it's not only self-published authors who are concerned about digital piracy. In April 2019, Philip Pullman—a best-selling author and president of the British Society of Authors—joined with other well-known authors, including Nobel laureate Kazuo Ishiguro and Margaret Drabble, to call on the British government to take action against online book piracy.[2]

Digital piracy is a serious business, but it's not the only kind of copying authors are concerned about. What if an author cuts and pastes bits and

LEGALSPEAK: RIGHTS, DEFENSES, AND REMEDIES

Most legal cases involving copyrights will break down into four issues: (1) *rights* (protection the law gives you); (2) *infringement* (interference with those rights); (3) *defenses* (legal excuses for infringing rights); and (4) *remedies* (what the court gives you to compensate you for your loss or damage). The copyright holder has to establish that she owns a valid copyright, that the right has been infringed, and that she's entitled to a remedy (issues 1, 2, and 4), while the alleged infringer has to raise any relevant defenses, or excuses, such as fair use (issue 3). As the copyright holder, you'd also want to think about how to rebut any defenses the alleged infringer might raise (we'll talk more about defenses in chapters 4 and 5) and what remedy you want—money and/or an *injunction*. An injunction is an order that requires or prevents another person from acting in a particular way. For example, you might seek an injunction preventing further sale of infringing books.

Don't let the jargon cause you sleepless nights. This is basically just how lawyers organize the facts of a particular case to present it in court. Remember that most copyright cases are actually settled out of court.

pieces of various authors' works, cobbling them together with her own work to make a new work? This is becoming more and more prevalent in the digital age. For example, around 2013, a self-published romance novel went on sale under the title *Amazingly Broken*, credited to the author Jordin B. Williams, which turned out to be a pseudonym. Soon after the book hit the market, readers discovered that it was largely a compilation of passages taken from two previous best-selling romance titles: *Easy* by Tammara Webber and *Beautiful Disaster* by Jamie McGuire. Those authors retained a copyright attorney and eventually settled with the creator of *Amazingly Broken* after threatening a copyright infringement action. They succeeded in having the infringing book removed from sale. However, not all authors understand their rights in a situation like this, especially where the infringing work is not a word-for-word copy of a single entire book.

There are even less clear-cut cases of copying where elements of plot and character are repurposed for a new work. Sometimes this will be a copyright infringement under the reproduction or distribution right, and sometimes it may be a fair use (see chapters 4 and 5). An unauthorized Harry Potter lexicon was found to be a copyright infringement, even though only a small portion of J. K. Rowling's work was copied (see sidebar).

It's possible that a retelling of someone else's story in which the characters or plot are sufficiently similar to the original will also be a copyright infringement, as in the case of Alice Randall's *The Wind Done Gone* (see sidebar). You don't necessarily need to copy the exact words of the original text to have infringed copyright. However, as Tess Gerritsen has noted (in the blog post quoted in chapter 1), basic character and plot elements are usually not copyrightable. In order to successfully argue copyright infringement in relation to a character or plot element, that aspect of your story has to be sufficiently distinctive and original to your own work.

Questions of copyright infringement can also arise in relation to books that, at first glance, seem to be quite different in terms of genre, setting, or overall plot. For example, Chaz Reetz-Laiolo, an ex-mentor and romantic partner of best-selling author Emma Cline, accused Cline of copyright infringement (and plagiarism) with respect to passages she allegedly copied in her best-selling novel *The Girls* from a screenplay he had been working on, *All Sea*. While the two works were set in different time periods and places, and involved significantly different themes, he identified similarities in plot points about the motivations and character journeys of the protagonists of each work. The copyright claim wasn't successful. The judge said that the two works weren't sufficiently similar for the purposes of a copyright infringement claim.

COPYRIGHTING CHARACTERS AND PLOT ELEMENTS

Judges interpreting copyright law have struggled over the years to work out whether, and in what circumstances, characters and plot elements may be copyrightable. Remember that copyright law is supposed to protect original *expression* rather than underlying ideas. But, of course, limiting copyright protection to word-for-word literal copying doesn't give much comfort to authors in cases where other people rearrange their words to avoid verbatim copying. That's why copyright law developed the "substantial similarity" test for infringement, which was used in the Harry Potter lexicon and *Wind Done Gone* cases. The substantial-similarity approach allows elements of plot and character that are sufficiently original and distinctive to obtain copyright protection.

The judge in the *Wind Done Gone* case said that the best way to think about the copyrightability of plot elements and characters is to consider them as existing on a spectrum between abstract ideas and protectable expression: "At one end of the spectrum—the stock scenes and hackneyed character types that 'naturally flow from a common theme'—are considered 'ideas,' and therefore are not copyrightable. . . . But as plots become more intricately detailed and characters become more idiosyncratic, they at some point cross the line into 'expression' and are protected by copyright."

Unlike the Harry Potter lexicon or *Wind Done Gone* cases, the situation involving *The Girls* couldn't have been argued under the derivative works right because Cline's work was not a retelling or adaptation of Reetz-Laiolo's work. She wasn't trying to retell his story. Reetz-Laiolo simply argued that Cline had, without authorization, borrowed from his screenplay important plot and character elements for her own story.

WHAT CAN YOU DO IF YOU THINK SOMEONE
HAS COPIED YOUR WORK?

Whether your concern is with verbatim copying or with the use of specific elements of plot and character from your work, there are a number of things you can do before you have to worry about going to court. Your first steps should be to attempt to locate the person doing the copying and to stop them directly if you can, as well as to target the places where their copies are being distributed and stop distribution of those copies (again, if possible).

If you can identify and locate the infringer, you may want to write to them directly and ask them to stop, while also potentially threatening a copyright infringement action if they don't. Sometimes, particularly in the online world, it's difficult to identify or locate an infringer. Many infringing authors write under pseudonyms and are often hard to track down.

Of course, if you can find the infringer, especially if they are in the United States, a letter or email asking them to stop and threatening legal action may have some impact. You may even consider hiring a lawyer to send a more official-looking letter on their legal letterhead (this will cost you something, but it shouldn't be exorbitant).

Perhaps even more useful than threatening the actual infringer is asking a number of online booksellers and any other websites that are hosting infringing material to remove the material from sale. Legally, under the Copyright Act, most digital content providers (like Amazon) are required to remove infringing works from sale when they receive notice of the infringement from the copyright holder. To expedite this process, many online companies have developed online forms you can fill in to report copyright infringement (Amazon's version is available at www.amazon.com/report/infringement).

Independent authors sometimes complain that online booksellers like Amazon don't always act promptly when they receive a copyright infringement notice from an individual writer—as opposed to, say, a publishing house—but legally they are required to remove infringing works if you give them notice. Again, a letter from a lawyer on legal letterhead may expedite this process. If an online bookseller fails to respond to a notice to remove an infringing work for sale, they may later find themselves *secondarily liable* for copyright infringement. *Secondary liability* is a way to hold someone responsible for enabling copyright infringement even if they didn't do the copying themselves.

Finally, if you're publishing with a traditional press, you may not have to face these headaches alone. Large publishing houses typically have their own legal departments to deal with copyright infringement and, if your work is important to them (e.g., if your work is making them money rather than languishing on a backlist), they may be prepared to spend their resources on protecting your copyright and sending takedown notices to Amazon and other e-tailers.

COPYRIGHT AND PLAGIARISM

Now that we've talked about how to enforce your copyrights, we should probably compare copyright infringement to plagiarism, so that you understand the difference more clearly. As I noted at the beginning of this chapter, copyright infringement is about copying (regardless of attribution) while plagiarism is about giving credit where credit is due (regardless of word-for-word copying). This means that one can infringe a copyright without committing plagiarism. A good example is digital piracy of the kind faced by Saare. Her work was copied *with attribution*. The pirates weren't taking credit for her work, just selling it, or making it available online, in competition with her own sales. Pirated movies, songs, and video games are another prevalent example of copyright infringement without plagiarism.

One can also plagiarize without committing copyright infringement—for example, by taking someone else's idea and rephrasing it but failing to give them credit. This is often of significant concern in academic settings. It comes up in situations where subsequent researchers reference or use a prior researcher's work without properly attributing it to the earlier researcher.

Finally, there are cases where both copyright infringement and plagiarism are committed simultaneously. An example is Shillady's book about Hillary Clinton, mentioned at the beginning of this chapter. Shillady engaged in both copyright infringement and plagiarism, although he was not sued for the copyright infringement. Similarly, in the *Amazingly Broken* case, the copyright infringer, who had cut and pasted slabs of other authors' work, failed to give credit to those authors and, in fact, took credit for that work himself.

The most important thing to know about the difference between copyright and plagiarism in the United States—I've mentioned it before but it's definitely worth saying again—is that there's no broad law against plagiarism in the United States. While there is a very limited federal law about giving credit to original creators, it only applies to limited classes of works of visual art, including paintings and some prints and photographs, and not to book manuscripts.

As we saw in the Shillady example, sometimes a public allegation of plagiarism will cause enough of a stir that the book in question is removed from the market without anyone ever having to think about copyright infringement. Another particularly high-profile example occurred in 2006 with the publication of a young adult novel by a debut author and Harvard undergraduate student, Kaavya Viswanathan. The novel, *How Opal Mehta Got Kissed, Got Wild, and Got a Life*, hit the *New York Times* best-seller list. Soon after its release, however, it was recalled by the publisher—Little, Brown and Company—and the author's contract for a second book was canceled after she was accused of plagiarizing from the work of other authors, including Salman Rushdie and Meg Cabot. Viswanathan may or may not have infringed those other authors' copyrights, but the accusations of plagiarism were enough to make the publisher take action before the matter went any further. Sometimes a public allegation of plagiarism will get quicker results than the threat of a copyright infringement action.

MOVING ON . . .

Before we turn to fair use, we should touch on work-for-hire and other similar situations, where you write something on commission and usually don't end up holding copyright in it. Undertaking these projects can be a good way to launch, or supplement, a writing career, as long as you understand what you're getting into. The next chapter talks about these kinds of arrangements and what they mean for copyright ownership, other rights you may be giving up, and responsibilities you may be taking on.

CHAPTER THREE

Writing for Someone Else

Ghostwriting, Freelancing, "IP," and Works for Hire

Author Jobie Hughes describes himself on his website as "the author of three novels, two of which were #1 New York Times Best Sellers and have sold over five million copies worldwide."[1] However, neither his website nor his Amazon or Goodreads author pages list those best sellers. The only book featured is a subsequent stand-alone title, *At Dawn*.

What about the best sellers? Why doesn't he talk about them? Why aren't they for sale on his Amazon page? Because he wrote them for a *book packager*, a company that creates manuscripts in house by contracting projects to writers who may or may not obtain authorial credit or royalties, and who may not be contractually permitted to publicly associate themselves with their work. Hughes's experience was with Full Fathom Five, which describes itself as a "content creation company." His story is a cautionary tale about some of the riskier aspects of writing works on commission for someone else. American copyright law has a specific *work for hire* doctrine, which refers to particular examples of writing works in which copyright will belong to someone else. Basically, this doctrine can apply in two situations: works created under an employment contract and certain works made under commission. The publishing industry tends to use the term *work for hire* more broadly than is currently contemplated in the Copyright Act to include things like ghostwriting, writing for a book packager, and other forms of freelancing. This book largely uses the colloquial, industry definition of the term, but I've attempted to draw a clear distinction between the legal usage of the term and industry usage where necessary.

Book packaging and work-for-hire projects come in all shapes and sizes. Many deals between authors and book packagers are actually very beneficial to the authors. A notable example is Nicola Yoon's best-selling young adult novel *Everything Everything,* written for Alloy Entertainment and adapted into a motion picture. However, the deal Hughes made with Full Fathom Five was unfortunately not one of the author success stories, although it was certainly a success story for Full Fathom Five.

Hughes is, in fact, the author of the first two books in the popular young adult science fiction series *The Lorien Legacies,* which is a creation of Full Fathom Five. The books are published under the pseudonym "Pittacus Lore," a character in the series. The project is the brainchild of James Frey, a self-described "bad boy of American literature"[2] and founder of Full Fathom Five, who contracted with Hughes to pen the first two books. The contract, however, was pretty unfavorable to Hughes. He was forbidden to publicly mention his association with the series or his authorship of the books, which is why he does not list these titles on his website. Full Fathom Five also retained the copyrights in the books, which enabled the company to continue the series after parting ways with Hughes, including a movie adaptation of the first book. Hughes was also, by all accounts, not compensated particularly well for his work on the series.

Hughes's experience with Full Fathom Five will certainly worry authors who are considering taking on these kinds of projects. However, writing for other people is not always a bad strategy, provided that you enter the arrangement with your eyes open, and have an attorney or agent scope out the contract if need be. These projects can be a great way to practice meeting deadlines, honing your craft, and making some guaranteed income while working on your own original projects. It all depends on the circumstances and on the contract terms offered.

Even within Full Fathom Five, it appears that not all the contracts are as problematic as Hughes's. Not all of Full Fathom Five's work is uncredited. There are a number of authors whose names appear on Full Fathom Five titles and who are credited as the authors on the company's website. They do not appear to hold copyright in their work, but again, that's not unusual for a book packager, and it's certainly not illegal.

Writing on commission is nothing new. The practice has been around for decades if not centuries. If you've ever read a *Hardy Boys* or *Nancy Drew* novel, you've read a book produced by a packager. This chapter focuses on the ups and downs of writing works on commission for other people and, in particular, answers the following questions:

What is a *book packager*? What are the advantages and disadvantages of writing for them?

How does writing for a book packager differ from writing an *"IP" (intellectual property)* project developed in house by a publisher?

How does *ghostwriting* differ from other works written for other people?

What about *freelance* journalism? Do I get to keep my copyrights if I'm a freelancer?

Do I get *royalties* if I write a work on commission for someone else?

If I sign a non-disclosure agreement, can I mention my writing on my C.V., or on my website?

How much creative control do I get if I write a work for someone else?

I've raised a lot of questions here, and most of them will be answered in terms of your specific contract. We'll talk more about particular types of contract in chapters 6 and 7. What the publishing industry typically refers to as "work for hire" contracts generally come in one of three flavors: (1) writing for a book packager, (2) writing an IP project developed in house by a publisher, and (3) ghostwriting. Some journalism is also written on a work-for-hire basis. All of these arrangements are pretty much variations on the basic concept explained in the next section.

WHAT IS A WORK FOR HIRE?

A *work made for hire* or *work for hire* is a concept that's largely unique to American copyright law. Works for hire are works made under an agreement that allows the party commissioning the work to hold the initial copyright in it. In other words, it reverses the usual situation, in which the author owns the copyright and thus can license or sell it to other parties, like publishers or media outlets. With a work for hire, the author never owns the copyright and typically has no control over what is later done with the rights.

The legal concept of a work for hire is actually more limited than the way the term is used in the publishing and general entertainment industries. Legally speaking, work-for-hire arrangements arise in one of two ways: as a work made by an employee within the scope of her employment or as a work specially ordered or commissioned in certain cases that are set out in the Copyright Act. In the industry sense, however, works for hire are basically *any* arrangements for creating any kind of creative work (movies, art, sculpture, music, etc.) where the creator will not own copyright in the work at the date of creation. These arrangements include books that have been commissioned by a book packager, by a publishing house, or under a ghostwriting contract. To figure out whether you or your publisher owns copyright in your work, it's necessary to look at what your contract says. We'll consider contract issues in more detail in chapter 6.

WHO IS AN "EMPLOYEE" UNDER THE WORK-FOR-HIRE DOCTRINE?

The strict legal definition of *work for hire* in the United States is limited to two particular categories: creating in the employee context or certain forms of work on commission listed in the statute. In the first context (works created as an employee), most employers do have a clear policy on intellectual property ownership that employees sign, but not always.

Courts have tried to establish rules about ownership of intellectual property for situations where there is no contract or where the contract is unclear. In particular, courts have attempted to explain the difference between an employee (whose intellectual property usually belongs to the employer) and an independent contractor (whose work may or may not belong to the commissioning party, depending on the intention of the parties).

The Supreme Court tried to explain the concept of an "employee" in this context in the case of *Community for Creative Non-Violence v. Reid* in 1989. Here, the Court said that the term *employee* typically means someone who is in a regular, salaried employment relationship with an employer. This would mean that a newspaper article written by a staff journalist for publication in the paper that employs the journalist would be a work for hire, so copyright would automatically belong to the newspaper/employer. The copyright for a piece written by a freelance journalist, on the other hand, may or may not be owned by the journalist, depending on the terms of her contract for the piece.

WORK FOR HIRE VS. ASSIGNING YOUR COPYRIGHT VS. JOINT COPYRIGHT OWNERSHIP

There are a number of situations where an author may not hold copyright in her own work, including work-for-hire scenarios, situations where the author assigns her copyright to a publisher, and situations where she jointly

Writing for Someone Else

holds the copyright with her publisher. The latter arrangement, called *joint copyright ownership*, is basically the same as jointly owning any kind of property. Just as you can jointly own a car or a house with your spouse, another family member, or a friend, you can jointly own a copyright with someone else: a publisher, a friend, a family member, a coauthor, or a book packager.

Yes, you did read that right. Increasingly, book packagers are opting to hold joint copyright with the authors they hire to develop projects for them. For example, Alloy Entertainment, a book-packaging and television-development arm of Warner Bros., and one of the leading book packagers in the United States, shares copyrights with some of its authors. Katie Cotugno's popular young adult romance novel *99 Days* and its sequel *9 Days and 9 Nights* are Alloy projects written by Cotugno. Alloy and Cotugno jointly hold the copyrights. HarperCollins, in turn, has a license to publish these works, granted by Alloy and Cotugno jointly. *Everything Everything* by Nicola Yoon, mentioned earlier, is also an Alloy project, and Yoon, too, shares copyright with Alloy.

FEES, ROYALTIES, AUTHORIAL CREDIT, AND CONTROL

We'll consider book-packaging arrangements, ghostwriting, and in-house IP projects for publishing houses below. However, before we look at the nitty-gritty of each kind of arrangement, it's worth bullet-pointing a general overview of other stuff you may want to look out for in these kinds of arrangements. Again, it's important to keep in mind that there's nothing inherently wrong or illegal, or even unethical, about these arrangements. Some of them can be very lucrative and helpful to authors.

Outside of questions about copyright ownership (which will usually *not* belong to you in a work-for-hire or similar arrangement), a work-for-hire contract will usually contain clauses about the following:

- How the author gets paid (flat fee or royalties or a combination of both)
- Authorial control over revisions (how much say you get over the content of the final product)
- Authorial consultation on cover design and other formatting issues
- Authorial credit (whether your name will be on the book and whether you're allowed to claim authorship in public, like on your website)
- If your name is not on the book and you're not allowed to claim authorship, whether you're allowed to mention your authorship of the book in more private professional materials, like a résumé, as opposed to publicity materials, like your website
- How closely you have to follow any guidelines or plans for content provided by the commissioning publisher and whether the publisher can hire someone else to revise what you wrote, if they're not happy with your work

If any of these issues are particularly important to you and are not included in your contract, you should discuss them with the person who offered you the contract to see if new terms can be added to address your concerns. If you have an agent or attorney, they can handle this for you.

Because there's no uniform standard for how these arrangements can and do work, it's often difficult to find information you need on typical market practices on a range of relevant issues. That's largely because many of the specific terms of these contracts will vary widely from project to project, company to company, and writer to writer. Often the best way to learn what you need to know, including whether your contract terms are reasonable, is to talk to other authors who've worked on similar projects at the same or similar companies.

Writing for Someone Else

You can also talk to your agent if you have one. Some agents actually assist their authors in finding work-for-hire projects and have a good idea of reasonable market terms for different projects. If you're offered a work-for-hire contract and you don't have an agent, it may be a good idea to seek representation at that point. Some agents may be happy to take you on as a client and negotiate your work-for-hire contract in exchange for their standard royalty (the agent's expertise may be worth it).

Alternatively, if you're a member of a writers' organization like the Authors Guild, it may provide legal assistance for members. You might want to consider joining such an organization at some point in your career in any event. We'll discuss the advantages in chapter 13. Usually the fees required to join these organizations are pretty manageable. It may simply be a question of finding the most appropriate organization for your writing needs. For example, if you're a romance writer, it probably makes sense to join the Romance Writers of America (usually a reliable advocate for its members, though a recent rift has fractured the organization). If you're a children's author, you may want to join the Society for Children's Book Writers and Illustrators (SCBWI). Some authors' organizations require you to already be a published author before you join (e.g., Science Fiction and Fantasy Writers of America). Others, like SCBWI, may provide different levels of membership for published versus unpublished authors.

While there are no uniform standards for work-for-hire arrangements, an expert in the publishing field may at least be able to tell you if the contract you've been offered is out of left field. During the controversy surrounding Jobie Hughes's work for Full Fathom Five, another writer, Suzanne Moses, who had been offered a contract by the company, released a copy of her contract publicly after consulting several attorneys. One of her attorneys said he "had never seen a contract like this in his sixteen years of negotiation."[3] If you find yourself in a similar position, it's probably a good idea to consult an agent, attorney, or other expert.

CAN AN AGENT FIND ME WORK FOR HIRE?

Many agents work with book packagers, who often consult them for recommendations of writers for particular projects. Some agents manage their author-clients' careers in a combination of work-for-hire and original projects. Don't be afraid to go out and ask for help from the people who know the industry best. If you have an agent and are interested in work for hire, ask them to keep their ears open for any opportunities for you. If you don't have an agent but are offered a work-for-hire contract, maybe look for an agent to negotiate the deal for you. That agent may later represent your original work as well.

Three great online resources for finding reputable agents are Writer's Market, Publishers Marketplace, and QueryTracker. They all require payment of a membership fee. If you're worried about mounting career expenses, you can definitely choose one rather than signing up for all three. They will give you lots of useful information about which agents specialize in what projects and how to contact them. You can also sign up for *Publishers Weekly* emails to learn which agents are making deals in particular genres, and how often. That can be a useful source of information on who to ask for help and possible representation.

DIFFERENT FLAVORS OF WORK FOR HIRE: BOOK PACKAGING, IP PROJECTS, AND GHOSTWRITING

There are three main situations where you might be faced with the prospect of writing a book as a work for hire: (1) book packaging, (2) an IP project developed in house by a publisher, and (3) ghostwriting. These are all variations on the same theme: a writer is engaged as a hired pen to write someone else's story or a story that someone else has developed initially but that needs a writer to flesh it out.

Book packaging, as we know, involves companies that develop ideas for books—sometimes just the kernel of an idea, sometimes more fully outlined—and then hire a writer, or team of writers, to flesh it out. Some examples of larger-scale and more well-known book-packaging projects include the middle grade *Warrior Cats* series, penned by a team of writers under the pseudonym Erin Hunter; and the *Hardy Boys* and *Nancy Drew* series, developed in the early twentieth century by the Stratemeyer Syndicate (an early book packager). A book packager licenses its projects to publishing houses for production and distribution. Sometimes the publisher ends up purchasing the rights itself. For example, the Stratemeyer Syndicate was ultimately purchased by Simon & Schuster, which has now contracted with another book packager, Mega-Books, to develop new content for the latter two series. Other times, the publisher continues producing the works under license, as has been the case with HarperCollins's publication of *Everything Everything*.

The advantage for a publishing company in purchasing, and then owning, the series itself is that it takes complete creative and financial control over the series and associated merchandising, as well as movie, television, video game, and other adaptations made from the books. Some publishers have recently begun to cut out the middleman altogether and simply develop their own projects in house. These are typically referred to as *IP projects*, although that term is also applied to projects developed by book packagers.

An in-house IP project involves the publisher itself developing the idea for a new book or series (it may be an original idea or it may be based on another property the publisher or its parent company owns, like an existing movie or television series). The publisher then contracts with an author or group of authors to write a book or series based on the outlines it has developed in house. These arrangements tend to be similar to book-packaging arrangements for the authors. Typically, the author will not own copyright.

"IP" VS. INTELLECTUAL PROPERTY

The publishing industry has, in recent years, started using the term *IP* to refer to a brand they want to develop—for example, a series of books and associated properties. *Strawberry Shortcake* and *Spongebob Squarepants* are two good examples of this kind of IP. Sometimes the ideas start with existing characters and plots, and sometimes they're developed from scratch.

In IP situations, independent authors and other creative artists are engaged on a work-for-hire basis to write or develop aspects of the brand, like books, television treatments, merchandise, video games, and so on. Like the term *work for hire*, the term *IP* can be confusing because the way it is used in the publishing industry doesn't match the legal meaning of the term, which simply refers to a group of laws that protect property in information, comprising patents, copyright, trademarks, and trade secrets. If you ask a lawyer to define *intellectual property* or *IP,* she'll probably recite this list, but if you ask a publisher or book packager, she'll probably say something like "a project developed in-house that an author was hired to write."

In fact, it's not unusual for players in the publishing industry to define a term differently than the technical legal definition of the term. So if you're ever talking to someone in the publishing industry about "IP" or "work for hire," be careful that you're not talking about completely different things! And if you ever need to hire an attorney, make sure the attorney understands the industry well enough to know the difference between *IP* and *intellectual property.*

Depending on the project, the author may or may not be credited, may obtain a flat fee or a cut of the royalties or both, and may or may not be permitted to identify herself as being associated with the book(s).

An obvious advantage for a publishing house or associated entertainment company in developing these kinds of projects is that the publisher and its related companies can handle all the television, movie, and video game adaptations and franchising without having to negotiate separately with a book packager, author, or agent. For example, if I write a best-selling children's book series that my agent has placed with a traditional publisher, that publisher will typically have to negotiate separately with me and my agent for film, television, movie, and/or merchandising rights. That means the publisher will likely end up paying me more than if it had developed its own project in house and dictated all the contract terms related to commercialization of the different aspects of the project.

Another typical kind of arrangement you might face in your career is ghostwriting. This is typically a situation where a person wants to write an autobiography or memoir but doesn't have the technical writing skills or the time. She might ask a professional writer to be her "ghost"—in other words, to write the book for her. Often celebrities and other well-known personalities hire ghostwriters to tell their stories, but ghostwriting contracts aren't limited to famous people. Anyone who has a story to tell but doesn't have the skill or the time may choose to hire a ghost.

It's often difficult to identify ghostwritten books because the ghostwriter is typically not credited as the author. The book is usually released under the name of the person the book is about. As with book packaging and in-house IP, this is usually an arrangement between the person commissioning the book and the ghostwriter, where the writer gets a flat fee and/or a cut of the royalties. The whole point of ghostwriting is that the writer is just that: a "ghost." Typically the author will not be permitted to associate herself publicly with the project or claim authorial credit.

While the ghostwriter is usually not credited as the author on the cover of the book, some people who commission ghostwriters will make a point to thank them in the acknowledgments. One example is *Open: An Autobiography*, credited on the cover to tennis star Andre Agassi, but with significant involvement by Pulitzer Prize–winning author J. R. Moehringer. Despite the

GHOSTING VS. JOINT AUTHORSHIP

For celebrities who want to tell a story, either their own personal story or something fictional, one alternative to hiring a ghostwriter is to coauthor a book with an established writer. This practice has become quite popular in recent years. Examples include Bill Clinton coauthoring a suspense novel, *The President Is Missing*, with established author James Patterson; Malcolm X's daughter, Ilyasah Shabazz, coauthoring a young adult biographical novel depicting her father's teenage years with award-winning children's author Kekla Magoon; and the *Grandfather Gandhi* series of picture books about the life of Mahatma Gandhi, coauthored by his grandson, Arun Gandhi, with established children's author Bethany Hegedus.

The writing process in a coauthoring arrangement can take many forms, depending on the authors involved. In some cases, the established writer takes on the bulk of the writing, basing it on recollections, ideas, or other information provided by the coauthor. In other cases, the established writer may simply assist the less established writer with craft issues and might act as a general sounding board—more like an editor or a second set of eyes.

There are many other iterations of this relationship. The specific details of how the coauthors will work together may or may not be set out in their contract. However, the contract will likely say something about who owns the copyright in the finished work and who will be credited on the cover, in what order, and maybe even in what size of font. Occasionally, the details are made public, especially in a situation where the collaborators have a falling out, as was the case with Donald Trump and his coauthor on *The Art of the Deal*, Tony Schwartz. Although described as a "ghostwriter," Schwartz received a joint byline on the cover with Trump and reportedly received half of the book's $500,000 advance and half of the royalties. Later, as Schwartz became increasingly critical of Trump's politics, more details of the collaboration were reported in the press.

fact that Agassi is credited as the author and holds copyright in the book, and the book is billed as an "autobiography," Moehringer receives significant credit in the acknowledgments and the two men have been very open about their collaboration on the book in media interviews.

Kevin O'Leary, star of the reality TV show *Shark Tank* and a political commentator in Canada, has also used ghostwriters for a number of his books and is generous in acknowledging them, even though he is credited as the sole author of the books. For example, he has publicly thanked the senior producer of *Dragon's Den* (the Canadian version of *Shark Tank*), Lisa Gabriele, for ghostwriting his first book, *Cold Hard Truth: On Business, Money and Life*. In the acknowledgments section of his subsequent book, *Men, Women and Money*, he thanks both Gabriele and another ghostwriter, Bree Barton. He refers to them as "collaborators," which is the way Agassi and Moehringer typically refer to each other in media interviews about *Open*.

SHOULD YOU WRITE WORKS ON COMMISSION?

As the Jobie Hughes anecdote at the beginning of this chapter suggests, some contracts that involve working on commission for book packagers or publishers can be a trap for unwary writers. As a result of scandals such as these, writing projects like book packaging, ghostwriting, and in-house "IP" have gotten a bit of a bad rap, but they're not always bad news for authors. There are actually a number of potential benefits to writing under these arrangements.

As a general matter, there's usually nothing illegal about these contracts. Even the fairly strict and unfavorable early Full Fathom Five contract was probably quite legal as a matter of contract law. The question for you, as an author, is always whether you understand the terms you're being offered and whether what's being offered works for you. In terms of whether you should take on a particular IP or ghostwriting project, there can be advantages such as having the opportunity to flex your writing muscles, try out new ideas,

A BRIEF WORD ON FREELANCING

Because this is a chapter on writing for other people, it's a good idea to briefly mention freelancing. *Freelancing* is a fairly general term that refers to work you do, as a creative artist or otherwise, on an individual contract basis rather than as an employee. Thus, if you're writing a number of small projects on commission for others, you might refer to yourself as a freelancer. Freelancers are basically *independent contractors:* people who take on individual jobs and are typically paid per job rather than paid a regular wage by an employer.

The terms *freelancing* and *independent contracting* are more typically used in the publishing industry to refer to the work of freelance editors or journalists than to authors of books. As a cost-cutting measure in recent times, a number of publishing companies have outsourced editorial services to freelancers outside the company. Media companies, too, have increasingly outsourced journalism to freelancers, rather than keeping journalists on staff.

If you create content under a freelance arrangement, whether it's educational content, journalism, or other forms of writing, you'll want to ask the same legal questions about your contract as authors writing larger commissioned projects: Will you retain copyright in your work? Will you be paid a flat fee or a royalty, or a mixture? Will you be credited for your work? If not, can you take credit for the work in your professional or marketing materials, or mention it on your C.V.?

There are no right or wrong ways to enter into freelancing arrangements as a matter of law, and there's nothing wrong with freelancing. The best lesson for everyone is to be clear about what the arrangement entails and to make sure that at least the key terms of the arrangement are in writing. It doesn't have to be a formal, signed document. A series of emails is usually enough to create a contract, provided that it's clear what everyone is agreeing to.

and earn a bit of guaranteed income. In projects where you're credited as the author, you also have the advantage of helping to develop your reputation as an author. Writing *Everything Everything* for Alloy certainly made Nicola Yoon a household name in the young adult literary community.

If authorial credit is important to you, find out whether it's a possibility under the contract you're being offered. If you want to hold a share of the copyright, see if that's possible. The reality is that even though many of these arrangements are more or less "take it or leave it" contracts, there may be some wiggle room at the margins—for example, in terms of things like royalty rates, fees, or advances. Just remember that, as in any contractual negotiation, you can't always get what you want.

MOVING ON . . .

Now that we've looked at the weird and wonderful world of writing works on commission for others, it's time to turn to the fair use defense, which may be a useful legal justification for repurposing someone else's original content. The next two chapters examine different contexts in which you may raise the fair use defense in relation to your work.

CHAPTER FOUR

Fair Use Basics

Back in 2002, Google began an ambitious project to digitize virtually all the world's books to make them fully text-searchable by researchers and others. Originally called "Project Ocean" and then colloquially termed "Google Books," the idea was to create a virtual Library of Alexandria. So what happened? The project became mired in copyright infringement lawsuits. Even though Google ultimately won a big legal battle on the basis of fair use, the project eventually lost steam in the wake of the litigation. Google Books still exists today, but in a much more limited form than originally contemplated.

The copyright infringement issues came up because representatives of authors and publishers didn't like the idea of Google making digital copies of their work without paying for it. Understandable. We're all writers here. Many of the books Google had copied into its database were copyrighted. Not all of them. Many were in the public domain, and some were *orphan works* (books that are still copyrighted, but no one can identify or locate the copyright owner).

Both the Association of American Publishers, representing publishers, and the Authors Guild, representing authors, sued Google. The lawsuit with the publishers ultimately fizzled out after many years of protracted litigation and settlement discussions. A settlement was almost reached, but could not be finalized because of concerns that its terms would violate laws other than copyright law, like antitrust law and international copyright treaty obligations.

The lawsuit with the Authors Guild continued without the publishers' association. Google ultimately won, because of the fair use defense. The court said that Google was making fair use of the copyrighted books and could continue presenting snippets of text in book search results without permission, and without infringing copyright. By the time the case was decided, Google's system had been scaled down from the original plans to make entire books available online. Instead, the system only allowed users to locate snippets of books displayed on specific pages in the search results.

Was the court right in saying Google's project was fair use? Didn't the Authors Guild have a good point about authors getting paid for unauthorized copying of their books? Google said that its book digitization project would benefit all of us, including authors. After all, writers like being able to search for other people's work as a source of ideas and inspiration.

At the end of this chapter, I'll explain exactly why the court said Google's project was fair use, but first we need to understand a little more about how fair use works. As with all copyright issues, it's complicated. This chapter explains the nuts and bolts of fair use. While fair use isn't the only defense (or excuse) for copyright infringement, it is the one you're most likely to encounter as an author, so we're going to devote a couple of chapters to it. This chapter is a primer on the defense, and the next focuses on some particular fair use scenarios: parody, educational uses, and fanfiction. We'll also come back to fair use in later chapters on social media marketing and photographic permissions.

For now, let's turn to some common misconceptions about fair use. How often have you heard any, or all, of the following?

You can always copy other people's work for educational purposes (i.e., this is fair use).

It's okay to copy a line from a song or poem in an epigraph or chapter heading, but not within a chapter of a book.

If you put a notice on your work saying "this is a fair use" or "no copyright infringement intended," it will be a fair use.

Fanfiction is fair use, and so is parody.

If you only use *x* percent of someone else's work, it is a fair use.

It probably won't surprise you to learn that none of these statements is absolutely true all of the time. Most of them are true in some situations. As with so much of copyright law, a lot depends on context.

WHAT IS FAIR USE?

Fair use excuses you from copyright infringement in certain circumstances. Unfortunately for authors publishing in the United States, it's difficult to work out with any certainty exactly what those circumstances are. Many other countries have much clearer guidelines about when certain kinds of copying violate the law. The equivalent defense in those countries is typically called *fair dealing*, rather than *fair use*. In the United Kingdom, the copyright statute includes pages of detail explaining what kinds of copying are fair dealing, in comparison to the US Copyright Act, which includes one paragraph and a bulleted list of *fair use factors*. We'll go through those in a minute. The idea behind the American approach is that "less is more." Having a less detailed statute gives courts more leeway to deal flexibly with new fair use scenarios in practice—for example, when a new copying technology is invented.

It's worth noting that in recent revisions of the UK's copyright law, Parliament has started to include a little more flexibility, taking guidance from the American approach. Australia has now also adopted a more hybrid approach. Like the UK law, the Australian statute includes detailed guidelines about what is considered fair dealing, but Parliament recently added a new "flexible dealing" section to the Australian law. This section is more like the American fair use approach. It is intended to be more responsive to emerging technologies and copying norms by giving courts more flexibility to deal with these new situations.

What's so good about the American law that other countries are looking to it for guidance? It is precisely this flexibility that other countries are now beginning to emulate. Of course, the American approach comes at the cost of uncertainty, but that's intentional. Congress intended to preserve the ability of courts to respond to new situations when it included fair use in the Copyright Act for the first time in 1976. Before that, fair use had been completely up to the courts to develop. Retaining much of the courts' flexibility in this area means that Congress doesn't have to keep going back to update the statute every time someone invents a new technology that challenges how we think about copyright and fair use. With Google Books, Congress didn't have to weigh in on the issue at all. The courts had enough leeway to handle it.

In many other countries, parliamentary bodies have had to amend copyright statutes to deal with new technology. In the UK, for example, Parliament has updated the copyright law a number of times to address fair dealing in the digital age—for example, by adding a provision that making backup copies of protected software is fair dealing in the late 1990s, in response to the early days of the personal computer revolution.

The downside of the American system is that a case actually has to go to court before anyone knows for sure whether a particular use is a fair use or not. The American system has the advantage of flexibility, at the cost of some uncertainty. As we know, not all cases end up in court, and many that do are settled without a judge's ruling. As a result, we don't always know what the law truly is on any given fair use question.

HOW DO I KNOW IF SOMETHING IS FAIR USE?

Because of the flexibility in the American fair use doctrine, you often have to play it by ear with fair use questions. The Copyright Act, and what the courts have said in interpreting it, will provide some guidance, but often you (or your agent or attorney) simply have to make an educated guess, based on what's been said by courts in the past in other circumstances. For example, no one really knows if, say, parody is fair use as a general rule. Compare this with the approach in Australia, where the Copyright Act says explicitly that parody is fair dealing. In the UK, too, the copyright law states clearly that copying a work "for the purposes of caricature, parody or pastiche" is not copyright infringement. We'll look at parody in more detail in the next chapter.

Because of the uncertainty surrounding fair use in the United States, publishers will often ask you to get permission for anything you want to quote in your book—even small snippets, like single lines of a song or poem. If you have permission, there's no copyright infringement in the first place. If there's no infringement, you never have to worry about fair use. Many publishers would rather be safe than sorry, even when there's only a small amount of copying involved.

If you want to avoid the whole question about getting permission versus arguing fair use, often you can rework your manuscript so you're not actually quoting or copying someone. For example, you could describe a song, or refer to its title, instead of quoting the actual lyrics. You can generally quote titles of books, poems, songs, television shows, and movies because those aren't usually protected by copyright or even trademark law. We'll talk about titles in more detail in chapter 8.

LEARNING BY DOING: A CASE STUDY ON FAIR USE

Probably the easiest way to understand fair use is to work through a hypothetical example to see how the law operates in practice. For this exercise, I've decided to draw from a real situation that didn't actually go to court. We

AUTHOR ATTRIBUTION

Some people mistakenly think that giving credit to the original author when you copy her work amounts to fair use. As we learned in chapter 3, copyright isn't about attribution, or giving credit, at all. While giving credit is a good practice, it has nothing to do with copyright infringement. Of course, a particular copyright holder may give you permission to use her work if you promise to give her credit, but that's not fair use, it's a contractual license. In other words, she is contracting with you to use her words if you give her credit. Once you have actual permission from the copyright holder, even if that permission is subject to a condition (like attribution), you're not infringing copyright because you're not copying without authorization. Just make sure the person you get permission from is actually the copyright holder: for example, if the author of the other work has assigned her copyright to her publisher, you'll need her publisher's permission to copy it.

can look at it with fresh eyes and try to figure out how a court might have decided it.

In 2018, Vice President Mike Pence's daughter, Charlotte, and wife, Karen, wrote and illustrated (respectively) a picture book about the Pences' pet bunny, titled *Marlon Bundo's A Day in the Life of the Vice President*. When the book came out, so did a competing one entitled *A Day in the Life of Marlon Bundo*, written by Jill Twiss and illustrated by Gerald Kelley (under the pen name E. G. Keller). Promoted by comedian John Oliver, a vocal critic of the vice president's views on homosexuality, this book also recounted a "day in the life" of the bunny, but recast the titular rabbit as a gay character in search of a life partner whom he wasn't able to marry because of government policies. The latter book, unveiled on Oliver's TV show and heavily promoted by him through multiple platforms, could be characterized in many ways: a parody, a satire, a political commentary, or a fund-raising program. Proceeds from sales of the book were donated to LGBT-friendly organizations.

Even though the Pences didn't sue Oliver or the publisher, Chronicle Books, the situation raises the kinds of issues that fair use cases often struggle to address. These cases often revolve around the balance between the rights of the copyright holder and the need to support competing viewpoints and commentary on copyrighted works, including making fun of them. Of course, if the Pences had sued they would have needed to establish copyright infringement before anyone started talking about fair use, so for the purposes of this exercise, let's assume it's at least possible that *A Day in the Life of Marlon Bundo* infringes copyright in the text of Charlotte Pence's book and/or in Karen Pence's illustrations. Now let's look at what fair use law says and how it might operate in the Bundo situation.

The fair use part of the Copyright Act is found in section 107, directly following the section that talks about what rights copyright gives you (remember the section 106 rights we talked about in chapter 2?). If you don't like legal terminology, avert your eyes or skim over the next bit, but if you do want to see exactly what Congress said about fair use, here's section 107 in all its glory:

> [T]he fair use of a copyrighted work . . . for purposes such as criticism, comment, news reporting, teaching (including multiple copies for classroom use), scholarship, or research, is not an infringement of copyright. In determining whether the use made of a work in any particular case is a fair use the factors to be considered shall include—
>
> (1) the purpose and character of the use, including whether such use is of a commercial nature or is for nonprofit educational purposes;
>
> (2) the nature of the copyrighted work;
>
> (3) the amount and substantiality of the portion used in relation to the copyrighted work as a whole; and
>
> (4) the effect of the use upon the potential market for or value of the copyrighted work . . .

If you did read the whole thing, you may have breathed a sigh of relief when you saw the bit about criticism, comment, news reporting, teaching, and research being fair use. Doesn't this mean that everything in that list is automatically fair use? So if John Oliver's bunny book is regarded as, say, "criticism" or "commentary," it's a fair use, right?

Of course not. That would be way too easy.

Congress went on to say that courts have to look at that list of four factors *every time* they consider whether something is fair use, even if the use is for educational purposes, criticism, commentary, or news reporting. So the fact that you want to criticize or comment on someone else's work, or even make an educational use of someone else's work, won't automatically make it a fair use unless it also satisfies the four-factor test. Application of this test is typically very context specific. Let's look at how the test plays out in practice.

THE FOUR-FACTOR TEST

I know I said you didn't actually have to look at the specific words in the Copyright Act to understand fair use, but I lied! Well, not really. You don't have to decipher the precise words of the statute to understand the four-factor test, but you do need to have some idea of what the factors are. Here's a refresher:

1. The *purpose and character* of the use, including whether it's a *commercial use* or a nonprofit educational use

2. The *nature* of the copyrighted work

3. The *amount and substantiality* (you might think "significance") of the portion used

4. The effect of the use on a potential market for, or value of, the copyrighted work

The best way to understand how these four factors operate is to go through them one-by-one as a court typically does and look at what past

DISCLAIMERS—"NO INFRINGEMENT INTENDED"

Many people believe that if they include a disclaimer when they copy someone else's work, it will excuse them from copyright liability—for example, saying "This is a fair use" or "No infringement intended" when you post a fanfiction work or video mashup online. These disclaimers have no practical or legal effect. This is because there is no "intent" requirement in a copyright infringement claim. All a copyright holder has to do is establish that you *copied* their work. It doesn't matter what your intention was—whether you were acting in good faith, or whether you were saying complimentary things about the copyright holder or the work. The fact of copying, regardless of your intention, is enough to establish copyright infringement. In technical terms, lawyers call copyright infringement a "strict liability" wrong; that means you are "strictly liable" if you commit the infringing act, regardless of what you intended and regardless of whether you meant any harm to the copyright holder. Saying you didn't intend to infringe, or that you intended to make a fair use, is irrelevant. A court may take your intention into account in calculating damages for copyright infringement, but hopefully you never actually get to that point. Hopefully, you'll learn enough from these chapters to know how not to infringe another person's copyright in the first place.

courts have said about each of them in the process. Bear in mind that judges don't apply the factors in a precise or mathematical way. It's usually not as simple as "Three factors favor the copyright holder and one favors the defendant so the copyright holder wins." Part of applying the factors flexibly is the ability of courts to give different weight to each factor depending on the circumstances.

Let's put these four factors of fair use under the microscope, with the vice-presidential bunny in mind.

Factor 1: The Purpose and Character of the Use

What does the "purpose and character" of the use mean in legal terms? The Copyright Act doesn't give a lot of guidance. It only suggests that commercial use is less likely to be fair use, whereas nonprofit educational use is more likely to be fair use, but it doesn't define either of those terms. And what about all the uses in between commercial use and nonprofit educational use?

To make matters even more complicated, courts have added another wrinkle by asking whether the use is "transformative." What the heck is that supposed to mean? It's actually an attempt to explain what *purpose and character* means, to identify which uses are more likely to be fair uses. A *transformative use* is a use of the original material that adds new insights or understandings to it. Alice Randall's retelling of *Gone with the Wind* from the slaves' perspective is arguably a transformative use because it recasts our understanding of the original story. It invites us to consider a wholly different perspective on the story.

You can contrast a transformative use with a purely *consumptive* use, a complex-sounding term courts have used that actually has a pretty simple meaning. (And, no, it has nothing to do with a wasting disease.) In the fair use context, a consumptive use is simply a typical consumer-oriented use. A good example is home video recording, an issue that came up in the 1980s when the Supreme Court was asked to decide whether early Betamax video recorders (remember those?) were being used to infringe copyright in movies broadcast free-to-air on television.

Home video recording is a straightforward example of a purely consumptive use of a copyrighted work. People recording the movies weren't adding any new insights or understandings to them. They were simply "consuming" them (i.e., watching them) later in time than the original broadcasts. The court decided that home video recording on Betamax devices *was* a fair use but *not* because it was transformative. It was obviously a consumptive use. The court held that it was fair use for other reasons, and largely because, at the time (early to mid-1980s), judges didn't believe that home taping would negatively impact the commercial market for copyrighted video entertainment. Judges may not feel the same way today.

Let's go back to our vice-presidential bunny. Is John Oliver's book commercial? Arguably, yes. Even though the proceeds are donated to charitable organizations, it is being sold commercially to the public. It's definitely not being sold for nonprofit educational purposes. It might be possible to say there's an element of "education" behind it, in the sense that it perhaps educates people about Mike Pence's views on LGBT issues. However, even if the book is regarded as educational, it's unlikely to be regarded as for a "nonprofit educational purpose" because the book is sold commercially.

Nonprofit educational purposes have actually been defined pretty narrowly by the courts in recent years. Even a nonprofit organization typically can't claim that all its copying is fair use. For example, in a case against Georgia State University, a nonprofit educational institution, a group of academic book publishers sued the university for making digital coursepacks for students that included copies of chapters of their copyrighted books. The university had not asked for permission. Instead, it claimed fair use. The court said that the university's copying was *not* a nonprofit educational use because the costs of the coursepacks were subsidized by student fees.[1]

What about transformative use in the bunny context? Does John Oliver's book recast the original book in a new way, shedding new light on the messages in the original book? Arguably, yes. It uses the bunny character to illustrate a side of the vice president's policies that Oliver finds troubling. In some ways, this is like Randall's retelling of *Gone with the Wind*.

Taking the first fair use factor as a whole, it's often difficult to get a clear answer as to who it favors in practice, the copyright holder or the copyist. Many uses of someone else's work are both commercial *and* transformative, like *The Wind Done Gone* and, arguably, *A Day in the Life of Marlon Bundo*. The first factor cuts both ways. What do you do when your book is both transformative and commercial?

You look at the other fair use factors, of course.

Factor 2: The Nature of the Copyrighted Work

The second fair use factor asks courts to consider the nature of the work being copied. This factor is actually much easier to understand than the first. Courts have defined *nature of the work* in two different ways over time. Today, courts may apply either or both meanings. The earlier cases referred to whether the original work had been published or not. Courts gave greater protection to unpublished work than to published work, on the presumption that the author of an unpublished work should be given the opportunity to commercialize it before anyone else makes money from it. In early fair use cases, *nature of the work* typically meant whether or not the work was published at the time it was copied. In the Marlon Bundo case, John Oliver timed his book to come out on the same day as the Pences' book, so this factor might have worked against him if a case had gone to court. He had not given the original book a chance to make money before he launched his own book.

More recently, however, courts have described *nature of the work* as relating to where the work falls on the copyright spectrum. Bear in mind that copyright covers a wide variety of things—from art, music, and literature to more scientific and functional works, like encyclopedias, dictionaries, maps, software code, technical manuals, and academic books. Courts are likely to be more deferential to protecting works at the more creative or artistic end of the spectrum than those at the more functional end. In other words, *nature of the work* now usually refers to how close the work is to the creative end of the copyright spectrum. This approach makes sense if you think about the main aim of copyright law: to promote innovation and knowledge throughout society. It makes sense to give people more leeway to copy and develop scientific and technical work than to copy artistic creations. In other words, it's for the benefit of society as a whole to have more access to, and use of, work that will enhance technological and scientific development.

What does this mean for authors in practice? It really depends on what you're trying to achieve. If you're writing scientific, technical, or general nonfiction, you may be drawing from other scientific, technical, or nonfiction work and may be able to argue fair use more easily than a fiction writer copying another writer's story. If you're a fiction author copying from other fictional work, you may have more trouble with factor 2 because you're copying a work on the more artistic end of the spectrum.

Factor 2 might be of limited help to John Oliver's Bundo book, if he were ever sued over it. The work that he and the author and illustrator copied, assuming they copied enough to be liable for copyright infringement (see factor 3 below), does fall on the more artistic or creative end of the copyright spectrum. It's an illustrated picture book, rather than a scientific or reference work. While it does have some nonfiction content—the bunny is real, and many things the bunny does in the book are based on what actually happens in a typical day in the vice president's life—it's clearly not a book at the more technical or functional end of the copyright spectrum. It's a children's book that uses a fun character to teach young readers a little about what the vice president's job entails.

Factor 3: How Much Did You Copy?
The third factor, like the second, isn't difficult to understand. It's the one about how much you copied. The only wrinkle here is that courts will consider this question both as a matter of quantity and a matter of substance. If you take a large amount of the original work without permission, that's an easy question (i.e., it's a large quantity). But if you copy a small portion of someone else's work, but it's a really significant part, that may also count against you.

The leading case in which a small quantity of copying was found to be a significant aspect of the overall work was the 1985 Supreme Court case of *Harper & Row v. Nation Enterprises*. The case involved a newspaper that had quoted a small section (three hundred to four hundred words) of President Gerald Ford's forthcoming memoir *A Time to Heal*, a book of around five hundred pages. The book dealt with the president's decision to pardon former president Richard Nixon. While the amount of words copied was tiny compared to the size of the book as a whole, the Court said that those particular quotes amounted to "the heart of the work," so the third fair use factor worked against the newspaper in the case. The words quoted were effectively President Ford's explanation for the pardon, which was the main reason anyone would have wanted to buy the book.

To apply the third factor to the Marlon Bundo example, the court would actually have to put the two books side by side and see what, and how much, was copied. Unlike the *Time to Heal* case, the issue in Bundo wouldn't be about taking a small part of a much larger work. The question would be whether the Oliver book's use of similar content—illustrations, structure, word choice, and so on—would be enough for factor 3 to weigh against fair use.

Factor 4: The Effect of the Use on the Copyright's Value

The fourth fair use factor is the one that's likely to create the most headaches. It deals with the impact of your use of someone else's work on the value of, or market for, their work. There is often some overlap between factor 4 and the commercial-use aspect of factor 1. Courts often consider the two together for that reason. Think about it logically. If you're making a commercial use of someone else's work (factor 1), you're more likely to be impacting the market for their work (factor 4). One question courts often ask is whether your work will be a *market substitute* for the original. In other words, will consumers buy your work instead of the original? If that's the case, you're less likely to have a valid claim that your work is a fair use.

For example, if I'm a musician and I make an unauthorized cover version of your copyrighted song, people might buy my song instead of your original song, so my use is less likely to be fair use. My song becomes a market substitute for yours. However, if I write a parody of your song—like Weird Al Yankovic's parodies of, say, Michael Jackson's songs "Beat It" ("Eat It") and "Bad" ("Fat")—people probably won't buy my song instead of your song. In fact, people will only be interested in the parody if they already know the original. Even though a parody may be commercial, it often won't negatively impact the market for the original, and might even increase interest in it. Interestingly, Weird Al actually does get permission from copyright holders for his parodies, even though he technically might be able to rely on fair use.[2] If you can get the copyright holder's permission, it's often safer to do so to avoid any doubt.

Let's think about that pesky bunny again here. It's possible to categorize Oliver's book as a parody or a commentary on the Pences' original book, and, for that reason alone (putting aside strong political divisions influencing people's purchasing decisions), Oliver's book is unlikely to be a market substitute for the original book. People probably wouldn't have bought his book *instead of* buying the Pences' book. Oliver clearly capitalized on the imminent release of the Pences' book to draw attention to his own work, but the people who purchased his book probably did so to make a political statement against the administration and/or as a fun way to support the charities that would benefit from the proceeds.

The Availability of Licensing under the Fourth Factor

One tricky question that's come up in recent years about the fourth fair use factor involves the possibility of licensing the original work: in other words, if you had asked for permission to use the work, would the copyright holder have given you a license? Some courts have said that if licenses are readily available, you should be required to pay the license fee instead of using the work for free and claiming fair use. The court in the Georgia State University coursepack case noted that licenses to copy many of the books in question were readily available from the publishers, so the university should have paid for licenses, rather than copying without permission.

In many situations, licenses won't be readily available, but where they are available and you don't pay for a license, factor 4 may weigh against your use being a fair use. This is because factor 4 talks about the effect of your work on the market for the copyrighted work. If the copyright holder *could have* obtained license revenues from your use, but you avoided payment and instead copied without permission, you've deprived them of that profit. In other words, you've negatively impacted their licensing market under factor 4.

Thinking about parody situations like John Oliver's Marlon Bundo book, a license wouldn't likely be available there. In the next chapter, we'll talk more about why parody, in particular, doesn't lend itself to licensing. But basically, not many copyright holders will let other people pay to make fun of them.

PUTTING IT ALL TOGETHER

Remember that none of the fair use factors works in a vacuum. Courts will consider all of them in most cases, although certain factors may be more compelling in some cases. Having gone through them all, what do we think a court might say about Marlon Bundo? John Oliver's book is both transformative and commercial under factor 1, so that doesn't give us a lot to go on. It copies a simultaneously published work that's at the more creative end of the copyright spectrum under factor 2, so that weighs against fair use. We're not actually sure how much was copied under factor 3 without a closer examination of both books, so we don't know exactly how this factor would play out. But we do know that the work is unlikely to cut into the market for the original work under the fourth factor.

Overall, factors 1 and 4 together might weigh in favor of fair use, factor 2 would weigh against, and we're not sure about factor 3. There's probably a good chance that Oliver's book would be fair use as a parody for reasons we'll look at in more detail in chapter 5, but we can already see from this general discussion that a number of the fair use factors support fair use. To come to a clearer conclusion, we'd need more information on other factors, and on how particular judges might weigh those factors in practice.

Before we turn to a more specific look at parody, educational use, and fanfiction in the next chapter, let's do a few quick exercises to make sure we understand the basics of the fair use defense, including answering the question raised at the beginning of this chapter, about why Google Books was found to be fair use.

Example 1: Google Books

If you've forgotten the details of Google Books, take a look back at the first few pages of this chapter. Now let's think about why the court said Google Books was a fair use.

You might want to try to figure it out for yourself before reading on. Think about (1) the purpose and character of Google's use, including whether the use was transformative; (2) the nature of the books copied; (3) the amount copied; and (4) the impact of Google's use on the market for, or value of, the books copied.

Got an answer yet? Let's compare it with what the court said . . .

FACTOR 1 The court said that Google's copying was transformative because it allowed for deep text searching (or full text searching) of the books. It was unclear at the time whether Google could, or would, make money from the project through advertising or by charging fees, but the court didn't focus on commercial use and instead emphasized transformative use. Courts are allowed to do that. Remember, the defense is meant to be applied flexibly.

FACTOR 2 The court said this factor was "not dispositive." In other words, it wasn't very helpful for the fair use analysis in this particular case. Many of the books Google copied were at the more artistic end of the copyright spectrum, but many were also more scientific or technical, so the second factor really wasn't much help.

FACTOR 3   The court said that even though Google copied the entire works (i.e., a large *amount* of copying), that amount wasn't excessive in light of what Google was trying to achieve. There was no way for it to make a fully text-searchable library without copying entire books.

FACTOR 4   Here, the Authors Guild had argued that Google impacted authors' markets for the books in two ways: (1) by serving as substitutes for the original books and (2) by posing a security risk that hackers could obtain unauthorized access to entire books without paying for them. The court disagreed. According to the court, the digitized books were not substitutes for the original books because Internet users could only see snippets of the books in their search results. They couldn't download entire books. Also, Google put significant security measures in place to prevent hacking, so it was unlikely that hackers would be able to download entire books without paying for them.

How close was your answer to what the court said? Don't worry if it wasn't close. This is all meant to be flexible. The flexibility gives people more scope to argue fair use (which can be comforting to authors) but creates more uncertainty unless and until a court actually decides a particular issue (which can be frustrating).

Example 2: The Seinfeld *Trivia Book Case*
In a case involving an unauthorized trivia book based on the popular TV series *Seinfeld*, a court held that the book infringed copyright in the show and was *not* a fair use. Here's how it applied the fair use factors.

FACTOR 1   The trivia book was not transformative because it didn't add any new insights or understandings to the television show. It merely repackaged information from the show. It was also a commercial use.

FACTOR 2   The copyrighted work (the television show) was at the more artistic/entertainment-oriented end of the copyright spectrum, so this factor also worked *against* fair use.

FACTOR 3   The court seemed to punt a little bit on this question, focusing more on other issues like transformative use, but it did note that the trivia guide used 643 questions based on the television show and thus seemed to draw a substantial amount of content from it.

FACTOR 4   While there was no authorized *Seinfeld* trivia book on the market at the time the case was decided, the court held that the unauthorized trivia guide usurped a potential market for an authorized trivia guide.

Ultimately, in the court's view, all four factors weighed against fair use. Again, another set of judges might have decided differently. Flexibility leads to uncertainty.

Example 3: Snippet Copying
Here's an invented case, but one that's very relevant to authors and often comes up in writing workshops. What do you think should happen in a situation where the author of a novel wants to quote two lines from a forty-line song lyric? Should it be considered fair use? Think about the following:

> *The purpose and character of the use.* It's definitely commercial.
> Presumably, the author wants to publish the novel. Is it transformative? Hmm. That's a tough one. What do you think?
> *The nature of the copyrighted work.* Is the song at the more creative/artistic end of the copyright spectrum? (Probably, especially if it's a popular song lyric.)
> *The amount copied.* Only two lines out of forty were copied, but does it matter if they are key lyrics, like a repeated chorus that underlines the meaning of the song—for example, Madonna's "We are living in

a material world / and I am a material girl"? (Oops—I just copied those lines without permission. Is *that* a fair use? What do you think?)

The impact of the copying on the value of, or market for, the original song. The book won't be a market substitute for the song, but has the author deprived the songwriter of license fees she could otherwise have asked for?

There's no clear answer to this question and it's always going to be fact-specific, depending on what you copied from where. It also depends on whether the copyright holder wants to sue or not. Charlotte and Karen Pence didn't sue John Oliver for his Marlon Bundo book, although they may well have been quite upset about it. That doesn't mean that his book is or isn't fair use. We just don't know for sure until someone takes the matter to court.

When you want to copy a couple of lines of a poem or song, your publisher will often ask you to get permission for avoidance of doubt. However, a lot of books are published with quoted lyrics where no permission appears to have been granted. Usually, if permission has been granted, there's a copyright acknowledgment somewhere in the front matter or back matter of the book.

MOVING ON . . .

In the next chapter we'll consider some specific fair use situations and how courts have dealt with them: parody, educational use, and fanfiction. While the answers in those situations are not necessarily very much clearer than the examples given in this chapter, at least you can see what courts have said in the past about some of these situations.

CHAPTER FIVE

Specific Fair Uses

Parody, Fanfiction, and Educational Use

In the summer of 2018, best-selling comic author Andrew Shaffer released the first in a new series of novels depicting Barack Obama and Joe Biden as a crime-fighting duo in the vein of Sherlock Holmes and Dr. Watson, but with more of an action-adventure feel. The novel, *Hope Never Dies*, was billed as both *parody* and *fanfiction* and was pitched largely to an audience of Democratic voters feeling nostalgic about the Obama administration. The novel is a parody because it makes fun of the close relationship between the two men, often described in the press and social media as a "bromance," and it's fanfiction because it riffs on people and issues in the public imagination and presents them in a new way. While questions about parody and fanfiction are difficult to unravel in the fair use context, those issues don't arise in relation to this novel. Can you guess why?

Because there's no copyrighted work here to begin with. *Hope Never Dies* is based on real people, not on an existing copyrighted work. No copyrighted work means no copyright infringement, which, in turn, means no need to talk about fair use. This novel pokes good-natured fun at real people, who happen to also be public figures, so there's little chance of a defamation action either. We'll talk about defamation in chapter 10.

While *Hope Never Dies* doesn't repurpose any existing copyrighted works, it is a good example of what parody and fanfiction are all about, and why they can be important, not merely entertaining. Parody, in particular, also enables us to take a new and sometimes humorously critical look at how we feel about important issues. The Marlon Bundo example from the previous chapter is another instance of this.

In this chapter we'll look at copyright's fair use defense in the context of parody and fanfiction, as well as educational uses. All of these uses are usually of some benefit to society, and most of us want laws that allow us to poke fun at, rework, or think critically about a whole host of issues. The question is how well copyright law strikes an appropriate balance between protecting copyright owners and promoting other socially desirable uses of their work.

As we learned in chapter 4, the fair use defense is intended to be applied flexibly, which is supposed to support and encourage socially beneficial uses of copyrighted works. But we're still stuck with those four fair use factors, even when we deal with parody, education, or fanfiction. There's no law in the United States that says, "If you're making a parody or an educational use, it's a fair use."

However, there have been cases where American courts have said that particular parodies, fanfiction, or educational uses are, or are not, fair uses. These cases are all context-specific (of course) and all rely on particular applications of the four fair use factors we discussed in the previous chapter, but at least they give some guidance as to what issues the courts think about in these situations.

PARODY AS FAIR USE

Let's start with parody, because it's where American fair use law is perhaps the most developed. Remember: there are no hard-and-fast rules to say that all parody is fair use. It's always a question of applying the fair use factors set out in chapter 4. We already looked, in that chapter, at one book that's arguably a parody: *A Day in the Life of Marlon Bundo*. But there are many other examples. Think about *Pride and Prejudice and Zombies* by Seth Grahame-Smith. It copies pretty much the exact wording of Jane Austen's classic novel and inserts additional material about zombies. It's funny in its own right, and also makes fun of how seriously we take Victorian novels, to an extent. It's not a copyright infringement, though. Is that because it's a fair use?

No. It's not a copyright infringement because Jane Austen's work is now in the public domain. Do you think it would be a copyright infringement if the novel were still protected by copyright?

While there's no clear answer, it's a fun exercise and will help you review the four fair use factors. Let's see . . .

FACTOR 1   *Purpose and character of the use.* The use is clearly *transformative*, isn't it? It recasts the work in a new light by incorporating zombies and gory humor. However, the use is also commercial. So the first factor would cut both ways.

FACTOR 2   *Nature of the work copied.* The work copied is both published and toward the artistic end of the copyright spectrum, so this factor would suggest infringement rather than fair use.

FACTOR 3   *Amount copied.* The amount copied is just about the entire text of the original book, although a lot of material is also added. So this factor would suggest infringement rather than fair use.

FACTOR 4   *Impact on the market for, or value of, the copyrighted work.* The parody likely wouldn't negatively impact the market for the original work, even though it's a commercial use. It's not a market substitute for the original book. In fact, people would need to have bought, or at least read, the original book to understand the parody.

So, fair use?

Remember the case involving *The Wind Done Gone*, Alice Randall's retelling of *Gone with the Wind* from the slaves' point of view? (We talked about it in chapter 2.) The court described Randall's book as a "parody" when it applied the fair use test. According to the court, a parody includes not only reworkings of an original that make fun of the original, but also those that comment on or criticize the original in some way. In that sense, Randall's work was clearly a parody of *Gone with the Wind*. By recasting the story in a different light, told by characters not significantly represented in the original work, the book was a commentary on the original with critical elements and thus was a parody in the legal sense.

The court said that even though Randall's book was a parody, not all parody is necessarily fair use. It always depends on application of the four-factor test. As we saw in chapter 2, the case was settled before we had a chance to find out definitively whether *The Wind Done Gone* was a fair use. But at least we know it *could* have been a fair use, and that it was a parody for copyright purposes.

It could go either way. I wonder what Jane Austen would have thought.

This example highlights some issues that come up again and again for courts in considering parody cases. For one thing, parodies are usually both commercial and transformative. Think about fair use factor 1. You always have to *transform* a work in some way in order to make fun of it (like making Michael Jackson's "Bad" dancers into "Fat" dancers). If you just copied it without doing anything transformative, it wouldn't be funny.

The leading Supreme Court case on parody and fair use is the 1994 decision involving rap group 2 Live Crew's parody of the famous Roy Orbison song "Pretty Woman." The parody's lyrics referred to women who are big, hairy, bald, and "two timin'." The lyrics were obviously very different from

Orbison's version. However, the exact same drumbeat and bass line were used in the parody, and the melody line was recognizable despite the changed lyrics. Ultimately the court said that the parody here may be a fair use, noting that in parody cases, the focus should be on transformativeness, the extent to which the parody alters the original with "new expression, meaning and message."

Parodies usually riff on works toward the more artistic or creative end of the copyright spectrum. Think about fair use factor 2 here. It's not usually that funny to parody a scientific or technical work, or someone else's copyrighted software code. Of course, it is possible to parody more functional copyrighted works. A great example is Diana Wynne Jones's *The Tough Guide to Fantasyland*, a book that parodies the popular *Rough Guide* travel series of books but is actually a craft book about overdone tropes in fantasy writing. The *Rough Guide* series is more at the functional or technical end of the copyright spectrum, but Jones parodies it masterfully here.

Another issue specific to parody in the fair use context relates to the third fair use factor: how much of the copyrighted work the parodist has used. This has always been a challenge for courts in parody cases. In the "Pretty Woman" case, the Supreme Court said that the parodist should use no greater amount of the original work than necessary to conjure up the original in the minds of the audience. But that's a really subjective question, and the answer will differ from case to case, depending on the facts.

PARODY VS. SATIRE

A related question is whether you can call something a parody when it borrows from an existing work to make fun of *something else*. Courts have had a very hard time with what they have described as the difference between *parody* and *satire*. Parody involves spoofing the actual thing you're copying, like John Oliver's team making a cute family pet into a character struggling with same-sex marriage policies. But what happens if you copy, say, the dis-

MORE ON INJUNCTIONS

Many copyright cases involve injunctions—court orders that either prevent a publisher from releasing a book or order the publisher to remove an existing book from sale. Injunctions can be *preliminary* or *permanent*. A preliminary injunction is kind of like an "emergency" order made before the full case is heard in order to prevent the copyright holder from suffering damages that may be difficult to recover later. If the allegedly infringing book has been for sale for months or years before the final case is heard by the court, the damages could become significant. Courts will often try to avoid this by making a preliminary order to prevent sale until the case can be decided in full. A *permanent* injunction, on the other hand, is made at the full hearing of the case and is the final order based on all the evidence brought before the judges.

In copyright cases, it's very common for the parties to settle the dispute after a preliminary hearing: the earlier stage in the litigation when the court decides whether to grant a preliminary injunction. The court's decision on the preliminary injunction is often a useful guide as to what might happen at the final hearing. Armed with this knowledge, the parties often have greater guidance and incentives to help settle the case before a final hearing. It also saves them the various costs of keeping the litigation going.

tinctive illustrations in a book to make fun of something else entirely? This is considered satire and is usually not protected as a fair use.

It's exactly what happened in a case regarding a spoof of the O. J. Simpson trial written in the distinctive wordplay style, and with the distinctive illustrations, of a Dr. Seuss book. The book was called *The Cat NOT in the Hat!* and was subtitled "A Parody by Dr. Juice." The court said this wasn't a parody at all because the book didn't make fun of Dr. Seuss, but rather used Dr. Seuss to make fun of something entirely unrelated.

Of course, the court did what all courts do in fair use cases: applied the four-factor test. Ultimately it decided the book wasn't a parody because it didn't transform the original works it copied. It had nothing to do with Dr. Seuss or any of the stories he'd told, according to the court. It simply used Seuss's famous style to draw reader attention in the marketplace. If you find that interpretation of fair use odd, you're not alone. Many lawyers and copyright researchers have criticized the decision, and the distinction the court made between parody and satire, but for better or worse, that's the law we're stuck with. You can contrast this case with a more recent parody case involving Dr. Seuss's beloved *Oh, the Places You'll Go!* (discussed in chapter 12). That case was a clearer parody of the actual Dr. Seuss book itself, rather than riffing on the book to make fun of something else.

In the "Dr. Juice" case, Dr. Seuss Enterprises (the company that now owns copyright in the Dr. Seuss books) had asked the court for an *injunction* to prevent the commercial release of the book. Remember that an injunction is an order a court can make to prevent the sale of a book. The court here *enjoined* (prohibited) Penguin Books, along with the audio book producer, Dove Audio, from releasing the print or audio versions of the book. That means they were unable to make any money from the work they'd done producing the books.

Because of these serious and potentially costly risks, your publisher is usually going to ask you to obtain permissions for anything you want them to publish if you borrow from someone else's work. If you don't, they face this kind of litigation. Your publication contract will likely say that you will *indemnify* them (pay them back) if they get sued over what you write for them. We'll look at these contract clauses in chapter 6.

LICENSE TO PARODY?

A final point to make about parody is related to fair use factor 4, and the potential market for the copyrighted work. Recall from the previous chapter

SO IS PARODY FAIR USE OR NOT?

As with everything else related to fair use, there are few clear guidelines for parody. We know that not all parody is fair use, and that satire (using someone's work purely to make fun of something else) is technically not parody. As with all other fair use situations, the best way to figure out if something is fair use is to make your best guess based on what courts have said so far.

You can also look at copyrighted works that are parodied a lot, which may be an indication that the copyright holder for those works doesn't mind parody so much and isn't likely to sue you. That's not a legal question, just a practical exercise that might help calculate the likelihood that you'd be sued over a parody of a particular work. Next time you're in the humor section of a bookstore, take a look to see what kinds of parodies are being sold. Then flip inside the front covers and see if they have copyright permissions or not. If they don't have permission, you might see a notice like "This book is a parody and has not been prepared, approved, or authorized by the creators of [the copyrighted work] or their heirs or representatives."

That notice doesn't give any legal protection but does make it clear, or at least reasonably clear, that the publishers of the parody seem to be claiming parody as a fair use. As we already know, saying something is a "fair use" or a "parody" or is "intended to be" a fair use or parody doesn't have any legal effect in practice. Remember, writing "parody" on the cover of the book didn't help "Dr. Juice" with *The Cat NOT in the Hat!*

If you're a fan of Margaret Wise Brown's iconic children's book *Goodnight Moon* (illustrated by Clement Hurd), you might be surprised at the number of parodies you find, including *Goodnight Bush, Goodnight Democracy, Goodnight Marketers, Goodnight Lab, Goodnight Goon,* and *Mad* magazine's *Goodnight Batcave.* Most of these are labeled as parodies and look very much like the original book at first glance. If you look inside the front cover, most of them note that they are unauthorized parodies. All of these books may well be fair uses as parody, but that's no guarantee the copyright holders will never sue for copyright infringement.

that courts tend to say that if you want to use someone else's work, you should get a license if you can. Otherwise, you're arguably depriving the copyright owner of potential licensing fees it could have made from the work. Courts have also recognized that copyright holders generally won't give out licenses to make fun of them and so it's not fair to ask parodists to get licenses, or to hold it against them if they don't. This is precisely what the court said about *The Wind Done Gone*. You can't expect parodists to get licenses, so you shouldn't hold that against them under factor 4 of the fair use test. It's very unlikely that the Pence family would have given John Oliver a license to produce and promote his parody book, particularly given their opposing political views, so it wouldn't make sense to penalize him for not getting a license if the case went to court.

FANFICTION

One situation that has come under the spotlight in recent years is whether *fanfiction* is fair use. Fanfiction (or "fic") is basically a form of derivative work based on an existing work such as a book, a movie, or a television series. As the *Hope Never Dies* example demonstrates, you can even write fanfiction about real people, and copyright infringement isn't usually a problem there, because there's no copyrighted work that's being reimagined.

Usually fanfiction is written by, you guessed it, fans of the original work. Fans may want to write a version of the work where two characters become romantically involved in a way that doesn't happen in the original—for example, Kirk-Spock romances in classic *Star Trek* fanfiction. Sometimes a fan wants to reimagine the story in a different setting, or even combine two existing worlds into one—for example, putting the *Star Trek* characters into the *Star Wars* galaxy far, far away.

Sometimes a work may be retold in a way that isn't at all complimentary to the original—for example, the "Buffy vs Edward" video mashup of scenes from the TV show *Buffy the Vampire Slayer* and the movie *Twilight*. A *mashup* is a compilation or "mashing up" of two or more existing things to create something new. A lot of rap music, for another example, "mashes up" existing songs while adding new elements.

The point of the "Buffy vs Edward" mashup was to criticize the then popular view that an innocent teenage girl being pursued by a deadly vampire (in *Twilight*) was sweet and romantic. The mashup showed the kick-ass vampire slayer Buffy being stalked by the vampire hero of *Twilight* (Edward) and ultimately staking him. The entire mashup was composed of scenes from *Buffy* and *Twilight*, so the work involved a lot of copying, but the copying was for the purpose of creating something new: new insights on the original *Twilight* story.

There was no formal litigation over the mashup. However, the owners of copyright in the *Twilight* movie (Lionsgate) sent a "takedown" notice to YouTube to remove the video, which it did. Ultimately, after going through a *notice and takedown* procedure (see sidebar), the video was reinstated. There is a good argument that the video is fair use because, even though the works copied were on the creative end of the copyright spectrum (fair use factor 2),

+   the mashup wasn't commercially released, so it wasn't commercial under fair use factor 1, and wouldn't have interfered with a market for either of the copied works under factor 4;

+   a license likely wouldn't have been available from either copyright holder with respect to factor 4 (like parody, critical commentary of this kind is not likely to be licensed by the copyright holder); and

+   the mashup was only about six minutes long, so it didn't borrow substantial amounts from either *Buffy* or *Twilight* under factor 3.

Ultimately, after the notice and takedown battle, Lionsgate backed away from fighting about it, and the video is still available on YouTube.[1]

NOTICE AND TAKEDOWN PROCESS

One of the changes made to the US Copyright Act in the late 1990s was the insertion of quite a complicated update called the Digital Millennium Copyright Act (DMCA). This update added a bunch of things to the statute, most of which we don't have to worry about for the purposes of this book. A lot of them had to do with supporting distributors of digital movies, television shows, digital music, and e-books from hacking of encryption codes that prevent unauthorized copying. You probably know from your own video streaming services, or your DVD or Blu-ray collection, that you can't copy content without hacking into the digital locks the distributors put on them. Parts of the DMCA make it illegal to try.

One thing the DMCA does that is more relevant to authors is the *notice and takedown* section. This part of the statute says that if a copyright holder gives notice to an online service provider, like Amazon or YouTube, that content on its website infringes a copyright, the provider has to remove the potentially infringing material or face liability for copyright infringement itself. If you see unauthorized copies of your work on Amazon—either complete pirated copies or another book that copies large parts of your book—you can ask Amazon to remove the book from sale, and it may face copyright infringement liability if it doesn't.

If the person who posted the content objects to it being taken down, and convinces the website that it isn't infringing, she may ask for the work to be reinstated, which is what happened in the "Buffy vs Edward" situation. The notice and takedown procedures don't tell you whether or not anything posted online is a fair use, but it does give copyright holders the ability to take quick and cheap action to fend off copyright infringements.

While "Buffy vs Edward" may or may not be considered technically a form of fanfiction, the same fair use test applies. This video is also a useful guide for other artists of mashups who are creating more fan-oriented works. If you like *Outlander*, the time-traveling romance book and TV show, there are any number of video mashups of popular songs paired with video and photo stills from the show. Likewise, the Internet is full of fanfiction websites for particular fandoms where authors post their own versions of books, shows, or other source material they love, or love to hate.

IS FANFICTION FAIR USE?

As with parody, there are no clear guidelines saying that fanfiction is, or is not, fair use. It will depend on the circumstances and the application of the four fair use factors. There are some common issues that tend to come up with respect to fanfiction:

Most fanfiction is noncommercial and transformative. Most of it is done for the love of it rather than to make money, with some high-profile exceptions we'll talk about in a minute. (Think about fair use factor 1, on commercial and transformative uses.)

Most of the works used as the basis of fanfiction are at the more artistic or creative end of the copyright spectrum. (Think about factor 2.)

Most fanfiction will, by definition, take a significant amount from the original work, at least in terms of copyrighted characters and recognizable plotlines. (Think about factor 3.)

Most fanfiction won't negatively impact the market for, or value of, the original copyrighted work. (Think about factor 4.)

If you were doing a mathematical equation here, the fair use scales would look pretty evenly balanced. Factors 1 and 4 will typically support a fair use claim, while factors 2 and 3 will typically work the opposite way. However, as we know, that isn't how fair use works. A court may decide that one factor, or set of factors, is more important in a given case than others. It may be that, in the fanfiction context, courts will be more swayed by factors 1 and 4, relating to commercialization and the impact on the market for the original work.

Many people think noncommercial fanfiction is pretty harmless and that, if it has any impact on the market for the original work, it's to increase attention on the work in a positive way. How many people decided to revisit their favorite 1980s movies and video games after *Ready Player One* was released? (Of course, Steven Spielberg's company didn't rely on fair use in making the movie; he licensed the works he used.)

In terms of market impact, factor 4 also looks at the availability of a licensing market. If the copyright holder could have asked you to pay for a license to write your fanfiction, arguably, you shouldn't be able to do it for free, right? When we looked at parody, we learned that courts generally don't believe there would be a licensing market available for parody because most copyright owners wouldn't let people pay to make fun of them. Does that work differently for fanfiction? It's hard to know.

Some authors, like Anne Rice, have prominently stated that they "don't allow" fanfiction, which suggests that there wouldn't be a licensing market for fan-made works based on her books.[2] Other authors, like Stephenie Meyer (still sticking with vampires) have expressed mixed feelings about fanfiction.[3] Meyer hasn't sued E.L. James for *Fifty Shades of Grey*, which started out as *Twilight* fanfiction. Hugh Howey, author of the best-selling *Silo* series of science fiction novels, has actively encouraged fans to write fanfiction based on his work, and to sell it commercially without paying him any license fees.[4] And Author Neil Gaiman has written on his blog: "As long as people aren't commercially exploiting characters I've created, and are doing it [i.e., writing fanfiction] for each other, I don't see that there's any harm in it, and given how much people enjoy it, it's obviously doing some good. It doesn't bother me. (I can imagine a time and circumstances in which it might. But it doesn't.)"[5]

It's difficult to draw any conclusions about whether, as a general matter, there would be a licensing market available for fanfiction or not. So much depends on the attitude of particular authors or publishers, and their views differ widely. Hugh Howey jokes that his lawyer was "no doubt reaching for his heart medication" when Howey started talking about ownership in words being a strange concept, an argument supporting his own views that people should be allowed to make money from fanfiction, without needing a license or permission to do so.[6]

There have been some attempts to create formal licensing schemes for fanfiction—for example, Amazon's Kindle Worlds program, which operated for about five years before closing down in 2018. Kindle Worlds was a licensed fanfiction platform allowing fans to write works based on the "worlds" included in the program. These worlds included popular TV shows and books whose copyright holders had granted Amazon a license to allow its customers to write fanfiction and sell it commercially via Kindle Direct. However, the licenses came with restrictive terms about what fans could and couldn't write in particular fandoms. Additionally, fan authors weren't allowed to mix elements from different worlds in the same work. The licenses also made it clear that the copyright holders of the original works, rather than the fan authors, would own copyright in all the fan-made works. It was an interesting experiment, but it wasn't particularly successful—maybe because of the restrictive licensing terms.

While we've not yet seen much litigation involving fanfiction in the publishing industry, the question of fanfiction and fair use has come up in other industries. For example, in the *Axanar* case, Paramount Pictures sued the makers of a *Star Trek* fan film (a prequel story line to the original series) for copyright infringement. Paramount convinced the court that the fan film

SCHOOL VISITS AND COPYRIGHT PERMISSIONS

If you have published your book with a traditional publisher (rather than self-publishing) and want to make copies of, say, a chapter for a school visit, you probably will have to seek permission from your publisher if you've assigned copyright to them or granted them an exclusive license over your copyright in the book (we'll look at those license terms in chapter 6). Most publishers won't mind some copying for classroom use, because it's good marketing and publicity for the book. However, most contracts will require you to get the publisher's permission even to copy chapters of your own book for a classroom visit or other presentation—for example, giving a workshop at a writing conference.

was not a fair use. In making this decision, the court was swayed by the following facts:

+ the fan film was to be commercially released;

+ the costumes were custom-made to replicate the original Star Trek costumes; and

+ the characters closely matched some of the original characters, and the plotline was very close to plotlines referenced in the original *Star Trek* series.

Obviously, these issues are very specific to that particular project. If the fan film wasn't going to be commercially released, would the court have decided differently? A lot of people mistakenly say that if an unauthorized use isn't commercial, it will be considered a fair use. We know that's not true, because it's only one of the issues a court will consider in determining fair use, but it's not a bad guideline. At the very least, copyright holders are usually less bothered by unauthorized uses that don't commercially compete with them.

EDUCATIONAL USES

Educational use has become a pretty complex part of copyright law, which makes life difficult for teachers, researchers, and others involved in academic pursuits. Luckily for us, many of the wrinkles that have arisen about educational uses of copyrighted works won't specifically apply to our writing.

The main situations in which authors may confront fair use in an educational setting include the following:

+ writing an educational book and/or accompanying materials (workbooks, website, etc.) and quoting from other educational works in the process;

+ copying material from your work for school visits (if you write books for younger readers);

+ copying handouts to distribute at presentations, workshops, or conferences; and

+ responding to requests from educators, researchers, or scholars seeking permission to use your work (e.g., in classroom handouts or coursepacks).

When you think about these kinds of uses in light of the four fair use factors, a handful of common issues are likely to arise, including these:

Nonprofit educational uses are more likely to be fair uses under factor 1, but courts have pretty narrowly interpreted what *nonprofit* means in this context, as we saw in the Georgia State University coursepacks case in chapter 4.

The nature of the work copied may well be more on the scientific, technical, or functional end of the copyright spectrum in the educational-use context with respect to factor 2.

There will often be a readily available licensing market for a lot of educational work, at least in terms of academic texts, for the purposes of factor 4.

You may hear people referring to educational fair use guidelines and saying that you are allowed to copy x percent of a book for educational purposes, or one chapter, or something like that. However, this is not based on the Copyright Act itself. While the fair use provisions of the statute do talk about copying for classroom purposes, the law doesn't say how much can be copied for those purposes and, again, the answer relies on an application of the four fair use factors.

It's also important to be aware that occasionally, when people refer to guidelines like this, they're actually referring to guidelines from other countries, many of which do have clearer laws about how much you can copy for educational purposes. Be careful if you simply search the Internet for guidelines, because if you accidentally stumble on guidelines from other countries, they won't necessarily reflect the law in the United States.

MOVING ON . . .

Having looked at how fair use works in the United States, hopefully you now see that, while the law is complicated and uncertain in many areas, it also has the flexibility to accommodate new kinds of uses. Additionally, in practice, you can avoid a lot of problems by simply seeking permission to use someone else's work. In the next chapters, we switch gears to look at contracts related to your copyrights and how best to protect your interests in your work.

BEST PRACTICES GUIDELINES

Speaking of guidelines, they can be quite useful in the United States because of the law's flexible approach to fair dealing, and because many court cases are settled before we get to find out what the law on fair use actually is in a particular situation. A number of organizations have embarked on projects to create "best practices" handbooks for various fair use scenarios, like journalism, documentary filmmaking, educational settings of various kinds, and so on. These best practices are drafted to help people in those industries or settings to have at least a basic grasp of the norms within the industry on fair use, and the ways in which the law might apply to different kinds of uses that are standard within the industry.

One organization that has created such guidelines is the Center for Media and Social Impact at the School of Communications at American University. If you check out their website (http://cmsimpact.org/codes-of-best-practices/0), you will find user-friendly sets of guidelines for fair use in journalism; online video; media studies publishing; teaching, research, and study; poetry; documentary filmmaking; and visual arts, among others. Again, you can't rely on these guidelines as statements of the law, but they will give you some background as to what kinds of conduct should arguably be accepted as fair uses in particular contexts.

Another organization that has become active in publishing guidelines on matters of interest to the publishing industry is the Authors Alliance. In 2017, they published a handbook on fair use for authors of nonfiction and academic work.* This handbook is more lengthy than some of the Center for Media and Social Impact's guidelines, and it also provides a number of practical examples of situations that may be regarded as fair use.

---

* Brianna L. Schofield and Robert K. Walker (Eds.), *Fair Use for Nonfiction Authors: Common Scenarios with Guidance from Community Practice,* available at www .authorsalliance.org/wp-content/uploads/2017/11/AuthorsAllianceFairUseNonfiction Authors.pdf.

CHAPTER SIX

Contracts with Agents and Publishing Houses

In 2018, best-selling Australian author Kate Morton won a lawsuit against her first agent, Selwa Anthony. Anthony had sued Morton, claiming that the author owed Anthony outstanding commissions for deals Anthony had brokered. Morton, in return, claimed that Anthony owed her money for overpayments of the agent's commission. After the end of the agency relationship, Anthony had continued to take commission from ongoing sales of Morton's books for deals she'd brokered for Morton. While perpetual (i.e., forever) commissions like this are common practice in the publishing industry, Morton didn't realize Anthony would keep taking commissions after the termination of the agency relationship. Most author-agent contracts allow for perpetual commissions on the theory that it's reasonable for an agent to reap the benefits of a deal she has brokered.

The problem in this situation was that Morton never signed a formal agency contract. The agreement was purely verbal. There was no written record of its terms. Verbal contracts are usually valid and enforceable, but it can be difficult to figure out what the parties intended, which is why it's always a good idea to get things in writing, even if that writing is only a series of emails. Ultimately, the court accepted that a verbal agency relationship existed between Morton and Anthony, but that it did not include

THE PAROL EVIDENCE RULE/"ENTIRE AGREEMENT" CLAUSES

Because contracts can be made in so many ways—verbally, in exchanges of emails, over the telephone, or in more formal documents—contract law has developed a rule that if the parties say that a particular written document is their "entire agreement," that choice will be enforced. You often see clauses in agency and publishing agreements that say something like "This is the parties' entire agreement and it supersedes all previous discussions or agreements." If your contract contains a clause like this, it means that you can't go back to previous discussions or emails and say they're part of your agreement. If an agent or acquiring editor has said something important to you in an email and it's not in the final written document, ask for the contract to be redrafted to include it, or it won't be part of your agreement.

While these *entire agreement clauses* (also called *merger clauses* or *integration clauses*) may seem unfair, they're actually intended to avoid confusion about what you agreed to. If a term is written in the document, it's in the contract. If not, it's not part of the contract. There are some exceptions to this, often when clarifying ambiguities. Courts will sometimes look at typical conduct in an industry, or prior discussions between the parties, to clarify the meaning of something in the contract. However, generally speaking, if your agreement contains a merger clause, all the important terms should appear in that document. If not, the *parol evidence rule* prohibits a court from looking at a term outside the "four corners of the written document."

If your agency or publishing contract *doesn't* include a merger clause/entire agreement clause, it's much easier to argue that terms outside the final document, like things said in emails before signing the contract, are part of your agreement. However, most agents and publishers will include this clause in the final version of the document, so you can't argue that those other things are part of your contract.

perpetual commissions on deals Anthony had brokered for Morton, so Morton didn't owe Anthony any additional money. In fact, Anthony was ordered to pay Morton $500,000 because she had failed to handle the foreign sales of some of Morton's books appropriately.

This chapter focuses on traditional publishing contracts: contracts with agents and traditional publishing houses. Chapter 7 will turn to contracts you may sign as a self-published author, such as contracts with Amazon's Kindle Direct publishing program (often referred to as KDP). Because contracts are simply business agreements, they can be drafted pretty much however you want. As long as neither party has been fraudulent or deceptive, the agreement will likely be valid and enforceable. That's why it's a good idea to have an attorney—or agent—look over any contract before you sign it. Of course, before you *have* an agent you may have to rely on an attorney or legal consultant of some kind. We'll talk about who might advise you best, and most cost-effectively, in chapter 13.

Bear in mind that most author-agent contracts are relatively standard in terms of what they say, and they are usually no more than two or three pages. For publishing contracts—where the money is actually negotiated and rights are transferred—hopefully your agent will be a good advocate and help you obtain the most favorable terms possible from the publisher. You may still want to have an attorney look over a publishing contract, and that's okay. If anyone tries to pressure you to sign quickly without reading the contract properly, that's a red flag.

Note that a lack of negotiating power, which is typical when signing with an agent or publisher, usually isn't enough to convince a court that the contract was created through fraud, deceit, or duress. As long as you—the author—understood what you were signing, and the agent or publisher didn't trick you, or talk you out of seeking legal advice, or refuse to answer any of your questions (all red flags), the contract will likely be valid.

UNDERSTANDING YOUR CONTRACT IS
YOUR RESPONSIBILITY

It's important that you understand your contract, and it's your responsibility to make sure you do. If you understand what you're signing, it's very difficult to come back later and say you didn't mean to enter into an agreement on those terms. Best-selling romance author Mary Kuczkir, writing under the pen name Fern Michaels, learned this the hard way when she entered into an unfavorable (to her) contract with her then attorney, Martin Friedman, appointing him to additionally take on the role of her agent, when she parted ways with a prior agent. Under the terms of the new agreement, Friedman charged a flat fee for legal services connected with Kuczkir's publishing contracts as well as taking an 11 percent commission for publishing deals he brokered. Kuczkir tried to get out of the contract by saying it was unfair and that Freidman had taken advantage of her in securing her agreement to unfavorable terms. The court didn't agree. The judge said that even if the contract ultimately wasn't to her liking, she knew what she was doing when she signed the contract, and her attorney hadn't tricked her into signing it. In other words, you'll be held to the contract you signed in most cases, so make sure you understand what it says and what it means.

In the coming pages, I'll talk you through the kinds of terms you're likely to see in standard agency and publishing contracts. However, it's important to keep in mind that these contracts vary over time and between different authors, agents, and publishers. There's no single way to draft a contract, so you'll want to be aware of the basic terms you're likely to see in practice, but also appreciate how much these terms can vary from contract to contract.

WORKING WITH AGENTS

Let's start by talking about contracts with agents, because most traditionally published authors start out by securing an agent, who then sends their work out to publishers on submission. Some authors do it the other way around: get a publishing contract first and then look for an agent to negotiate the deal. That's fine too. As with everything else publishing-related, there's no "one size fits all" way to go about these things.

We've already talked a bit about the form of your contract with your agent—written or verbal or a combination of the two. We also noted that often you, as an author, especially if seeking your first agent, typically don't have nearly as much negotiating power as the agent. If the agent doesn't want to give you a written contract, you may have to decide whether you're happy with a verbal agreement or if you'd like to find another agent. Most verbal agreements these days are supplemented by some kind of writing, even if it's only a handful of emails or text messages.

Agents typically sign a client on the strength of a single manuscript, although some agents will want to look at, or talk about, your larger body of work before signing you. Make sure to ask whether the agency contract is limited to one book or will cover multiple projects. Will the agent continue to represent you if she doesn't sell your first project? Some agents will want to start with a single project, see how it goes, and then take it from there. That's not a bad way to start out. It gives both of you an easy out if the author-agency relationship doesn't work well.

Most agency agreements can be terminated by either party for any reason, perhaps with a notice period (e.g., two weeks, one month, or six months). Many agreements will include a fixed period, usually renewable, for the agency relationship to remain in place—for example, twelve months, which will automatically renew for another twelve months unless one of you decides to end the relationship.

It's probably not worth getting too worried about agreements that lock you in for a particular period unless that period is unreasonably long (say, five to ten years). You'll probably get a sense within the first six to twelve months whether your agent is committed to selling your work, how communicative she is, how responsive she is to your concerns, and so on. If the contract is for twelve months, or even eighteen or twenty-four months, that's probably fine. It usually takes about that long to work together on editing a project, sending it out on submission, and seeing how it goes.

Even if you want to terminate a contract before it formally expires, that's not usually a problem in practice. If the agency agreement isn't working well, there's generally nothing wrong with both of you (author and agent) agreeing to end things. The only situation in which an agent may not want to end the relationship at your request is if, say, she's in the middle of a submission round of your work. She may ask you to wait until that round of submissions plays out before ending your agency relationship. Of course, if she sells a manuscript during that time, you will be tied to her for that deal, even if you later move to another agent.

What Isn't in the Agency Agreement

You may have a lot of questions for your agent that won't actually be written down in your agency agreement, or at least not in any detail. That's generally okay, as long as you understand what is, and what isn't, a formal part of the contract. For example, your written contract may not specify exactly how many editors the agent will send your work to at a time, how often she'll pass on editor feedback to you, whether she'll give you a list of editors she's approached, and so on. In terms of the agreement itself, these issues will probably fall under a more general clause that says something along the lines of the agent promising to use her "best efforts" to sell your work.

These kinds of clauses leave a lot to the agent's discretion, but this approach also makes sense if you think about how hard it would be to draft

YOUR AGENT IS A FIDUCIARY

Literary agents are in a fiduciary relationship with clients because legally fiduciary duties apply to *all* agency relationships. In any situation in which someone acts as a formal legal agent for someone else (like a trustee or your investment adviser), they are a fiduciary and are legally obliged to act in your best interests. While literary agents don't often get sued for breach of fiduciary duties, it has happened. For example, in 1983, author Kitty Kelley successfully sued her agent, Lucianne S. Goldberg, in relation to claims of fraudulently misrepresenting the amount of royalties owed under a book contract Goldberg had brokered.

In 2013, graphic novel author Alex Grecian unsuccessfully sued his agent, Ken Levin, for breach of fiduciary duty (and breach of contract), arguing that Levin had put his own interests ahead of Grecian's when attempting to secure film and television deals for Grecian's work. Grecian argued that Levin appeared to be interested only in securing deals with production companies in which Levin himself had an interest and that he also wanted to receive a producer credit for the work. At the *summary judgment* stage (a point in the litigation before the full case is argued), the judge didn't feel there was enough evidence to support these claims.

In 2018, in a much-publicized criminal case, accountant Darin Webb, employed by the literary agency Donadio & Olson, was charged with fraudulently embezzling money from the agency's clients, including *Fight Club* author Chuck Palahniuk. Webb was tried and sentenced to two years in prison. The agency subsequently filed for bankruptcy. While this was a criminal action, and the agency subsequently went bankrupt, it likely had also infringed its fiduciary duties to its clients by not adequately supervising Webb's activities over client funds.

precise contract language that covers every single thing the agent might or might not do for you on a daily basis. Because agents will typically contract to use their "best efforts," and because they are also *fiduciaries*, courts will look at what "best efforts" means in practice in any given situation if a problem or legal dispute arises.

A fiduciary is a person who acts on behalf of another person in a relationship of trust and confidence. Literary agents owe fiduciary duties to their clients in the same way that company directors owe fiduciary duties to shareholders, and as investment advisers owe fiduciary duties to their clients. Fiduciaries are required by law to act in the best interests of their clients and not to make profits at their clients' expense. That doesn't mean they can't take money from their clients as compensation for their services, but it does mean they can't put their own financial interests ahead of their clients'.

Because literary agents' interests are generally closely aligned with their clients' interests, they usually don't face situations of putting their own interests ahead of yours. When you make money, they make money (by taking their commission). Their commission is their "skin in the game," so that's a good thing for you.

Commission

Standard literary agency agreements set out commissions usually around 15 percent for books sold in the North American market. The percentage will tend to vary on foreign market sales, because your agent will likely have to engage the services of a foreign agent or associate who will also take a commission on those sales. That additional commission will cut into your share of the pie, but hopefully this will be balanced out by the increased sales in those foreign markets.

The actual payments can be made in a number of ways. Sometimes a publisher will send all advances and royalties to your agent and she will cut

BAD AGENTS: WHAT'S A CLIENT TO DO?

We know that agents are fiduciaries and are supposed to act in their clients' best interests. What happens when something goes wrong? It doesn't happen often, but it does happen. In 2018, for example, the children's book publishing world was rocked when it came to light that literary agent Danielle Smith, who ran her own agency, Lupine Grove, had lied about submitting her clients' work to publishers and even about receiving significant offers, which she counseled clients to refuse. Some of her clients said that she even forged emails from editors, which she forwarded to them. The deceit allegedly went on for many years and affected a large number of authors. Ultimately, she closed her agency. She likely breached the "best efforts" clauses in her contracts, assuming she included those clauses. She definitely breached her fiduciary duties to her clients. She may also have broken general laws relating to commercial misrepresentation and deceptive conduct. What's the upshot for the clients? Unfortunately, these laws didn't help them out much.

Even if Smith had breached the law, what would the clients actually get if they sued her? How would they prove to a court how much money her deceptions cost them? There would be no way of showing how much money any client might have received if a deal had actually been made, or whether a deal would have been made if Smith had done her job properly.

This is why it's always a good idea to do your homework before you sign with an agent. Use online services like QueryTracker, AgentQuery, and Publishers Marketplace, or the magazine *Publishers Weekly,* to scope out agents with good reputations. If any agent offers you representation, talk to some of their other clients to get the lowdown, and look at *Publishers Weekly* and Publishers Marketplace and see what kinds of deals and how many deals they've made in recent years.

Unfortunately, doing your research isn't a cure-all. These steps likely wouldn't have helped Smith's clients, because she had a good reputation as an agent when she first started, and it was only later that her unethical conduct came to light. But if you do your homework, you lessen the chances of a problem down the track.

a check to you for your payment minus her commission. Some publishers will agree to make separate payments to you and your agent so that you get paid directly by the publisher (minus the commission, which the publisher sends to the agent). Some publishers will pay the entire royalty to the author, and then the author is responsible for sending the commission to the agent, although many agents might not agree to such arrangements.

Contracting with Multiple Agents

If you write in multiple genres, you may need to think about whether you need different agents for different genres. Many agents focus on particular market segments, such as nonfiction, mystery, romance, or books for young readers. If your agent doesn't represent some of the genres you write, you may want to consider having a second agent. For example, some authors who write both fiction and nonfiction have different agents because selling nonfiction is often quite different from selling fiction. Not all agents do both.

Many agents won't mind if you have another agent to represent something that she doesn't represent, but you should ask first before you seek another agent. Some agents prefer that you don't have another agent, and that's fine too, but you should both be up-front about what that means for you and your career. If your agent is at an agency with multiple agents working in different genres, she may be able to refer you to a colleague for work she doesn't represent herself. She may also be happy for you to submit your other work to publishers yourself if she doesn't want to submit it. Just try to stay on the same page, so to speak, to avoid bad feelings as a result of miscommunication or misunderstandings.

The End of the Agency Relationship

If you (or your agent) ultimately decide to part ways, there are a handful of things you should keep in mind, not the least of which is the perpetual commission issue mentioned in the Morton and Anthony example at the beginning of this chapter. For one thing, you want to know what rights and

WHAT ABOUT SEQUELS?

One very difficult issue that can arise if you leave an agent is what happens to negotiations and commissions in relation to sequels and other books included in the initial publishing contract—for example, a contract for a duology, trilogy, or other multi-book deal. The initial contract may oblige you to write the sequels or other books for the same publisher.

When your (first) agent negotiates the original deal, the agency agreement usually contemplates that she'll also take commissions on the later books covered by that original contract. You may be okay with that, because she brokered the original deal. However, the downside is that, if she's not your agent anymore when you write the second book, she may not have much interest in negotiating the contract and securing any better terms for you than you had in the first contract. She can simply take her commission for that next book without having to do any additional negotiating work. Your new agent won't be able to negotiate that contract either, because she's not the person who made the original deal.

It's a difficult problem and one I hope you never have to face, but if you do find yourself in this situation, it might be a good idea to call in a lawyer to see if you can (a) seek permission from the first agent for the new agent to negotiate new contract terms, and maybe share the commission between them; (b) have the lawyer negotiate the new contract on your behalf for a flat fee (and then the first agent would take the commission); or (c) come up with some other way around the problem, depending on the circumstances.

Many authors become frustrated because they assume (incorrectly) that their new agent can handle contracts for sequels or other books in multi-book deals negotiated by the prior agent. It can be a rude awakening to find out that this is generally not something your new agent will be able to do for you.

obligations you and your agent will have in relation to each other going forward, even after your agreement ends. It's likely that your agent will want to take ongoing commissions for deals she's brokered for you. You may also run into a situation where your agent hasn't sold a project and you want to take that project to a new agent. Questions may arise about who the prior agent submitted the project to, and whether she's obliged to disclose that information to you for the benefit of your new agent. If your new agent doesn't know who the old agent submitted the work to, she may end up sending it to the same people, which could be embarrassing for you and her.

These are issues worth thinking about when you first sign with an agent. No one wants to enter into an agency relationship assuming the worst, but you do have to plan for it. Try to get in writing some idea of what will happen at the end of the relationship, in terms of projects your agent has sold and those she hasn't.

WORKING WITH PUBLISHING HOUSES

While contracts with agents are likely to be only two or three pages long, contracts with publishing houses (after the agent makes a deal) tend to be longer. That's because these contracts deal with the specific rights you're selling or licensing to the publisher, as well as setting out your obligations in terms of preparing the manuscript for them.

The good news is that if you're working with an agent, she should be able to handle the negotiations and explain the contract to you. If you're not working with an agent, this is a good point in your career to think about either finding an agent or engaging the services of a lawyer—more on how to do that in chapter 13. Here, I'll set out the kinds of terms you're likely to see in a standard publishing contract, and the questions that you, or your agent or attorney, may want to raise about them.

Your publishing contract will usually cover the following issues, although not always in the most user-friendly way: (a) the rights you're giving to the publisher; (b) the obligations that you and the publisher have in relation to each other when preparing the book for publication and sale; and (c) procedural issues related to the contract itself—things like the entire agreement clause (see sidebar) and the law that governs the contract. (Many traditional publishing houses are based in New York, so many contracts are governed by New York law.) Sometimes this third category of clauses includes a mandatory arbitration clause saying you agree to take any disputes with the publisher through an *arbitration* process, an alternative form of dispute resolution outside court, which is often quicker and easier than litigation and also has the advantage of confidentiality. You may not realize this, but court proceedings are typically open to the public, and final judgments are publicly available. Going to court really is airing your dirty laundry in public.

What Rights Are You Giving to the Publisher?

You or your agent will likely spend the most negotiating time on the rights you're giving to the publisher. This is probably not something you should attempt on your own unless you're really comfortable with contract and copyright law. If you make mistakes here, or misunderstand what you're giving away, you may find yourself in trouble later if you realize you gave a lot more than you meant to.

You're definitely going to give the publisher a license or an assignment of the copyright in the book manuscript itself. Assignments of copyright that last more than five years are required to be in writing under copyright law, but all your publishing agreements will likely be in writing, so you don't have to worry too much about that particular quirk of the Copyright Act. You may need to think about whether to go with a *license* or an *assignment*—while they sound similar, and often work similarly in practice, they're legally not the same thing.

An assignment is basically an outright sale, as when you sell your car or your house to someone. Once you assign (or sell) the copyright, you don't own it anymore, and you can't dictate what the publisher can or can't do with your work. A license, on the other hand, gives permission to publish and distribute the book on the terms you set out in the agreement. Remember the kinds of licenses we talked about in the copyright chapters? Creative Commons licenses, for example, are licenses that allow other people to use your work without paying you any fees or royalties, provided that you follow the license terms—which may include, for example, a provision that you make your work available for free to others.

A general rule of thumb is to avoid outright copyright assignments and instead seek to give a license to the publisher. Outright copyright assignments are problematic because you've given away everything to the publisher and will have little say in what they do with your copyrights. Most publishers will agree to a license rather than a full assignment of copyright. One exception is academic publishing, where, at least in some academic fields like law, assignments are the industry norm. This makes a certain amount of sense if you keep in mind that most academics aren't expecting to make a lot of money from their academic publications. Their compensation comes from their academic positions. Academic writing is part of the job. It bolsters their professional reputations and helps with promotions, raises, and the like. The entire publishing model for academics is different than that for commercial nonfiction and fiction authors.

If you license your work to a publisher, which is typically what happens in commercial fiction and trade nonfiction, you also have to decide (or your publisher may dictate) whether the license is an *exclusive license*. An exclusive license is like an assignment of copyright, in the sense that the publisher will become the only person who can commercially exploit the copyright in the work—the license is exclusive to them. A regular license, one that is not exclusive, will allow you simultaneously to license the work, or particular rights in the work, to different people. That kind of license is not very common in book publishing, although you may see it when you publish short stories, personal essays, or freelance journalism.

Magazines and journals often don't require an exclusive license but may ask for *first publication* rights—the right to publish the piece before anyone else. Then, after that, you may be free to publish in other places without infringing the license you gave the first publisher. If, for example, you publish a short story in a literary magazine and later want to republish it in your short story anthology, you may have no legal problems if you only gave a first publication license to the magazine. The magazine may simply ask for attribution in the anthology (e.g., "This story first appeared in *The New Yorker*").

While you're definitely going to give your publisher rights to publish and distribute the work in book form, whether under a license or an assignment, there are lots of other rights you may or may not decide to give away. These include film and television adaptation rights; merchandising rights; rights to make prequels, sequels, or other derivative works based on your original manuscript; foreign rights—that is, rights to sell the work in markets other than North America; e-book and audiobook rights; rights to make editions for the print handicapped; and rights to make abridgments or condensations or to include your piece in an anthology.

Not all contracts deal with all of these rights. A lot depends on context: what you're selling and what kind of additional markets the publisher typically works in, outside of standard book publishing. These context-based complexities are why having an agent or attorney is a good idea at the negotiation stage.

A general rule of thumb is to give away as little as you reasonably can in the initial contract—or at least in the first pass of negotiations—on the theory that all the different rights can be worth significant amounts of money separately. Why give away *merchandising* or *world* rights up front when you could charge more for them later, perhaps at a later stage of the negotiations? Merchandising rights include the rights to sell toys and other paraphernalia based on the characters and situations in your book. World rights are the rights to publish the work globally.

FOREIGN RIGHTS VS. TRANSLATION RIGHTS

It's important to understand the difference between foreign rights and translation rights. While the two are related, they mean different things. *Foreign rights* are the rights to sell your book outside the North American market (which comprises the United States and Canada). *Translation rights* are the rights to sell your work in translation. For example, if you wrote your book in English, you may license your English-language rights to one publisher and your Spanish translation rights to another. It's likely that those Spanish-language editions would then be sold in Spanish-speaking countries, bringing foreign rights into play alongside the translation rights. However, that's not always the case. Translated versions of books are also sold in the United States. You've probably seen foreign-language translations of popular books at your local bookstore or library. Additionally, English-language versions are sold overseas—for example, there is a demand for English versions of books throughout Europe. So be careful, when talking about foreign and translation rights, that you understand fully which rights particular publishing houses may be asking for.

Another question you might ask is whether the publisher you're negotiating with can make the best use of the rights they're asking for. If your publisher has a large sales presence in North America but a limited record of selling in other markets, why give them foreign rights? You or your agent may find another publisher down the road who would be a much better candidate to sell your work in foreign markets.

Negotiating Royalties

Royalties can be another challenging area for an author to negotiate. While there are some industry standards in different fields, contracts vary between publishers, authors, and genres. This is another area where an agent or attorney can be invaluable in explaining how your royalties work, and how they'll be calculated under the contract you've been offered. Sometimes royalties are calculated with reference to the publisher's net profits (the money they make on selling your book after they've deducted their costs), sometimes they're based on the list price of the book (the book's regular retail price), and sometimes it's a combination of the two. Often the royalties are paid on a sliding scale. Your royalties may increase after a certain number of copies are sold.

While negotiating royalties is not for the faint-hearted and is best done with the assistance of an agent or attorney, some useful guidelines can be found online, including in a comprehensive free guidebook created by the Authors Alliance, *Understanding and Negotiating Book Publication Contracts*.[1] Also be aware that your royalties will likely vary depending on format: e-book royalties are often higher than royalties on traditional books. Royalties on audiobooks and other rights will also vary widely.

The Authors Alliance guide gives examples of the kinds of contract clauses you may see in your publishing contract that are related to different ways royalties can be calculated. For example, where the royalties are based on the retail price for the book, the royalties clause may look something like this:

> The Publisher shall pay the Author a royalty of ten percent (10%) of the retail price thereof on the Work.[2]

While this language sounds very jargony, it just means that the author will get a 10 percent royalty based on the retail price of each book sold. If, on the other hand, your royalty will be based on the overall income the publisher receives in relation to sales of your book, regardless of the price for which the book is offered for retail sale, the royalty clause may look more like this:

> The Publisher shall pay the Author a royalty of twenty percent (20%) of the revenue received by the Publisher attributable to the Work.[3]

The percentage may be higher here because it is based on the wholesale price at which the publisher sells books to distributors and booksellers, which will be a lower price than the retail price. If the retail price is twenty dollars, but the publisher sells the books to distributors for fifteen, the royalty here is based on what the publisher actually receives, so a higher percentage typically goes to the author than if royalties were calculated on the basis of the retail price.

There are many different ways to calculate royalties, and they may differ for different forms of the book (hardcover vs. paperback, e-book, audiobook, trade paperback, etc.). In practice, royalties clauses can be lengthy and complex.[4] The length and complexity of these clauses are a good argument for working with an agent, who can typically explain what's being offered and whether it seems reasonable under current industry standards.

Advances

An *advance* is an amount of money your publisher gives you up front, before the book goes into production. Your royalties are later deducted from the advance, so you don't actually get royalty payments until your book has *earned out* its advance. Typically, advances are paid in installments, usually two or three. The first installment is usually paid on signing the publication contract. The final advance is usually paid when you deliver the completed manuscript to the publisher. There may also be one or more interim advances, which are paid when you deliver certain portions of the book to the publisher prior to completion.

Because advances are actually part of your royalties—your compensation or payment for writing the book—your agent takes her commission out of both the advance and the royalties. For example, if you get a $10,000 advance on a book, and your agent takes a 15 percent commission, you'll actually get $8,500 in your pocket. Then neither you nor your agent will take any further payments until the book has earned out, at which point you start receiving royalties and the agent starts deducting her 15 percent commission from those royalties.

Many books never earn out, which means that technically you owe the publisher money. Many publishing contracts allow the publisher to ask you to return the portion of the advance that isn't earned out. It's not all that common for a publisher to actually ask for this money, but it can happen. Also, if something goes wrong in the publication process and the book doesn't end up being published, sometimes the publisher will ask for a return of the advance. Again, it's not all that common, but it does happen, especially if the reason for the failure of the book to go into publication (or distribution) is the fault of the author—for example, if the author doesn't finish the book or doesn't finish it to the satisfaction of the publisher.

A typical *advance clause* often looks like this:

> The publisher agrees to pay the Author as an advance against all Author's earnings accruing under the terms of this Agreement the sum of X, of which Y is payable on the signing of this Agreement and Z is payable on the delivery of the final manuscript.[5]

This clause (cribbed from the Authors Alliance's guidebook) is an example of an advance payable in two parts: the first when the author signs the publishing contract and the second when the author delivers the final manuscript to the publisher. This clause doesn't say anything about the return of the advance if the book doesn't earn out. The Authors Alliance points out that in most cases a publisher won't seek repayment of the advance if the book doesn't earn out, but will simply not pay any royalties. However, there are situations where a publisher may take repayment from sales of future books.[6]

Your Obligations to the Publisher

You'll find yourself agreeing to do, and not to do, certain things under the publishing agreement. For example, there will likely be something in the contract about your obligation to deliver a satisfactory manuscript to the publisher by a particular date. If you're a fiction writer and have already written the manuscript prior to submission, this won't be a big deal. However, if you're a nonfiction or academic author, you'll probably have a bit of writing to do before the delivery date comes around. Even if you're a fiction author, the publisher may have asked for revisions prior to delivery of the final manuscript.

The contract will also likely say something about what happens if you fail to deliver the manuscript on time, or if you deliver a manuscript that doesn't satisfy the publisher. If you fail to deliver at all, you might be able to negotiate an extended date. If you deliver something that doesn't satisfy the publisher, you may have to negotiate an opportunity to rewrite the manuscript if that's not in the original contract. The Authors Alliance guide includes information about your, and the publisher's, obligations to make sure that the publisher is satisfied with the manuscript you have delivered, and the options in place if the publisher is not satisfied.[7]

Some contracts will say that the publisher is permitted to find someone else to rewrite the manuscript if you fail to do so or refuse to do so. These are clauses you want to watch out for. Again, a good agent can help here. You want to be wary about handing creative control over your work to someone else, even though, ultimately, you probably will need to let the publisher have final say over the content of the manuscript prior to publication.

The same goes for editorial revisions during the production process. The contract will likely contain clauses about the extent to which the publisher can make editorial or other changes to your manuscript and the extent to which you get approval over those changes. These can be difficult situations, particularly for authors seeking to obtain creative control over their work, so it's important to make sure you understand what you're agreeing to up front to avoid misunderstandings later on.

The publisher will also likely get final say over the format, cover, and jacket design, and will likely arrange any additional artwork (unless you're

MORALITY CLAUSES

In the age of the #MeToo movement, several authors have found their agents or editors cutting ties with·them because they don't want to be associated with authors who have, or are getting, a bad reputation in the industry. Historically, contracts with agents and editors didn't contain clauses allowing for termination of the arrangement on morality grounds, so when an agent or editor wanted to stop working with an author, they relied on other contractual clauses. As we know, agents can usually cancel a contract for any reason with notice to the author. Publishers can rely on other clauses, such as clauses about not submitting satisfactory work to the publisher.

It can be difficult for an author to prove that the publisher actually canceled a contract because of morality concerns rather than concerns about satisfactory writing. For example, in 2017, Simon & Schuster dropped publication of an already announced autobiography by Milo Yiannopoulos because of concerns about comments the author had publicly made about pedophilia. Simon & Schuster said they had canceled the contract because they were not satisfied with the quality of the manuscript. Yiannopoulos sued Simon & Schuster, saying that the cancelation was based on the publisher's concerns about his public statements, not about the quality of his writing.

In the wake of #MeToo concerns, and of situations like that involving Yiannopoulos, many agents and publishers have started including *morality clauses* in their contracts with authors. These clauses typically state that the contract may be terminated if the author breaches acceptable professional standards of conduct. It's not clear how easy these clauses would be to enforce in practice because their terms are somewhat vague, especially in defining acceptable professional standards of conduct. However, the inclusion of these clauses in publishing contracts does shine some light on issues that have been of concern to the industry in recent years.*

* For more on morality clauses, see Jacqueline Lipton, "2018: The Year of the Morality Clause," Authors Alliance blog, June 6, 2018, https://www.authorsalliance.org/2018/06/06/2018-the-year-of-the-morality-clause/.

an author–illustrator or author–photographer, or otherwise providing your own art). You may want to ensure a clause in the contract that requires the publisher to consult with you on design and marketing issues, but they're unlikely to give you full veto power over these aspects of the production and marketing process.

The publishing contract will also likely require you to obtain all permissions and clearances to use any material quoted in your work that is protected by other people's copyrights, trademarks, or other interests. You'll likely also be asked to give the publisher an indemnity (promise to compensate them) if they're sued over anything in your book that, say, infringes a copyright or trademark or is defamatory or breaks any other laws.

You may want to try to negotiate with your publisher to limit your potential liability to nonfrivolous lawsuits (i.e., legal claims that have a reasonable basis). You may also want to see if you can carve out additional legal expenses from your indemnity—for example, by saying that if the publisher wins the case, you shouldn't have to compensate them for attorney's fees and other costs. You may also want to ask whether you can be covered by your publisher's legal liability insurance. Again, these are all difficult issues for which you might want to seek the advice of an agent or attorney. The free Authors Alliance guidebook cited above may also be useful on these issues.

Rights Reversion

Your publishing contract will—or at least should—explain at what point(s) your rights will revert to you. In other words, in what circumstances can you take back the rights you gave the publisher? If you assigned copyright outright, there may not be a rights reversion clause because you effectively sold everything you had to the publisher. That's another reason why outright assignments are to be avoided. You have to get the publisher to agree to assign the rights back if the publisher owns them under the original contract. There is a provision in the Copyright Act that allows for termination of a transfer with notice to the publisher, but it can't be exercised until thirty-five to forty years after the original transfer, depending on the context, so it's not all that helpful to authors who are concerned that a publisher isn't actively promoting or selling their book in the shorter term.

Most traditional publication contracts only contain licenses to the publisher, often exclusive licenses. It's easier to get a rights reversion in these situations. The contracts themselves usually set out the circumstances in which rights will either (a) automatically revert to the author or (b) revert to the author if the author gives notice or makes a request for reversion.

The most common rights reversion situation is where the publisher is no longer publishing or distributing the book. Traditionally this was referred to as the book being *out of print*. Today, however, with digital publishing, it's arguable that many books are never technically out of print, provided that an e-book or *print-on-demand* version remains available. With print-on-demand, a physical copy of the book isn't actually made until an order for a copy comes in. Digital printing technology enables this to be done fairly quickly and cheaply by storing electronic templates of the text and cover design that can be printed in response to an order.

Because it's hard to know today when a book is actually out of print, a lot of publishing agreements include an additional term explaining what "out of print" means—for example, if the book is no longer advertised in the publisher's catalogue or if a particular number of books hasn't been sold during a set period. This is something to watch out for in your contract. Make sure it's clear when the book will be considered out of print, so that you can get your rights back from the publisher—for example, so that you can self-publish or offer the book to another publisher.

WHO ARE THE PARTIES TO EACH CONTRACT?

Before we leave our discussion of traditional publishing contracts, it's worth adding a brief note about who is contracting with whom when an author, an

AGENTS AND SELF-PUBLISHED AUTHORS

It's becoming increasingly common for successful self-published authors to sign with agents to handle particular aspects of their work. For example, an agent may sell foreign rights or film and television rights for an author who has successfully self-published her work and wants to maintain creative control over the original work. Self-published author Hugh Howey, whom we met in chapter 5, writes about how important his team of foreign rights agents has been in expanding his career internationally.[*]

An agent may even expand domestic sales of a successful self-published author in the same geographical market as the self-published version. For example, agent Jane Dystel sold traditional publishing rights for Tammara Webber's self-published best seller *Easy* to Penguin in 2012.[**] Dystel also handles Webber's subsidiary rights, including foreign rights, in books Webber has self-published in North America.[***]

[*] Hugh Howey, "The Value of Awesome Agents," May 15, 2012, www.hughhowey.com/the-value-of-awesome-agents/.

[**] Jason Boog, "Tammara Webber Lands Two-Book Deal after Self-Published Bestseller,"October4,2012,www.adweek.com/galleycat/tammara-webber-lands-two-book-deal-after-self-published-bestseller/59556.

[***] Maryse's Book Blog, "An Interview with Tammara Webber," November 21, 2012, www.maryse.net/behind-the-books-interviews/behind-the-books-an-interview-with-tammara-webber.html.

agent, and a publisher are involved. Your contract with your agent is a simple author-agent agreement as described above, under which the agent agrees to represent your work to the best of her ability. You are not usually granting any rights to the agent in any of your work. You're simply giving the agent the right to act on your behalf to make deals. If the agent asks to own rights in your work, that may be a red flag, and may limit you in what you can do with that work later on if you move to another agent.

Your contract with a publisher is also a contract between you and one other person or company. Your agent is typically not a party to this contract, even if she has brokered the deal. She has no rights or legal obligations under that contract. All the legal obligations are between you and the publisher. The agent may sign the publishing agreement to acknowledge that she will receive notices and payments on your behalf, but she has no significant legal obligations or responsibilities under that contract.

Some agents have established small publishing companies through which they actually publish work of their clients in certain circumstances—for example, books they really believe in but can't find a publisher for in the traditional marketplace. Be careful, if you enter into these kinds of contracts, that you understand in what respects the agent is acting as an agent versus acting as a publisher. When the agent becomes your publisher, she may not owe you fiduciary duties in that capacity. You should make sure you have separate contracts for the agency arrangement and the publishing arrangement.

MOVING ON . . .

In the next chapter, we look at self-publishing contracts for those who want more creative and financial control over the publishing process. Remember that you don't necessarily have to choose between the two types of publishing. Many successful authors, like Hugh Howey and Tammara Webber, happily navigate a hybrid career involving elements of self-publishing and traditional publishing. If you have an agent and want to self-publish some projects, just make sure your agent is happy with this approach to avoid misunderstandings and problems down the line.

CHAPTER SEVEN

Self-Publishing Contracts

In July and August 2018, Amazon removed books by at least six self-published authors from its Kindle Direct Publishing (KDP) platform. One of the most popular and effective ways for an independent author to launch a career, KDP enables e-book sales through Amazon's Kindle Store. High-profile self-published author J. A. Cipriano, along with a number of other independent authors, learned that his books had been removed when he received an email from Amazon saying that his author account had been terminated due to manipulation of KDP services in breach of his contract with Amazon. Unable to sell books on Amazon, he was forced to find other, less far-reaching, avenues to distribute his books.

In July 2018, in a blog post addressing his fans, Cipriano wrote: "As some of you most likely have noticed, I am no longer published on Amazon—you'll find a few of my paperback titles, but not much more than that. Amazon severed our relationship without any useful information and no re-course [sic] of action for me to take. All that I know is I was kicked to the curb and it's not a great feeling."[1] Later in the post, he explained to his readers that he was struggling to figure out how to sell books in the wake of his problems with Amazon: "Over the past few weeks, I haven't been publishing anything new because I am trying to figure out my next steps towards getting you my books and I appreciate your patience and understanding. Once this mess is resolved, I'll be back to work."[2]

Cipriano was in an unenviable situation. In 2016, he had quit his day job to devote himself to full-time writing as an independent author. Two years later, he found himself with no steady income and with little explanation from Amazon as to specifically what had caused his account to be terminated. Attempts to obtain clarity from Amazon were met with form emails.[3]

Amazon heavily polices the KDP system and removes books from authors it thinks are trying to game the system. For example, the Kindle Unlimited program, part of the self-publishing platform, pays authors on the basis of numbers of pages read, rather than numbers of books sold. Theoretically, authors can manipulate that system by including bonus content at the end of their books, with a hyperlink at the beginning that readers click to go to the additional content. When a reader clicks the link, it looks like she's read the entire book when, in fact, she may only have read a few pages before going directly to the end. Another way of gaming the system is to program bots (simple pieces of software code) to "read" the books and rack up the page counts that way.

Under its contracts with KDP authors, Amazon reserves the right to remove books when it believes an author has acted improperly. The contract also covers the way Amazon deals with complaints and concerns when books are removed. The current agreement says that all disputes or complaints have to go to arbitration, rather than litigation in court, and on Amazon's terms. There's nothing inherently wrong with arbitration, as we mentioned in chapter 6, but it can be costly for an author if, say, Amazon requires them to go to Seattle (where Amazon's headquarters are located) to participate in an arbitration.

Amazon's contracts also prohibit class actions. This means that every author is effectively on her own, even if she has the same claim as a large group of other writers. Authors can't pool resources and fight a

Self-Publishing Contracts

court case together. If the matter does end up in court, Amazon requires the litigation to be in Seattle, which may be cost-prohibitive for many writers.

Where does this leave Cipriano, and others in similar situations? Amazon apparently believes that Cipriano gamed the system, although he says it hasn't provided specific details about the problem. Cipriano may have violated his Amazon contract, but there's no way to know for sure—it's a matter of private agreement between Amazon and the author. It is clear that Cipriano and many others face struggles in continuing as independent authors.

What's the lesson for the rest of us? Obviously, it's important to understand the contracts you're signing, whether with a traditional publishing house or a self-publishing platform. As an independent author, it's also important to appreciate the risks that may arise if you lose a major online distributor. At the moment, it's statistically true that the inability to sell on Amazon is likely to be fatal to an independent author's career. While self-publishing gives you the advantages of almost complete creative and financial control over your work, it does come with its own risks.

Moreover, while traditionally published authors typically have little bargaining power, especially early in their careers, those working with self-publishing platforms like Amazon typically have no bargaining power at all. They are generally faced with "take it or leave it" contracts, which may contain unfavorable or problematic terms.

This chapter examines some of the major legal challenges and advantages of self-publishing, focusing on the most popular platforms, like KDP and Smashwords (for e-books), Audible (for audiobooks), and KDP/CreateSpace or BookBaby for *print-on-demand* physical books. Print-on-demand is a system of publishing, enabled by digital technology, that allows a company to store digital files of your book and to create a hard copy when a customer places an order. It avoids the production and warehousing of large numbers of books that may not ultimately sell.

Many companies besides those listed above can help you prepare your book for publication. As with everything involving digital technology, this is a fast-moving sector—for example, both CreateSpace and Audible were independent companies before they were purchased by Amazon. As of this writing, CreateSpace has been completely subsumed into Amazon's KDP program, whereas Audible still has its own online presence separate from, but linked to, Amazon. When one company takes over another, the services offered and the prices charged for them typically change. Thus, it's difficult to talk in anything more than generalities about any given type of self-publishing. The key is always to look at the contract terms and prices offered by any service and do your best to understand them, even if it means hiring an attorney on a one-off basis to explain the contract to you.

Bear in mind that an attorney likely won't be able to negotiate terms of a self-publishing contract for you, because of the "take it or leave it" nature of these contracts. In legal jargon, these are *contracts of adhesion*, meaning that the author has no chance to negotiate the terms. Therefore, hiring a lawyer to explain those terms can be an expensive way to learn what your rights are under a contract you can't change. In chapter 13, we'll talk about some cost-effective ways to seek legal advice if you need it.

Be aware that many digital publishing and distribution platforms offer associated services like editing, formatting, cover design, marketing, and publicity. Again, you need to look at the contract offered and the levels (and kinds) of services to be provided at any particular price point in order to figure out what works best for you. The bottom line is that for authors who want to work independently, it's important to do your homework: read and understand the contracts, and get help if you need it; talk to others who have used the same companies; and check online reviews, if any, of the companies you're thinking of working with.

EVEN BIG-NAME AUTHORS CAN RUN INTO TROUBLE SELF-PUBLISHING

We've seen how removal of books by Amazon can be devastating for independent authors who rely on services like KDP for their livelihood. Even big-name, traditionally published authors can have problems when they venture online. In 2018, for example, *New York Times* best-selling author Cassandra Clare decided to launch a new self-publishing venture along with several of her writing partners, many of whom are also best-selling traditionally published authors. The plan was to self-publish, as e-books on KDP, a series of short stories related to Clare's well-known *Mortal Instruments* series. After self-publishing the short stories digitally, they would later be repackaged in a traditional volume and sold by Clare's publisher, Simon & Schuster.

Almost as soon as the first story was released for preorder on KDP, Amazon removed the listing, believing (wrongly) that a big-name author like Clare would never self-publish, and that someone else must have been impersonating her. Amazon relatively quickly re-listed the book after complaints by Clare and her fans. However, the disruption was significant, and Clare publicly raised concerns that the de-listing may have erased a large volume of preorders for the first story.[*] Independent authors aren't the only ones who face problems on popular digital platforms like KDP, although the costs are likely much more significant for them than for more established authors.

[*] Alex Green, "Cassandra Clare's Latest Book Temporarily De-Listed by Amazon," *Publishers Weekly*, April 9, 2018, www.publishersweekly.com/pw/by-topic/childrens /childrens-industry-news/article/76560-cassandra-clare-s-latest-book-temporarily-de-listed-by-amazon.html.

A NOTE ON TERMINOLOGY: *INDEPENDENT* VS. *SELF-PUBLISHED*

One thing that continually confuses authors, and everyone else for that matter, is the terminology of digital publishing, particularly terms like *independent author* and *self-published author*. Before the Internet and Amazon, an "independent author" was typically an author who published with a small independent press. These presses are a subset of traditional publishers, but outside the "Big Five."[4] In other words, they are smaller presses that usually publish fewer books per year, with smaller editorial staffs and perhaps more limited distribution. Many of these presses specialize in particular genres or have particular literary goals. For example, Graywolf Press, headquartered in Minnesota, describes itself as "a nonprofit publisher of fiction, nonfiction, poetry and genre-defying literature whose aim is to foster new thinking about what it means to live in the world today." More recently, the term *independent author* has also come to mean authors who self-publish their work. In this context, *independent* means independent of any traditional publisher, including the smaller independent presses.

If that isn't confusing enough, the Internet has also enabled many new, even smaller independent publishers to get off the ground, often focusing on e-book sales. These companies offer traditional-looking publishing and distribution contracts, but often on less favorable terms than a more traditional publisher. Sometimes the terms may *look* more favorable than a traditional publishing contract, but the newer publisher has much more limited marketing and distribution reach, which leads to lower overall royalties because of lower sales figures. Authors who publish with these companies, too, often call themselves independent authors.

In this chapter, I'll use the term *self-publishing* when I mean someone who takes complete editorial and financial control over their work, as compared with someone who works with a smaller independent press. However, I do occasionally use the term *independent author* when I'm talking about the

WHAT'S A "HYBRID AUTHOR"?

Digital publishing has caused us to rethink existing terms, like *independent author,* as well as to come up with some new terms for different models of authorship. One term that gets thrown around a lot, with little agreement on its meaning, is *hybrid author.* Usually, this term refers to writers who both self-publish and traditionally publish. For example, Hugh Howey, whom we met in chapter 5, started out as a self-published author and then moved into a more hybrid situation, with an agent and traditional publisher working on some of his projects. Sometimes an author starts out with traditional publishing and then writes a book or series that is too "niche" to attract a traditional publisher. In those cases, the author might become a hybrid author, sticking with publishing houses for work with wide-ranging commercial appeal and self-publishing other work. An example of an author who has done this is Liz Coley, who has successfully navigated both traditional publishing *(Pretty Girl 13)* and self-publishing with her *Tor Maddox* middle grade series and a number of other books. Another author who has taken a similar journey is A. G. Howard, author of the traditionally published best-selling *Splintered* series (reworkings of themes from Lewis Carroll's *Alice in Wonderland*) alongside the self-published *Haunted Hearts Legacy* gothic romance series.

Hybrid publishing can also refer to the somewhat unusual form of publishing in which a publisher shares both the up-front publication costs *and* the royalties with the author. This model is a hybrid between traditional publishing, where the publishing house covers the up-front costs and allots the author royalties on sales, and the pure self-publishing model where the author covers all the up-front costs and takes the lion's share of the royalties. One publisher that has been relatively successful with hybrid publishing contracts is John Hunt Publishing in the United Kingdom. John Hunt offers various levels of cost splitting with authors, including one publishing model that looks more like traditional publishing because the author pays nothing up front.

aspects of self-publishing that give an author more control over their work and their careers.

A good way to draw the line between self-publishing and the more ambiguous concept of the independent author is to note that, strictly speaking, self-published authors pay all publishing costs up front, even when working with a service that does the formatting, cover design, editing, marketing, and so on. In these cases, the author, while paying more up front, typically takes a much larger share of the royalties when the book is sold.

At the end of the day, it doesn't really matter what label you give yourself, as long as you understand your legal rights and obligations under any contracts you sign. This chapter focuses on those who self-publish in the sense that they control, and are generally paying for, all the publication costs and ultimately take a higher share in the royalties than under a traditional publishing contract.

BENEFITS AND CHALLENGES OF SELF-PUBLISHING: IS IT RIGHT FOR YOU?

Given the concerns about one-sided KDP contracts that I mentioned in the introduction to this chapter, why would anyone ever *want* to self-publish? The most obvious reason is to retain creative and financial control over your work. Authors who self-publish get a lot more control than traditionally published authors over things like the pricing, cover design, and format of the book; the timing of its publication; and the release and timing of new editions, revisions, prequels, and sequels. These independent authors don't have to worry about finding the perfect agent or the right publishing house, or fitting into anyone else's idea of what will sell in a particular market. *New York Times* best-selling author Jessica Park puts it this way:

> Publishers pay terribly and infrequently. They are shockingly dumb when it comes to pricing, and if I see one more friend's NY-pubbed ebook priced at $12.99, I'm going to scream. They do minimal marketing and leave the vast

THE STIGMA THAT HAUNTS SELF-PUBLISHING

There's still some stigma in the industry about self-publishing, although it's definitely waning. The negative view of self-publishing largely arose because of the similarities between early self-publishing and old-fashioned *vanity presses*—companies that published hard-copy books for authors, where the author covered the entire cost of publication. Authors then sold the books at events, books festivals, and out of the trunks of their cars. Because there was often little or no editorial oversight of this kind of work—and no established, accepted marketing channels for it—books published by vanity presses gained a relatively bad reputation. Today, some self-published books probably do resemble this model and may be of poor quality, while others are of terrific quality and are very successful.

If you're a successful independent author, you can probably pick and choose, down the track, whether you want to start working with an agent and/or a traditional publishing house, and you'll likely have a lot more bargaining power than a debut author. However, if your self-published books don't do well, they're unlikely to get you in the door at traditional publishing houses. In other words, if your reason for self-publishing is that you're getting a lot of rejections from agents and traditional editors, you may want to think hard before you decide to self-publish. If the agents /editors are rejecting your submissions because they think your writing needs more work, you may need to hone your craft first, rather than releasing books that aren't as good as they could be into an already competitive self-publishing marketplace. If, on the other hand, the agents/editors think your work is strong, but too "niche" to appeal to a wide market, it may be a good idea to self-publish. Self-publishing may help you find whatever market is out there, even if that market isn't big enough to attract a traditional publisher.

majority of work up to the author. Unless, of course, you are already a big name author. Then they fly you around the country for signings and treat you like the precious moneymaking gem that you are. The rest of us get next to nothing in terms of promotion. If your book takes off, they get the credit. If it tanks, you get the blame.[5]

Clearly, tempers run high and attitudes vary widely about the benefits and perils of self-publishing. When asked to weigh in on the controversy involving the removal of Cipriano's and others' work on KDP, Park acknowledged that Amazon isn't perfect. "There are some people who abuse the Kindle platform, and that's slimy," she told a journalist. "But some of these cases sound to me like KDP has misinterpreted something or is not communicating well, and it's shutting off accounts with insufficient explanation. They [Amazon] built this world to let people publish and encouraged them to get their work out there. So I really don't know, but I am frustrated for them if they've truly not done anything wrong."[6]

Now that we've covered the pros and cons of self-publishing as a commercial matter, let's turn to some of the legal issues that can arise in this context. We'll start out with e-books as the most popular form of independent publishing and then move on to print-on-demand and self-published audiobooks.

SELF-PUBLISHING AN E-BOOK

If you self-publish, you can choose which formats to sell (e-book, audiobook, and/or print). There's no rule that you have to sell your book in all possible formats. Many independent authors rely solely on e-book sales. You don't have to be an expert in self-publishing to know that Amazon is the clear market leader here. While there are other services like Smashwords and Draft2Digital, it's Amazon that holds the lion's share of the e-book market, controlling an estimated 70 percent of all e-book sales.[7]

No matter which company you deal with, you'll be asked to agree to their terms of service, often by simply clicking a button that says "I Agree." Even if this doesn't feel sufficiently formal to make a contract, it is legally binding, so it's important that you read and understand the terms offered, and think about whether they'll work for you.

One of the major issues to be aware of in these contracts is that most of them say the service provider—whether Amazon or anyone else—can change the contract terms in the future without consulting you. They usually send you notice of an update and/or make it available on their website, but there's generally nothing legally wrong with a contract that allows a service provider to change the terms at its own discretion. Think about the contracts for your bank accounts, insurance, or cell phone service. They generally do the same thing, and it's typically legally enforceable.

We've already mentioned some of the potentially problematic terms of the KDP publishing contract—for example, the idea that you commit to arbitration rather than litigation and that, if you litigate, you have to appear in court in the State of Washington and you can't bring a class action against Amazon. There's nothing inherently illegal about any of these terms. Courts will generally uphold terms like this even though they are very favorable to the service provider. Lack of bargaining power is not typically regarded as sufficient to challenge these contracts legally, so it's hard to argue that you didn't understand the contract or that you weren't given an opportunity to negotiate. In most cases, courts won't accept those arguments unless you can show that the service provider tricked or deceived you in some way. If they made the terms available to you up front and you "agreed" to them (by clicking the "I Agree" button), that's not regarded legally as fraud, deceit, or trickery.

Some courts have even suggested that these "take it or leave it" contracts ultimately benefit customers. The idea is that if companies had to agree to, say, go to court in any state in which a customer made a complaint, this would be very costly for the company, and it would ultimately pass on those costs to consumers through higher fees or lesser services.

Besides the clauses about arbitration and litigation, self-publishing contracts will include clauses covering many of the issues we reviewed in chapter 6 in relation to more traditional publishing contracts—for example, who bears legal liability in the case of a copyright or defamation claim (typically you do as the author) and who owns the copyright in the work (again, typically you do). In terms of legal liability, under self-publishing contracts, the author typically promises the self-publishing platform that the book doesn't infringe anyone else's legal rights, including intellectual property rights, such as copyrights and trademarks.[8]

In terms of copyright licenses/permissions, self-publishing platforms won't usually take *any* assignment or license of the copyright, except to the extent that they need your permission to distribute your copyrighted work online. This permission usually takes the form of a nonexclusive license to distribute the book digitally. For example, at the time of this writing, the KDP terms of service refer to a "nonexclusive, irrevocable right and license" to distribute e-books (as well as to make and distribute print-on-demand versions of books). Smashwords' terms of service similarly talk about the grant of a "nonexclusive worldwide right to digitally publish, distribute, market and sell" an author's books. In all cases, the author retains copyright in the work. The digital platform only gets a license to distribute the work online for the author.

Like traditional contracts, self-publishing contracts will also contain clauses about how royalties are calculated and paid. The key difference is that the share of royalties given to the author by, say, Amazon is significantly higher than under a traditional publishing contract. While the royalty scales vary, Amazon generally gives authors around 70 percent of the royalties, as opposed to the 5–12 percent you'll likely see in traditional publishing contracts. Traditional publishing contracts typically include varied rates for different formats. For example, those 5–12 percent rates may apply to physical books, and there may be a somewhat higher rate for e-books. Comparing Amazon to traditional publishers on royalties is a bit like comparing apples and oranges. Amazon's share of the profits might best be thought of as a fee for its distribution services. Bear in mind also that with self-publishing, you won't have an agent taking a commission out of your royalty payments. Different e-book distributors may offer special promotions or contractual terms from time to time that could affect your decision whether or not to launch your next book with them. For example, Amazon has had significant success with its KDP Select program, which is a part of KDP that requires authors to pull their books from all other e-book retailers in return for additional marketing and promotion initiatives by Amazon. If you sign up for these kinds of programs, you need to ensure that you follow their instructions, or you may risk termination of your account and removal of your books from their platform.

Another big difference between self-publishing and traditional publishing is that a self-published author gets to choose the sale price for her books and can usually change the price over time, or vary it from country to country. Most e-book publishing platforms allow the author to control these functions. KDP and Smashwords, for example, both give authors advice on their FAQ pages about how most effectively to price their e-books and how to deal with sales tax in different countries.

What E-book Platforms Don't Do for You

Independent authors who self-publish e-books are responsible for their own text formatting and cover design. Mark Coker, the founder of Smashwords, has provided a list of recommended and affordable formatting and cover-designing professionals for authors using Smashwords.[9] Remember, this is something that your publisher takes care of for you if you pursue the traditional publishing route. As noted in the previous chapter, you may not have final approval over formatting and cover design with traditional publishing, but you also don't have to organize and pay for these things yourself.

If you're thinking of working up your own cover design, keep in mind that you can't take any old image you find on the Internet and use it on your cover without ensuring you have appropriate permission. Remember what we learned in chapter 1: just because something is on the Internet doesn't automatically mean that it's in the public domain. Even if the image is available under a Creative Commons license, make sure you check that the terms of the license don't prohibit its commercial use. Using the picture on a book you sell commercially, even if you don't make a lot of money from it, is a commercial use. If you're confused about the public domain or Creative Commons, go back to chapter 1 for a refresher. You can also take a look at chapter 12, which focuses specifically on photographic permissions. Keep in mind that using someone else's art on your book without permission is unlikely to be a fair use because it's a commercial use that may well cut into the artist's market for the work. If you need a refresher on fair use, take a look back at chapters 4 and 5.

In self-publishing, you also have pretty much complete editorial control over your work. While most self-publishing platforms will have some rules about content, including not infringing other people's legal rights, and often some restrictions on areas like erotic content,[10] generally you have the final say over your manuscript. Of course, along with this control comes great responsibility. If the book is messy and filled with typos, it's all on you.

Self-published books in general, and e-books in particular, can be released whenever the author wants to release them. As soon as your book is formatted for your platform, you're good to go. You don't have to wait out an entire publication process. Of course, this means that you also have to gauge the best time to release your work. If it's a holiday book, you may not want to release it in July; if it's more of a summer read, you may not want to release it in the dead of winter. Again, you're in control of your own publishing journey, but that means you have to do your own research about formatting, cover design, marketing, pricing, and so on. This is appealing to many authors, but overwhelming to others. There's nothing inherently right or wrong about choosing to take one publishing path over another, or to go with a combination of traditional and self-publishing. The key is to understand what each demands of you and to be equal to the challenges.

PRINT-ON-DEMAND

Print-on-demand is an option you may want to consider as a self-published author. It enables you to sell hard copies of your book, usually through the same channels you use to sell your e-books. For example, Amazon offers distribution of print-on-demand versions of KDP authors' books. In order to take advantage of the print-on-demand option, Amazon requires its authors to do a little more work than is required to prepare an e-book for release. For example, a print-on-demand book will need a full cover with a spine, as well as a standard page size, and proper spacing of inside and outside margins. The formatting for hard-copy books obviously has to be a little more precise than that for e-books, which are only intended to be read on e-readers. Other service providers, like BookBaby, offer packages to help with formatting, cover design, distribution, and so on. BookBaby also provides its authors access to more than fifty additional distribution channels, including Amazon, Barnes & Noble, and Books-A-Million.

While it's not possible to cover the contract terms for each company that provides print-on-demand services, especially as the nature of the market is changing so quickly, it is worth noting some of the key elements common to current print-on-demand services. Most of these services basically piggyback on existing online distribution channels. Even though BookBaby says it can get your books into bookstores, the choice of what, say, Barnes & Noble will actually put on its shelves is up to that company's buyers. When a print-on-demand service offers you broad and global distribution of physical books, it typically means physical books ordered via online services. That's not nothing. Many readers who look for books on Amazon or Barnes & Noble online would prefer a physical book to an e-book, so the availability of print-on-demand books through these services may be worth the extra money or effort it takes you to prepare a physical version of your book.

If you are considering adding print-on-demand books to your e-book list, the best advice is to compare and contrast the currently available print-on-demand services, including checking their prices, how much help they'll give you with formatting and design, whether they'll send you physical or only digital proofs to approve before they sell any books for you, where and how they will distribute your books, and how quickly customer orders are likely to be fulfilled. Of course, you can also order print-on-demand copies of your books for your own stash to sell at events and book festivals, but that's unlikely to be your main source of revenue for the hard-copy books unless you do a lot of events that garner large crowds.

SELF-PUBLISHING AUDIOBOOKS

If you're already daunted by the idea of figuring out how to self-publish e-books, it may be overwhelming to think about the possibility of producing and distributing your own audiobook, but the technology and service providers are there if you want to try it. There is some evidence that audiobooks are a growing market for independent authors. As with most digitally based publishing platforms, Amazon is currently the leader of the pack with audiobook production and distribution. Amazon owns Audible, which is by far the leading retailer of audiobooks.

Audible provides services for independent authors who want to produce their own audiobooks and sell them online through its ACX platform (see www.acx.com). Audible gives you the option of narrating your own book or hiring a narrator. There are different royalty-split options available on Audible depending on whether you share royalties with a narrator, hire a narrator on a flat fee, or narrate your own book. Typically, Audible takes around 60 percent of the royalties and the rest are for you to split with a narrator or take yourself, if you either narrate the book yourself or pay your narrator a flat fee. Audible audiobooks are made available on Audible's own website as well as on Amazon's website and iTunes.

Audible isn't the only game in town for self-publishing audiobooks. Companies like Findaway Voices, ListenUp Audiobooks, and Author's Republic offer services to help authors produce and distribute audiobooks.

They typically also rely on the distribution channels used by Audible—that is, Audible, Amazon, and iTunes. However, they also distribute on other platforms that do not yet have the traffic that those "big three" have.

As with e-books and print-on-demand, the different kinds of contracts and their terms are too many and varied to cover in a single chapter. Additionally, they change rapidly as the market evolves. However, there are a few main ways in which contracts for self-produced audiobooks will differ from contracts for e-books and print-on-demand, and it's worth keeping an eye out for them when you consider contracting with any of these services.

For one thing, if you're producing your own audiobooks, you need to decide whether or not to hire a narrator. If you do, you'll be entering into a separate contract with that person for her services. At the moment, these contracts tend to be based on hourly rates for narration work, and you typically get a chance to audition potential narrators through a number of the services mentioned above. The contract with the narrator will need to make clear how much you'll pay, whether the narrator will receive a flat fee or share in the royalties, or both.

You probably also want to make clear in your contract that the narrator will receive no share of the copyright and will not be regarded as the author or copyright owner of any aspect of the audiobook. The ability of a narrator to assert authorship rights or copyright in an audiobook is unclear under American law, so it's not a bad idea to make this clear in your contract to avoid any doubt. If you use a standard audio-narration contract provided by one of the audiobook services like Audible, make sure it includes a term that states that the narrator is providing services on a work-for-hire basis and will not hold any copyright in the finished product. (If you're confused about work for hire, take a look back at chapter 3.) The current Audible contract does include provisions that protect the author's copyright in this way.[11]

If you narrate your own work, you don't have to worry about contracting with a narrator, but you will have to invest in appropriate recording technology and make sure you're confident that you can produce a recording that meets the standards set by whichever online distribution platform you're working with. These services, like Audible, typically have quite stringent requirements for finished recordings, related to things like sound quality, the length of the audio files, the inclusion of appropriate opening and closing credits, and the provision of a retail audio sample for customers. If you hire a narrator to read your book, typically the narrator has her own recording equipment and should ideally be familiar with the quality requirements of the audiobook distributors.

You may also want to make sure that you have the right to request a certain number of edits or revisions from your narrator if the work doesn't meet your satisfaction or the production requirements of your chosen audio distribution service(s). The current Audible contract requires the author and narrator to work in good faith on revisions and suggests that the narrator will make up to two sets of revisions to the first fifteen minutes (as well as revisions to the entire audiobook) at the author's request. The contract gives the narrator up to ten business days to make the revisions.[12]

The royalties you'll receive under a self-published audiobook distribution agreement with Audible, and most of the other companies mentioned above, are significantly less than those you'll receive on self-published e-books: usually 25–40 percent, depending on the distribution arrangement. Audiobooks are priced higher than e-books, though, so this can still be a decent amount of money. But you'll want to decide if the figures work for you.

Currently, Audible prices its audiobooks largely on the basis of their length and doesn't give authors the option of setting the price of their own audiobooks. This is a significant difference from self-published e-books on KDP, where authors can set their own prices. Audible generally estimates that a five- to ten-hour recorded book will be sold for fifteen to twenty dollars, a ten- to twenty-hour recording for twenty to thirty dollars,

ISBNS AND BARCODES

When I present workshops on legal aspects of self-publishing, someone usually asks me a question about ISBNs. These are the numbers, usually paired with barcodes, that uniquely identify books and, in particular, separate editions of books. They're used for marketing, cataloguing, and associated purposes. There is no particular legal effect attached to ISBNs. The system was created by the International Standards Organization (ISO). The ISO, headquartered in Geneva, Switzerland, coordinates with national standard-setting bodies to create uniform global standards for various industries. Today, individual ISBNs or blocks of ISBNs are sold by various agencies around the world. Usually each agency is dedicated to books sold in a particular territory. The US ISBN Agency is the official source of ISBNs for books sold in the United States and several of its territories.

Traditionally published authors don't have to think about ISBNs, because they are provided by publishers who purchase them from the ISBN Agency. Now, with all the newer self-publishing platforms emerging, independent authors often do have to obtain their own ISBNs because they are, in effect, their own publishers, and it's generally the publisher that's responsible for securing the ISBN.

Some independent publishing services, like Amazon, have their own systems, which are similar to ISBNs but don't work outside the respective service's platform. For example, if you self-publish e-books on KDP, Amazon automatically assigns you an ASIN (Amazon Standard Identification Number), which categorizes the book in the same way as an ISBN, but only for Amazon's distribution network. Thus, you may want to think about purchasing your own ISBNs as well, particularly if you publish outside Amazon. You can purchase your own ISBNs directly from Bowker, which is the official US ISBN Agency partner. Bowker provides you with a simple online contract: you provide information to them about your work, and they send you the ISBNs for it, along with the associated barcodes.

(Continued)

and books over twenty hours for up to thirty-five dollars. These are only current estimates provided by Audible, which retains full discretion on pricing.[13]

Another issue to be aware of with self-published audiobooks is that you must ensure that you have the audio rights before you go ahead and record. If you're a solely independent author, in the sense that all your work is self-published, this won't be a problem because you likely won't have assigned or licensed copyrights in any of your work to anyone else. Even if you self-publish on KDP, you retain your copyright as mentioned earlier in this chapter. However, if you have previously published some of your work traditionally and licensed or assigned copyrights, you need to make sure you have retained audiobook rights before you self-produce an audiobook version, or that you can get those rights back in order to produce your own audio version.

For example, if you have published a regular book version of your work or even published short stories in magazines, check that you haven't signed away any of your audio rights in the process. If your prior work is out of print, and you assigned audio rights when you originally sold it, don't assume you can automatically make an audiobook without securing a *rights reversion* (in other words, getting your rights back from the original publisher). Any contract you sign to self-publish an audiobook via Audible or any other service will likely require you to promise that you hold rights to make the audiobook, and you'll probably have to indemnify the service if you don't in fact hold those rights and an earlier publisher complains or threatens litigation.

Another trick with audiobook contracts is that the length of the contract term may be much longer than for, say, an e-book or print-on-demand arrangement. Audible currently takes a seven-year minimum distribution right for work sold through its services, so be aware that if you want to engage with the biggest audio distributor, you will be locking yourself in for a significant amount of time. By contrast, Amazon's KDP program allows you to withdraw e-books from distribution with five days' notice.

The bottom line if you're thinking about self-publishing audiobooks is that it's typically a larger commitment of time and money up front when compared to other forms of self-publishing (e-books and print-on-demand). The royalties are lower percentage-wise, but the retail price of audiobooks is much higher, so you'll have to make some calculations about whether it's worth trying out this publishing avenue. And it's worth repeating: if you go with the biggest player (Audible/Amazon), you will be locked into a seven-year distribution arrangement and they will control the pricing of your books.

MOVING ON . . .

While it's not possible to give a comprehensive explanation of every contract term you might see as a self-published author, hopefully this chapter has given you some direction about the main points to look out for in these contracts. In the next chapter, we turn to the often mystifying area of protecting author brands and reputations online, and the relevance of trademark law to authors. While legal issues related to author brands and trademarks don't come up nearly as often in practice as questions related to copyrights and contract terms, they do occasionally rear their ugly heads, so it's worth understanding the basics.

Protecting Your Author Brand

Trademark Basics

In April 2018, romance author Faleema Hopkins notoriously registered the trademark "Cocky" for her book series about the "Cocker Brothers." She then threatened, and ultimately sued, other romance authors for using the term in their book titles, arguing that their titles infringed her trademark. There was an uproar in the writing community and many questions were raised, such as:

Can an author register book or series titles as trademarks?
(The short answer is yes, but mainly for book *series*
titles.)

Can a fairly common word like *cocky* be protected as a trademark?
(Again, the answer is yes, but the word has to be sufficiently
distinctive.)

If these words can be registered as marks, do they have to be registered
in a particular font or color? (The answer is no. You can register a
simple word by itself as well as registering a version of it in a
particular size, font, color, etc. Hopkins had registered a stylized
version of "cocky" as well as the basic word.)

After unsuccessfully suing other authors, Hopkins ultimately surrendered her registration of the mark, so at least the Cocky situation is resolved. In early stages of the litigation, a judge suggested that if her trademarks were valid, they gave her little protection, because they were not particularly distinctive of her romance brand. They didn't distinguish her series from other romance series very effectively. However, the situation raised many questions, and generated a lot of misinformation, throughout the writing and publishing community, about what trademarks are and what they aren't, and how they apply (or don't) to our work as authors.

Trademark law is a little more complex in the United States than in other countries, because most other countries have *registration-based systems*, meaning that registration of the mark gives you trademark rights. The United States, by contrast, has a *use-based system*, in which ownership of a mark doesn't require registration. The American trademark system is similar to the copyright system in this way: there is a register, but you can own a mark you haven't registered. By the same token, registration isn't a guarantee of valid ownership. Rather, ownership of a mark is based on its *use* as a mark— you can't own a mark that you're not using commercially, regardless of whether you've tried to register it with the US Patent and Trademark Office (USPTO). Like copyright law, registration does give you certain advantages (like presumptions of ownership), so it's a good idea to register your marks. However, as we'll see, there are not many things authors can actually trademark. We'll talk about how to establish trademark *use* later in this chapter, but in short, if you can show that you're using a word, phrase, logo (etc.) as a trademark, you can claim ownership whether you're registered or not.

This chapter is about the application of trademark law to what we do as writers: when and how we can use marks to protect our brands, and how to make sure we don't infringe other people's trademarks. I'm also going to talk a little about other legal methods for protecting your author brand outside of trademark law, including aspects of unfair competition law, contract law, and a tiny bit of copyright law. Before we get into all that, we need to understand what a trademark is and how you can own a mark in the American legal system.

WHAT'S A TRADEMARK ANYWAY?

A trademark is technically a source identifier. All this means is that it's a word, phrase, logo, or other identifier that distinguishes one person's, or business's, products or services from another's. For example, when you see the big golden arches, you know you're at McDonald's, not Burger King. When you see sneakers with a distinctive swoosh on them, they're probably Nikes, not Adidas. That's basically what a trademark does: it serves as a signal to customers whose goods or services they're buying. It doesn't matter whether it's a word, a phrase, a symbol, or some combination, provided that the mark identifies the source of a particular product or service. In the United States, you can also register scents, sounds, and colors as trademarks. Think about the three distinctive NBC chimes. They're registered as a sound trademark (or sound mark).

Given the wide range of things that can be trademarked, you should now see why it doesn't matter whether an author tries to register a *stylized* version of a word or phrase as a series title, or simply the word or phrase itself. The real question is whether the word or phrase distinguishes her books from those of other authors, however it's visually presented.

REGISTERING A TRADEMARK
IN MORE THAN ONE COUNTRY

As with all intellectual property rights, there's no truly international trademark law. There are international treaties about trademarks, including the Paris Convention and the TRIPS Agreement, and there have been attempts to globally harmonize the trademark registration system to make it easier to register trademarks in multiple countries (see sidebar). Remember that most

TRADEMARKS VS. COPYRIGHTS

Some people confuse trademarks with copyrights. This is an easy mistake to make because they're both part of what lawyers call *intellectual property* (or *IP*). However, the two are quite different. Trademarks protect brands by helping customers identify the source of products or services, while copyrights protect the expression of a work, to ensure that the copyright owner receives economic rewards for licensing or selling it. Copyrights are limited to the author's life plus seventy years, as we saw in chapter 1, while trademarks can last indefinitely, so long as they continue to be *used as marks*.

Trademark protection is limited to the market for the particular goods or services the mark is associated with. This means that two or more people can own the same trademark in different geographic markets or different product markets. For example, the mark "Delta" is registered for both faucets and a major airline.

Copyrights protect most of what we do as writers. Copyright law protects the actual words we write against unauthorized copying. Trademarks, on the other hand, protect very little of what writers do. In the publishing industry, the biggest role for trademarks is for book *series* titles. Trademarks don't protect the words inside the book. Still, we often have to be careful about not infringing other people's trademarks—for example, if we want to write about a character who loves drinking Coke or driving a Porsche. We'll talk about those problems later in this chapter.

countries have registration-based trademark systems, which means that you must register the mark in those countries to own it. If you want your trademark protected in the United Kingdom, you have to register it there. To protect it in Canada, you have to register it in Canada. On the other hand, for your trademark to be protected in the United States, you have to *use* it before you can register it.

INTERNATIONAL TRADEMARK REGISTRATION

While there's no international trademark system, there have been attempts to streamline the trademark *registration* process internationally. If you hear someone talking about the Madrid System or the Madrid Protocol, that's what they mean. Those are two versions of an international attempt to help businesses register marks in multiple countries. The idea is to create a one-stop registration process for a trademark application that names all the countries in which the business wants to register the mark. The applications are then sent automatically to all the named countries for independent processing. Each country still makes its own decision on the validity of the mark, but at least the initial application process is easier.

These systems apply only to countries that have signed on to the treaties. The United States signed the Madrid Protocol, but not the earlier Madrid Agreement (which was the beginning of the Madrid System). If you apply to register a mark in multiple countries, either individually or under the Madrid System, there's no guarantee that each registration will be granted. For example, if your trademark conflicts with someone else's mark in the same or a similar market in a particular country, the application for that country may be denied. Some countries also don't allow trademarks to be registered for certain words, phrases, logos, and so on. For example, in the United Kingdom, there have always been prohibitions on registering marks corresponding with certain royal symbols (e.g., coats of arms). In the United States, there are restrictions on registering national and state flags as trademarks.

American law does allow *foreign trademark holders* to register marks here without using them first. This is a result of international treaties that cater to the needs of trademark holders in countries that don't require use to own a mark. The theory is that it would be unfair to expect, say, a Canadian trademark holder who owns a valid Canadian trademark to have to use it in the United States before registering it here.

TRADEMARK REGISTRATION
IN THE UNITED STATES

In the United States, you can't register a mark until you've used it for at least six months. When you apply for registration with the USPTO, you have to provide evidence of your use. Trademark examiners check to verify that you are making a genuine trademark use before they grant the registration. Because you have to provide evidence of use, and you have to identify relevant markets in which the mark is used, registration applications are much more complex for trademarks than for copyrights. While you don't need a lawyer to help you with a copyright registration (see chapter 1), you probably do need legal assistance if you want to register a trademark.

Trademark registration is also more expensive than copyright registration. As of this writing, a basic registration costs just under $300, not including attorney's fees, and the USPTO often asks follow-up questions to clarify issues like the particular market(s) in which you want to register the mark. There are also different market classifications—trademark attorneys know them well, but they may be confusing to the rest of us. If you hire an attorney, she'll charge for her work, but once you're already looking at the significant expense of registration, it may be worth the extra cost for the attorney's time and expertise.

Keep in mind that authors won't often have to deal with trademark registration because there's really not all that much we can trademark. We can't generally trademark our names or single book titles. The situation where an author is most likely to succeed in registering a trademark is for a book series title, like *Thomas the Tank Engine* or *Harry Potter*, because the series itself is an identifiable set of products from a particular source.

In January 2019, Chooseco LLC, publisher of the *Choose Your Own Adventure* series of interactive books and owner of the "Choose Your Own Adventure" trademark, sued Netflix for infringing its trademark in an episode of the science fiction series *Black Mirror* entitled *Bandersnatch*. The episode features a video game designer who says his work is based on a "Choose Your Own Adventure" book, fictionally titled *Bandersnatch*. Chooseco was concerned about the unauthorized use of the mark in an episode that links it with violence, drugs, murder, and mutilation of a corpse, among other things.

As this example demonstrates, the right to protect trademarks in book series titles can be important in the film and television licensing context, and is also important for merchandising (dolls, toys, games, etc.). Most of us don't ever get this far with our work. Anyone who does should probably consult an attorney for advice about registering trademarks and protecting the series' brand. While we've gone through a lot of nuts and bolts thus far about trademark law in the United States, the sad truth is that the law probably won't do much for you as an author—unless you create a popular book series.

REGISTERING A TRADEMARK BEFORE YOU USE IT: INTENT-TO-USE APPLICATIONS

I've already noted that you have to *use* a trademark to register it in the United States, but of course there's an exception. While you can't formally register a mark on what's called the *principal register* (the register of granted trademark rights) in the United States, you can register an *intent-to-use* (ITU) application on the *supplemental register*. This sounds like what it is: you are reserving your right to use the mark and will be granted registration on the principal register if you establish trademark use within six months of the ITU application. At that point, your mark moves from the supplemental register to the principal register, and your registered trademark rights date back to when you registered on the supplemental register. The ITU application system in the United States is largely an attempt to accommodate international treaty requirements. An ITU registration doesn't give you actual trademark rights, but it does put others on notice of your intention to register the mark, and of the markets you plan to register in. If your mark is later moved to the principal register, you can claim ownership of the mark from the time you first submitted the ITU.

WHY TRADEMARKS DON'T USUALLY PROTECT AUTHORS' NAMES

Generally, outside of celebrity contexts, the trademark rules on personal names (including pen names) are unhelpful to authors. The basic US rule is that a person's name cannot be registered as a mark unless it has obtained *secondary meaning*—that is, the person claiming the mark has to establish that customers really do see this name as the source of a product or service. You may already see why successfully claiming a trademark in a name is easier for a celebrity than for an average person. Even when a celebrity registers a trademark, it usually isn't accepted for registration as an author of books. For example, J. K. Rowling's name is registered as an American trademark in relation to "entertainment services" and online information related to news, games, and activities that involve her books. Even for famous authors, the USPTO usually doesn't accept registration of an author's name as a trademark simply for books she's written.

One reason why the USPTO takes this view may be to avoid confusing overlaps between copyright and trademark law. Each law says something about the source of particular items: copyright is focused on the author as the source of a protected work, while trademark law is focused on the commercial producer/distributor as the source of products or services. Allowing authors to protect their names as trademarks potentially confuses the two areas.

The Supreme Court faced this issue in a slightly different context in 2003 in the case of *Dastar v. Twentieth Century Fox*. The case involved a series of video documentaries about World War II based originally on a book, *Crusade in Europe*, written by President Dwight Eisenhower. Copyright in the book had been licensed to Fox so that it could produce a television miniseries based on the book. Fox failed to renew its copyrights in the series at a time when this was required under American law. As a result, a competitor, Dastar, was able to rework and repackage the series without infringing copyright. Fox sued Dastar for trademark infringement.

Fox's claim failed. The Supreme Court said that the question of authorship of a work is a matter of copyright law, not trademark law. Dastar's repackaging and sale of the work under its own trademark did not violate trademark law, because the idea of the "source" of a product under that law refers to the commercial *producer* or *distributor*. Dastar was the source of the repackaged videos in this sense, so its trademark did not mislead consumers. It would have been different if the copyrights hadn't lapsed. Fox could have successfully sued Dastar for copyright infringement for copying portions of its original miniseries, but it couldn't succeed under trademark law.

CELEBRITY AUTHORS

While most authors' names cannot be protected as trademarks, the publishing industry has, especially in recent years, developed a bit of a love affair with books penned by celebrities. Think about Jamie Lee Curtis's early forays into children's books like *I'm Gonna Like Me*, Chelsea Clinton's *She Persisted* series of children's books, and Michelle Obama's best-selling memoir, *Becoming*. There are also books by celebrity chefs like Jamie Oliver and Emeril Lagasse, and workout books by Jane Fonda. American trademark law doesn't allow just anyone to trademark their personal name, but if the name is associated with a franchise (like cooking, fitness, etc.) it may work as a source identifier and may attain trademark status. In these cases, the name of the celebrity as an author may be a trademark and may be registrable as such.

Another law that celebrity authors can use to protect their names, outside of trademark law, is the *right of publicity tort*. This is a law that allows well-known individuals to protect their names and likenesses against unauthorized commercial exploitation and use. One problem with relying on the right of publicity, rather than trademark law, is that the right of publicity is not federal law. It's state law and has developed differently in different states. Some states limit the right to living people, while others protect the names and likenesses of deceased celebrities (think Judy Garland, Elvis Presley, John Wayne). If the defendant isn't in the state where the celebrity, or her estate, wants to sue, there may be jurisdictional problems getting the defendant into the relevant court. In other words, it's usually easier for celebrities to rely on trademark law than on right of publicity law to protect their names as brands. We'll talk more about the right of publicity tort in chapter 9 when we consider privacy rights in relation to personal names and identities.

TRADEMARKS VS. DOMAIN NAMES

Many authors register Internet domain names for their professional web-sites, using either their own name or their book or series titles to direct the public to their pages. People often confuse the domain-name system with the trademark system because both involve protecting commercial forms of communicating with consumers about products and services. It's important to understand that domain names are simply part of an online addressing system and don't give you any particular legal rights in the name as a matter of intellectual property law. What you get under the domain-name system is effectively a contractual license with a registry (e.g., GoDaddy or iPage) to use the domain name for your website while you continue to pay the licensing fees. If the domain name you want is taken, you generally have to pick another one. You can try to negotiate with the person who already holds the name to see if they're prepared to transfer it to you, but this can take a lot of time and money.

Domain names can correspond with trademarks—for example, Nike is the trademark of the Nike Corporation, which has also registered the "nike.com" domain name. If you want to register a domain name that corresponds with your trademark and someone else has already registered it, there are ways to do that. The more expensive ways can involve suing for trademark infringement or dilution, and the cheaper involve either private negotiation or using the online arbitration system set up by the Internet Corporation for Assigned Names and Numbers (ICANN). That system is called the Uniform Domain-Name Dispute-Resolution Policy (UDRP). It's much cheaper and easier than litigating in court, but you have to establish trademark rights corresponding to the domain name for it to work. As we've already seen, generally authors can't establish trademark rights in their names and book titles, so the UDRP typically isn't all that relevant to them.

If the explanation of *Dastar* doesn't make sense to you, don't worry. You're in good company. A lot of lawyers find it confusing too. It's really just an attempt by the Supreme Court to keep copyright law and trademark law separate, and to encourage authors and creators to rely on copyright law to protect their intellectual property. It's enough to understand that as an author, you'll likely have very little, if any, involvement with the trademark system. Your publisher may assert trademark rights over some aspects of your books. If you publish with HarperCollins, for example, the HarperCollins trademark will be on your books as the commercial source, in the same sense that Dastar was the commercial source of the videos it had based on Fox's earlier work.

INDIVIDUAL BOOK TITLES

As with authors' names, trademark law doesn't do much to protect individual book titles because they don't tell customers anything about the source of the book in a commercial sense. The publisher is really the source of the product, rather than the author. With individual book titles, there's also a concern about scarcity. If only one person could ever use a particular word or phrase as a book title, over time, that would significantly limit what other authors could call their books. Trademark law isn't intended to give anyone a monopoly or absolute ownership over any word or phrase, so allowing one author to be the only person to ever write a book with a particular title could be very frustrating for later authors. If book titles were trademarkable, anyone who wrote, say, a murder/suspense book with a phrase like "smoking gun" in the title could theoretically stop anyone else from using that phrase in a similar, but different, title.

An example of this issue hit social media dramatically toward the end of 2018 when debut YA author Tomi Adeyemi accused best-selling author Nora Roberts of copying aspects of her book title, causing a flurry of invective across several social media platforms. Adeyemi's book, *Children of Blood and*

STUFF THAT CAN'T BE A TRADEMARK

While the United States doesn't have many limitations on what can be registered, there are some marks the USPTO won't accept. I've already mentioned restrictions on registering state and national flags as marks. There are also restrictions on misleading uses of geographic and descriptive terms—for example, names that falsely suggest that a product is made of a particular material (like lamb's wool, when it's actually synthetic) or that it comes from a particular place when, in fact, it's made somewhere else.

One of the hot-button issues in recent years has involved a section of the Lanham Act (the American trademark statute) that prohibits registering a mark that is *disparaging, scandalous,* or *offensive.* Disparaging marks are those that disparage a particular group of people, like the Washington Redskins mark in relation to Native Americans. In 2017, the Supreme Court held that the Lanham Act is unconstitutional to the extent that it prohibits registration of disparaging marks. The case involved Asian American rock band The Slants, challenging the USPTO's refusal to register the name on the grounds that it disparages Asian Americans. The Court held that the prohibition on registration of disparaging marks is unconstitutional under the First Amendment. In 2019, the Supreme Court said much the same thing about offensive and scandalous marks in a case involving the registration of the "FUCT" mark for a fashion line. None of this means a lot for authors—because we can't actually register much of what we do as trademarks anyway—but it is an interesting moment for American trademark law and free speech.

Bone, was a runaway best seller in the young adult fiction category, before Roberts's *Of Blood and Bone* hit the shelves. On seeing Roberts's book published, Adeyemi tweeted: "It would be nice if an artist could create something special without another artist trying to shamelessly profit off it."[1] Roberts contacted Adeyemi and explained that not only did she not copy the title, but, in fact, authors can't copyright or trademark titles. Moreover, a *New York Times* reporter found hundreds of book titles including the phrase "blood and bone."[2] Roberts's book was well into the production process, and the title had already been chosen, long before Adeyemi's book was released.

It may seem obvious why intellectual property law doesn't protect titles. However, even successful authors become confused about the issue, as the above example demonstrates. The bottom line is not to worry too much if you see other books with similar titles to yours out there. However, as a matter of marketing, if your book isn't yet released and you see lots of similar titles on the shelves, you may want to rethink your own title to avoid any potential reader confusion, or difficulties readers might face in finding your book.

CONTRACT AND UNFAIR COMPETITION LAW

As we've seen, trademark law doesn't protect much of what we do as authors. Can any other laws help us protect our author names and identities over the course of our writing careers? Honestly, not much. We've mentioned the right of publicity (see sidebar), but that only protects famous people and is difficult to rely on in a federal system because it is largely a nonuniform state law.

When you contract with publishers, you can include provisions about your right to be named as author of a work, but this usually isn't a problem, except when you're writing a work on commission and the publisher or book packager wants to release the work under a pen name (like Erin Hunter for the *Warrior Cats* books or Carolyn Keene for *Nancy Drew*). A contractual right to be identified as the author of the book doesn't stop other people from misusing your name, although people who make false and defamatory comments about you may be opening themselves up to a defamation action. We'll discuss the law of defamation in chapter 10.

If someone falsely identifies herself as the author of your book, American law doesn't give you much help other than under general federal and state laws related to *unfair competition*, which deal with misleading and deceptive trade practices. If you are concerned about this kind of situation and want to consider whether unfair competition laws might help you, it may be worth consulting an attorney who specializes in the area. While these laws are mainly about commercial misstatements in relation to products and services, there may be some application to authors.

Of course, as we saw in chapter 2, many situations involving false attribution of authorship will also involve copyright infringement. Usually, a person who falsely claims credit for your work will have *copied* some or all of your work, so a copyright infringement action may be an easier avenue to pursue if this ever happens to you. Again, once you start thinking about threatening copyright infringement, you might want to seek an attorney's advice (see chapter 13).

USING OTHER PEOPLE'S TRADEMARKS

As authors, we occasionally need to think about how we use other people's trademarks. Say your protagonist works at Starbucks, for example, or loves Rolex watches, or is hopelessly attached to her Mercedes. Could you be sued for trademark infringement?

The good news is that what we write, even in these situations, doesn't often infringe other people's trademarks. Simply referencing a mark in a descriptive, creative, or artistic way doesn't usually trigger trademark infringement liability. The point of a trademark infringement action is to prevent *consumer confusion* about the source of a product or service. If your book relies so heavily on someone else's trademark that a reader might believe that the trademark holder had actually sponsored it or was otherwise connected to it, you may be in trouble, but simply referencing a mark is generally fine.

Think about the 2013 movie *The Internship*, starring Vince Vaughn and Owen Wilson. It's an example of a creative work that so heavily relies on, and incorporates, the Google trademarks that it most likely would have infringed

TRADEMARK INFRINGEMENT AND DILUTION

You may have noticed that whenever I talk about infringing other people's marks, I mention consumer confusion. This is because the Lanham Act requires a trademark holder to establish a *likelihood of consumer confusion* as part of proving trademark infringement. If your use isn't likely to confuse consumers as to the source of a particular product, then you probably haven't infringed anyone's mark.

There are other sections of the Lanham Act that give trademark holders a right of action *without* proving consumer confusion. The most obvious example is *trademark dilution,* which allows the holder of a *famous mark* to sue another person for *blurring* or *tarnishing* the mark. That's a lot of legal terminology! Remember that this section only applies to famous marks, which are defined as those that are "widely recognized by the general consuming public of the United States" as the source of goods or services. This is supposed to be a significant hurdle for a trademark holder to cross in order to bring an action.

As to the two types of dilution, *blurring* refers to creating a lot of "noise" around the mark that prevents it from operating effectively as a mark. The example often given is that if someone used the mark "Nikon" on potato chips, this wouldn't confuse consumers about the source of the potato chips. No one thinks a camera company is likely to be making potato chips. However, it does perhaps lessen the strength of the original Nikon mark because now there's more "noise" around the mark in the minds of the consuming public. It's very unlikely that your reference to a famous mark in a book would have this impact, so you really don't have to worry too much about it.

Tarnishment means using someone else's mark in a way likely to damage the reputation of the mark—for example, associating it with something like drug use or pornography. Again, it's unlikely that many uses of a trademark in books will have this effect, but it's theoretically possible. An author

(Continued)

(Continued)

might, for example, focus an erotic novel on a sex game that hinges on unsavory uses of, say, Barbie dolls. In fact, Mattel has sued artists and entertainers for potentially harmful uses of Barbie dolls in the past, including the infamous "Barbie in a blender" case where an artist took photographs of nude Barbie dolls in various positions in kitchen blenders. Mattel sued under both copyright infringement and trademark law but lost the case on First Amendment grounds.

Google's marks if it hadn't been made with Google's permission and support. Moviegoers would likely assume Google was involved in the production, and indeed it was. Other situations when trademarks are used in books and movies with permission include cases where trademark owners have licensed the marks to the moviemakers. For example, a lot of well-known tech-related trademarks are depicted humorously in the 2018 release *Ralph Breaks the Internet*. If you sit through the end credits, you'll see a list of the licensed uses of the trademarks.

PARODY AND FAIR USE

Trademark law also attempts to protect descriptive and humorous uses of other people's trademarks in various ways. You'll often hear trademark attorneys talking about things like parody, fair use, and the First Amendment as ways in which trademark rights are balanced against other people's rights to refer to the marks in art, news reporting, and everyday conversation. We've seen these issues arise in the copyright context too. If you can't remember, go back to chapters 4 and 5 on fair use in the copyright context.

Fair use, parody, and free speech are treated a little differently—many would say more simply—in the trademark context than in copyright law.

USING A TRADEMARK IN A BOOK TITLE

Generally, it's okay to use other people's trademarks in your book title, provided that you're using the mark for creative/artistic purposes rather than to capitalize on the trademark holder's goodwill. While there aren't many cases that specifically deal with book titles, there are several on song and movie titles. American courts have given a lot of leeway to creative artists to use other people's trademarks in titles—for example, in cases involving the "Barbie Girl" song, made popular by the Danish music group Aqua in the mid-1990s, and the use of Ginger Rogers's trademarked name in a movie titled *Ginger and Fred,* about a pair of cabaret dancers famous for impersonating Ginger Rogers and Fred Astaire.

However, where a trademark is used solely to capitalize on the mark holder's goodwill and with little or no artistic relevance to the book, the author may be liable for trademark infringement, or possibly even trademark dilution. This happened in the case involving a parody picture book about the O. J. Simpson trial titled *The Cat NOT in the Hat!* As we discussed in chapter 5, the book played on the title of the famous Dr. Seuss book *The Cat in the Hat* and used illustrations highly reminiscent of the distinctive Seuss style. Dr. Seuss Enterprises (the company managing the trademarks and copyrights in the Suess books) sued under both copyright and trademark law and won on both fronts. The court said that there was no artistic or creative reason to draw on Seuss's work to parody the O. J. Simpson trial and the author had only done this to take advantage of Seuss's work. A series of complex and often confusing cases were decided after that, in which courts have tried to explain exactly when parody is excused under trademark and copyright law (also discussed in chapter 5). Writing parody is not for the fainthearted!

The bottom line is that a book title incorporating someone else's trademark won't usually infringe the trademark, but if you're concerned about a particular title you probably should seek legal advice. Of course,

(Continued)

Unlike the copyright law, the trademark law allows people to make fair use of a trademark without going into any particular legal test (think about that confusing "four-factor" fair use test from copyright law in comparison).

Trademark judges have generally accepted a range of uses as fair, including use in news reporting or in comparative advertising (comparing your product to someone else's), artistic uses, parody, criticism, comment, and noncommercial use. There are few hard-and-fast rules here, and different courts make decisions on the generally acceptable uses of trademarks in different ways. Not every parody will be ruled a fair use, nor will every comparative advertisement, but at least you know that if your use of someone else's mark is largely intended to be humorous or descriptive, or to comment on the trademark, there's a good chance that it won't be considered an infringement. Some judges, noting that these kinds of uses are generally unlikely to confuse consumers in regard to the source or sponsorship of goods or services, have said they generally cannot be considered trademark infringements in any event. If there's no infringement, you don't even have to think about fair use.

You can always try negotiating with a trademark holder for permission to use the mark, or you might think about inserting a *disclaimer* to note that your book wasn't approved or endorsed by the trademark holder. Disclaimers can be helpful in establishing that consumers would not have been confused by your use of the mark. If you tell your readers up front that you're not authorized to use the mark in question, there's a good chance they won't assume any sponsorship by the trademark holder.

If you're concerned that you're making such a significant use of someone else's trademark that you should get their permission, that's often not too difficult to do. Many companies are happy for you to use their marks (more publicity for them), provided that you're not using the mark in a way that's harmful to them. If you're going to be critical of them, they may not provide permission, but a critical use of a mark is unlikely to be a trademark infringement in any event. Consumers, after all, won't likely think that your criticism has been endorsed by the trademark holder. If you do consider seeking permission to use a trademark, keep in mind that the trademark holder may ask you to pay licensing fees, which may or may not be cheap, so you may want to consult an attorney first.

TRADEMARKS IN PHOTOGRAPHS
AND ILLUSTRATIONS

If your book contains photographs or illustrations, this is another area where trademark permissions can rear their ugly heads. We'll talk more about using photographs and illustrations, and the associated legal issues that can arise, in chapter 12. However, for trademark law purposes, if you want to include a photograph or illustration that incorporates someone else's trademark, you may need permission to do so—say, for a photo of a Coca-Cola bottle, or of a person in a Starbucks coffee shop with the company's logo prominently displayed.

As with referring to a trademark in the text of a book, the legal question here will be whether you're making a use of the trademark that's likely to confuse consumers about the source of your book. Most photographs and pictures that incidentally incorporate trademarks won't have that effect, so they likely won't infringe trademark rights. However, if you think the photographs or illustrations you want to use might infringe a trademark, it may be worth seeking an attorney's advice or seeking permission from the trademark owner. This will be a separate question from seeking a copyright permission from the person who owns copyright in the photograph to reproduce the image in your book.

MOVING ON . . .

Hopefully this chapter has given you some comfort about how much (really how little) most authors have to worry about trademark issues during the course of their careers. The next chapters turn to the laws related to privacy and defamation and the extent to which you can write about real people in your work.

Protecting Your Author Brand

CHAPTER NINE

Writing about Real People

Privacy Law

In 2017, a French court awarded 100,000 euros in damages to the Duke and Duchess of Cambridge, better known as Prince William and Princess Kate, for the publication of topless photographs of the princess, published in the magazine *Closer*. The decision was upheld by a French appeals court in 2018. The photos were taken by two of the magazine's photographers while the prince and princess were on a private vacation in France. The editor, publisher, and photographers were all held liable for breaching the royal couple's privacy under French law. The incident was very upsetting for the prince in particular. He released a statement noting that the episode reminded him of the circumstances surrounding the death of his mother, Diana, Princess of Wales. She had been harassed by paparazzi for most of her public life and died tragically in a car accident while being chased by photographers in Paris. Intrusions into a person's private life don't usually have such dire consequences. However, the public disclosure of intimate private information can be very hurtful, embarrassing, or upsetting, and can, in some cases, damage a person's professional reputation or career.

What are our obligations as writers to protect the privacy and reputations of people we write about? This question is very significant to journalists, as well as to those who write memoir, biography, and history. Even authors of historical fiction based on real people and events may be concerned about these issues. The laws related to individual privacy and reputation in America are largely state-based and piecemeal. There are no comprehensive federal laws on privacy or defamation in the United States. As a result, it can be difficult for authors to know, in any particular situation, which state laws might apply to them and what aspects of their writing could get them into legal trouble in any particular state.

This chapter focuses on privacy law. The next will tackle defamation. Because of the piecemeal, state-based nature of these areas of law, our discussions will be about common general principles rather than specific laws. You may need to seek formal legal advice if you find yourself facing a complaint about privacy or defamation in practice.

PRIVACY VS. DEFAMATION

There is some overlap between laws on privacy and defamation, and often a person upset by something you write will sue, or threaten to sue, under both. The key difference between privacy and defamation is that privacy laws protect an individual from access to, and use of, *true, but private,* information, while defamation is aimed at limiting the spread of *false* information that may harm someone's reputation. Defamation law is generally better understood than privacy law, at least in the United States, because defamation law has a clearer historical basis and background than privacy law.

Both sets of laws can run up against First Amendment arguments in America. The courts are often asked to balance a person's rights to her private life and/or reputation against the general right to free speech. This is particularly challenging in relation to public figures: politicians, famous athletes, and other public figures and celebrities have much more trouble convincing courts that their interests in their privacy and reputations

ANTI-PAPARAZZI LAWS

The aftermath of the death of Princess Diana in 1997, and some fairly egregious conduct by paparazzi subsequently (including stalking celebrities and putting them at risk of physical harm), led some countries, and at least one American state, to enact specific *anti-paparazzi laws* aimed at preventing risks to celebrities' well-being. California enacted its anti-paparazzi law in the late 1990s to protect celebrities from invasions of their private lives by freelance photographers. The law has been updated several times to extend liability to media outlets that publish photographs taken in breach of the law, and to reckless driving by paparazzi involved in celebrity car chases, as well as for hemming in celebrities and blocking their freedom of movement. In the United States, there are concerns that these kinds of laws may be unconstitutional in light of our strong First Amendment protections for free speech. However, the California laws remain on the books. Justin Bieber was one of the first celebrities to sue photographers under the car-chase provisions of California's law when he was fined for speeding while being chased by paparazzi.

override the public's right to know particular information about them. For example, a politician who takes a strong political stance against illegal drugs may be hard-pressed to convince a court that she has a right to stop a newspaper from publishing a story about her own drug problem.

This chapter focuses on privacy in particular, with a handful of cross-references to chapter 10 for situations where a specific privacy issue may overlap with defamation. Remember: defamation is about false statements that harm a person's reputation, while privacy violations are about intruding into someone's personal life and accessing or sharing true information about them.

For American authors, the news is pretty good on the privacy front, although it's perhaps less welcome news for the people we write about. Unlike the laws in Europe, American law is pretty weak and difficult to enforce when it comes to the protection of privacy. As already mentioned, most of our privacy law comes out of disharmonized state laws. There's no comprehensive federal legal protection for privacy, although there are specific federal privacy laws for particular industries—for example, HIPAA (the Health Information Portability and Accountability Act) limits what your health-care providers can do with your medical information.

One big reason behind America's fairly weak privacy law is the strength of our First Amendment protection of free speech. Historically, because speech is formally protected in the Constitution and privacy isn't, lawmakers have tended to prioritize the need to share information over the need to protect privacy. Additionally, Congress has no specific authority under the Constitution to make laws about privacy. This is why most of our privacy-protecting laws are made at the state level—which means that this body of law is not very well harmonized and is often difficult to apply in practice. Recently, there have been calls for Congress to create a more comprehensive national privacy law, partly to keep in step with developments in Europe. However, it's not yet clear that Congress can, or will, move in this direction. For now, at least, our situation in America is very different from that in many other countries (notably many European ones) where privacy is protected as a basic human right and constitutional right. Courts in those countries typically attempt to strike a clearer balance between the right to privacy and the right to freedom of expression.

A notable example of the European approach is *Google Spain v. AEPD and Mario Costeja González*, a case decided in 2014 under the European Union's Data Protection Directive of 1995, a precursor of its General Data Protection Regulation (GDPR, implemented in 2018). Mario Costeja González, a Spanish resident, had lodged an official complaint with the Spanish Data Protection Agency (AEPD) against a Spanish newspaper, *La Vanguardia*, and Google Spain in relation to the publication of a story about a real estate auction held ten years earlier to repay González's social security debt. The story had originally been published ten years earlier, when the news was fresh. However, the posting of the newspaper's archives on its website, and the way Google's search engine algorithm prioritized the article in searches for González's name, caused him concern. His complaint was based on Spanish laws implementing the Data Protection Directive (now replaced by the GDPR), specifically laws preventing the unauthorized processing and publishing of personal information. Theoretically, both Google and the newspaper could have been held liable for breaching the European law, but the AEPD upheld the newspaper's claim to a journalistic exception. Even fairly strict privacy protections, like those found in the European Union, do contain exceptions for legitimate journalism and situations where publication is in the public interest, though a detailed look at those laws is well beyond the scope of this chapter (a whole book could be written about it—and several have been). However, the AEPD simultaneously upheld González's complaint against Google and ordered the latter to remove the offending data from its search results. The court case named at the start of this paragraph was Google's attempt to reverse that ruling. The resulting ruling, by the Court of Justice of the European Union, established legal grounds for requiring search engine companies to consider individuals' requests for the removal of online information.

Because European countries typically take privacy so much more seriously than the United States, most of the privacy cases we read about, at least the successful ones, tend to come from foreign courts. Of course, even European courts will consider the balance between speech and privacy. An example is the case involving Prince William and Princess Kate, mentioned earlier. In interviews about the case, the lawyer for *Closer* noted that it was

PRIVACY VS. COPYRIGHT LAW

Because the United States doesn't have a strong privacy law, people concerned about protecting their privacy often resort to other legal arguments. For example, sometimes it's possible to use copyright law to protect privacy by claiming copyright infringement in relation to a photograph or published story that includes private information copied from another source. If, say, a magazine publishes an embarrassing photograph of me and I happen to hold copyright in the photo, I can always sue (or threaten to sue) the publisher for copyright infringement. The problem is that often when we're *in* a photo, we don't hold copyright in the photo. The person who holds copyright is usually the photographer (for more detail on copyright and photography, see chapters 1 and 12).

This problem arose in 2014 when actress Jennifer Lawrence and a number of other celebrities were left without effective legal claims against hackers who had leaked nude photographs online. Even though the photos were highly embarrassing, Lawrence and the other celebrities did not hold copyrights in them and so could not sue for copyright infringement. And although the photographs publicly exposed very private situations, the weak American privacy laws weren't much use here either. Defamation also wasn't a viable option because the photos were not photoshopped or doctored in any way; they presented true information. Remember that a successful defamation suit requires proof that false information was published (see chapter 10).

important for the press to report about the lives of the royal family as a general matter of free speech and freedom of the press. He noted that "it's of public interest to know that future heirs to the throne have a solid relationship and are getting on well. It's all part of the royal business."[1] However, the court ruled that publishing topless photos of the princess crossed an unacceptable line.

PRIVACY AND CONTRACT LAW

While most of this chapter is about tort law, it's worth knowing that in some situations, contract law may have a role to play in protecting privacy. For example, most social networks' terms of service require members to agree not to post private information, photographs, or videos about other people. However, even these contracts provide fairly weak protection for those individuals. What happens if a Facebook member posts private information about a friend without that friend's permission? For example, what if you post a picture of me apparently passed out drunk on the sofa with a beer can in my hand? I may be angry and hurt, but I can't sue Facebook for your breach of their terms of service because I'm not a party to your contract with Facebook. Of course, I could complain to Facebook and they may decide to remove the photograph, and maybe even suspend your membership, but it's completely up to them.

Another type of contract that may involve privacy (and defamation for that matter) is a publishing contract. As we saw in chapter 6, your publisher will probably include a clause in your publishing contract that you promise to indemnify them if they get sued for anything you write. This could include situations where they're sued for breach of privacy or defamation. The more usual cases arise in the defamation context (as we'll see in chapter 10).

AMERICAN PRIVACY LAW

Most American privacy law comes from a body of law developed at the state level, called *tort law*. Torts are civil wrongs, and these laws give individuals like you and me the right to sue others for various types of harm, including damage arising out of negligent conduct (e.g., car accidents), defamation, property damage, medical malpractice, and so on. In the privacy context, tort law revolves around intrusions into a person's private life through both

Writing about Real People

access to and publication of private information. Some privacy torts are part of state *common law* (i.e., court-made law) and others are in state *statutes* (laws written by state legislatures).

One interesting feature of these state laws is that they include special laws about celebrity privacy, as opposed to general privacy. The celebrity-focused privacy torts, often referred to as *right of publicity torts*, focus more on making unauthorized profits from using a celebrity's name, picture, or other likeness than on intrusions into their private lives. Celebrities can generally bring cases under both these special celebrity torts and the general privacy laws. You might remember that we mentioned these torts briefly in the previous chapter.

Over the years, there have been attempts to harmonize the state tort laws on privacy, generally spearheaded by the American Law Institute (ALI), an organization made up of legal experts and originally established in 1923 to help streamline and codify state laws in various areas. The ALI periodically issues "restatements" of different areas of law that state lawmakers can use as models to harmonize their laws with those of other states, and tort law is one of the main areas where the ALI is active. Its multivolume *Second Restatement of Torts*, developed between the 1960s and '70s, attempts to provide a uniform template for state privacy laws, among other issues (there is also a *Third Restatement of Torts*, but it doesn't cover privacy law). The *Second Restatement* includes four specific privacy torts:

+ intrusion into seclusion
+ appropriation of name or likeness
+ public disclosure of private facts
+ false light publicity

These torts are supplemented in many states by right of publicity torts, which are specific to cases that involve unauthorized profits earned by using a celebrity's name or likeness. Most states also have another tort, *intentional infliction of emotional distress*, which occasionally arises in relation to privacy but is usually not very successful. In fact, none of these torts are typically successful in practice. However, it's worth being aware of how they work, just in case anyone ever complains that your writing has violated their privacy rights.

Intrusion into Seclusion

The *intrusion into seclusion tort* basically prohibits anyone from intentionally intruding on the "solitude or seclusion" of another person or her private affairs or concerns, but only if that intrusion would be *highly offensive to a reasonable person*. Historically, this tort has been mostly about physical intrusions into a person's private space—for example, a photographer using a telephoto lens to capture pictures of someone sunbathing on their balcony. In the solitude of your own home, you would not expect to be photographed, and the intrusion may be highly offensive, particularly if you, say, sunbathe topless.

This tort won't generally affect much of what we do as authors, because writing about someone isn't an act that physically intrudes on their seclusion—unlike, say, snapping a photo of them in a private space. Your writing may expose details about their life they would prefer to keep quiet, but that's really a matter for the other privacy torts, the ones that focus on publication of personal information, rather than access to private information.

The Misappropriation Tort and the Celebrity Right of Publicity

The general *misappropriation tort* is very much like the celebrity right of publicity tort, but it applies to nonfamous people, so it makes sense to discuss the two together. The misappropriation tort prohibits a person from making a commercial profit by using the "name or likeness" of any other person (not necessarily a celebrity). The right of publicity tort effectively says the same thing, but for celebrities. Why do we need two torts that cover pretty much the same issue? Honestly, we probably don't, although courts do tend to interpret the two a little differently in practice, partly because public figures, in many ways, get less protection against unauthorized publication of information about them than private individuals.

We'll see more examples of this in chapter 10 when we contrast defamation claims involving public figures with those involving private individuals. One major difference between defamation involving public figures and the right of publicity tort is that defamation applies only to living people, whereas, in some states, the right of publicity tort extends to the estates of deceased celebrities. Estates of famous people like Elvis Presley, John Wayne, and Judy Garland have been very active in protecting the publicity rights, trademarks, and other intellectual property of those iconic individuals.

Both the general misappropriation tort and the celebrity right of publicity tort theoretically prohibit the unauthorized use of another person's name or likeness to make money. Arguably, if you write a book about someone without their permission, you're using their identity in this way. However, because of our powerful right to free speech in the United States, it's typically very difficult for the subject of a book (memoir, history, biography, etc.) to succeed in a misappropriation or right of publicity claim. If information published is false, there may be a successful defamation claim, and we'll talk more about that in chapter 10.

Generally, the misappropriation tort, where it has been successful, has applied to uses of a person's name or likeness that don't involve expressive works of art or literature. For example, many cases arise in the advertising area. If a company uses a photograph of a famous, or even a nonfamous, person in an advertisement without consent, that may be a situation where the misappropriation tort applies, because the company is taking unfair commercial advantage of the person in question. This is why if you—or your children—attend a public event or a class or workshop, you're often asked to sign a photo release permission in case the organizers take photos and want to use them for advertising, say, on their website. Without that permission, they'd technically be opening themselves up to misappropriation liability for using the photographs in that way.

Interestingly, for celebrities in particular, the right of publicity tort isn't always limited to names and photographs, but can cover other forms of "likeness." Some celebrities have raised right of publicity claims over soundalike voices used in advertisements. For example, when Bette Midler declined to allow the Ford Motor Company to use a recording of her singing in the background of an advertisement, they used a soundalike. She sued successfully under the right of publicity tort, on the basis that the ad falsely suggested that she had endorsed the brand. Singer Tom Waits succeeded in a similar case when the Frito-Lay company used a soundalike of his voice in one of their advertisements.

Public Disclosure of Private Facts

The *public disclosure* and *false light* torts are two separate laws that deal with similar things. The public disclosure tort basically prohibits a person from publicizing private information about another person if the publication would be *highly offensive to a reasonable person* and is *not of legitimate concern to the public*. Here, you can see the balance between privacy and free speech at play. If the matter is of legitimate concern to the public, the need to speak will trump the right to privacy. The publisher's conduct must also be highly offensive to a reasonable person, which has proved to be a very high bar in practice. It's almost impossible for plaintiffs to convince courts that the publication of true facts about them is highly offensive, although nude photographs might be an example of conduct that crosses the line into highly offensive territory.

This is the kind of tort that Jennifer Lawrence and other celebrities may be able to use when explicit photographs of them are stolen by hackers and published online. When hackers are involved, though, it's very difficult to find the people who engaged in the bad conduct. Even if they can be found, they may be in a different state or country. While, theoretically, the subject of a hacked photograph could sue the website(s) that published the photographs, we have a law in America, section 230 of the Communications Decency Act (CDA), which basically provides a safe harbor to websites that publish this kind of material when they are not themselves the original source of the material. In other words, if I post a harmful photograph of you on my Facebook page, you may be able to sue me for public disclosure of private facts, but you likely can't sue Facebook, because the company didn't create or post the photograph itself. Facebook also isn't required to remove the photo unless it is regarded as an actual creator or co-creator of the content. If Facebook is just passively hosting the material, section 230 generally makes it immune to liability, both for privacy-infringing torts and for defamation, in many cases.

This is different from the situation with copyrights in relation to Facebook and other online services, which *are* required to remove infringing material if you give them notice that it infringes your copyright. See chapter 2 for a refresher on the *notice and takedown* sections of the Copyright Act, which require online services to remove copyright-infringing material if you give them notice. For defamation and privacy, section 230 of the CDA operates in the opposite way: unless the online service provider is the creator of the content (or one of the creators of the content), it doesn't have to remove the content and is usually not liable for posting it.

While technically the public disclosure tort could apply to authors who expose private information about a famous or nonfamous person, the disclosure has to cross the "highly offensive" bar and the person in question has to be able to argue convincingly that the information was not of legitimate concern to the public (which is also a pretty high bar in practice, particularly if the person in question is a public figure).

False Light Publicity

The *false light tort* is similar to the public disclosure tort in many respects, and it has been argued that this tort is unconstitutional on free-speech grounds, so it's possible that some state courts won't recognize it. This law basically prohibits publicizing information about another person that portrays that person in a false light. It applies only when the impression given about the person would be highly offensive to a reasonable person and when the individual who published the information knew that she was giving a false impression or acting recklessly in publishing it.

You can probably guess from the description above how difficult this law is to apply in practice. There is no clear definition of *false light*, but it has to mean something less than "false information," because that would be defamation. Saying something untrue about a person is potentially defamatory, while saying something true that places the person "in a false light" can be considered false light publicity. Where do you draw the line? Better legal minds than mine don't know!

Even if the person you wrote about manages to argue effectively that what you published placed them in a false light, they still have to get over the "highly offensive" bar and deal with the jurisdictional problems that can arise in relation to all the privacy torts. In short, you're very unlikely to have to worry about this tort, even if you write something true about another person that they don't like.

A high-profile example of just how hard it is for even a celebrity to succeed in a case based on false light publicity is the litigation brought by actress Olivia de Havilland against the FX Network and other producers of the television miniseries *Feud: Bette and Joan.* In the series, de Havilland is portrayed in an unflattering light, particularly in a scene that shows the actress playing de Havilland being interviewed by a journalist and referring to her sister as a "bitch." De Havilland argued that the term she actually used in real life was "dragon lady"—she would never have said the "b" word. Her

Writing about Real People

COMPARISON OF AMERICAN PRIVACY TORTS

Here's a summary of the main features of the American state-based privacy torts for easy reference.

INTRUSION INTO SECLUSION
>Intentional intrusion
>Reasonable expectation of privacy
>Highly offensive to a reasonable person

MISAPPROPRIATION
>Making commercial profit
>Individual name or likeness
>Without authorization

PUBLIC DISCLOSURE OF PRIVATE FACTS
>Publicizing private information
>Highly offensive to a reasonable person
>Not of legitimate public interest

FALSE LIGHT PUBLICITY
>Publicizing information that places person in a false light
>Highly offensive to a reasonable person
>Not of legitimate public interest

RIGHT OF PUBLICITY
>Making commercial profit
>Famous person's name or likeness
>Without authorization

claim of false light publicity failed. The court said that a fictional portrayal of a real person was, by definition, untrue, so the fact that the portrayal wasn't faithful to every detail of de Havilland's real life could not be regarded as the producers acting with ill intent (called "malice" in legalspeak) in portraying her in a false light, as required under the tort in California.

The right of publicity claim also failed, even though the actress's name and likeness were used without her permission. The court looked at standard industry practice in the film and television industry and noted that while permissions to use famous people's names and likenesses were not uncommon, they were not required as an industry norm. Additionally, because the use of her name and likeness was creative and transformative, it was not a mere commercial misappropriation. While the tort itself says nothing about transformative uses being excusable, the court was prepared to impose this exception in practice. This sounds very much like the way courts have incorporated a concept of transformative use into the fair use defense in copyright law (for a refresher on that, see chapter 4) to protect creative work from legal liability.

Again, if you're an author engaging in a creative writing practice, you likely won't have very much to worry about in terms of these torts. Journalists may have more to worry about, but even for journalists, defamation law is probably of greater concern (and is discussed further in the next chapter). If you are ever threatened with litigation under any of the privacy torts, it's a good idea to seek legal advice. It could well be that a letter from a knowledgeable attorney explaining why your work doesn't infringe these privacy rights will end the matter.

Intentional Infliction of Emotional Distress

Before leaving the topic of the privacy torts, it's worth mentioning the "intentional infliction of emotional distress" tort. This is another tort that sounds really worrying in theory but doesn't have much bite in practice.

Basically, this tort law prohibits outrageous conduct intended to cause severe emotional distress. While theoretically you could argue that publishing something inflammatory about someone else is outrageous conduct intended to cause severe emotional distress, the tort usually doesn't apply to writing—it usually applies to immediate physical threats of harm or violence. Additionally, the emotional distress has to be very specific and must amount to more than just being upset, scared, or shocked. It would be very difficult for anyone to win a case claiming intentional infliction of emotional distress against an author.

ACROSS THE POND: THE EUROPEAN UNION'S GENERAL DATA PROTECTION REGULATION

Privacy is one of those things that various cultures across different countries feel quite differently about. As noted earlier, not only are laws *within* the United States varied when it comes to privacy, but such laws vary widely between the United States and other countries. Many of the European countries have powerful laws that protect privacy, bolstered by European Union-level regulations that reinforce those national laws. That's one reason we see more privacy cases reported from Europe, and why a lot more of them are successful than in the United States.

Over the years, you may have read about model Naomi Campbell's suit against a news organization for publishing photos of her leaving a Narcotics Anonymous clinic in London; Formula One racing boss Max Mosley's suit against a tabloid for publishing photographs of him engaging in an allegedly Nazi-themed sex party; and the suit brought by Catherine Zeta-Jones and Michael Douglas against a British newspaper for publishing sneak pictures of their wedding. Under British privacy law, such cases are often successful.

Many European countries are also parties to the European Convention on Human Rights, which raises privacy to the level of a basic human right, like the rights to free speech and personal liberty. Additionally, the European

THE RIGHT TO BE FORGOTTEN

Under the European Union's 1995 Data Protection Directive (now replaced by the GDPR), EU courts, including the Court of Justice of the European Union—the court that interprets EU laws—acknowledged the existence of a *right to be forgotten*. Basically, this right is related to allowing humiliating events from a person's past to stay in the past, and not to be relived endlessly on the Internet. While technically you have no right to prevent anyone from ever finding out about your past, you do have a right (in the European Union, at least) to expect certain information to descend into obscurity over time, as it would have in the days before the Internet.

For example, if you've been caught up in an embarrassing personal situation or a malpractice suit or a bankruptcy proceeding, European law acknowledges that, over time, you have a right for that past action not to define you. This right entitles you to request Internet search engines and other digital services that process massive volumes of personal information to delete or suppress certain past information from, say, online search results. While the information may still be available somewhere in an archive, it shouldn't be splashed across the first page of Google's search results if someone searches for you online.

This law has caused a great deal of difficulty for companies like Google, Facebook, and Wikipedia, which have had to go to great lengths to implement systems that allow users to make requests to remove personal information accessible over their services, and to evaluate the merits of those requests and remove information when appropriate. This right will likely have no impact on your writing, but it's worth knowing that if you're researching a subject for a book using a search engine in the European Union, you may not be getting as much information about your subject as you would if you used a computer in the United States.

Union has historically protected privacy, initially through its Data Protection Directive and more recently through the GDPR, which sets out mandatory standards for anyone who processes *data*—information about an identifiable person—to protect that person's privacy. Generally, the law requires a person's consent to processing or sharing information about them. If there is no consent, there has to be some other justification for processing or sharing the information, such as national security, legal need, personal use, or public interest (including journalism).

The privacy of all EU residents is protected by the GDPR, which means that, even in the United States, if you process or use personal data about an EU resident, you will likely be required to comply with the European regulations. This can come up for authors who, say, maintain a mailing list for their fans. If any of your fans are in the EU, you'll technically have to get their consent to include them on your mailing list and send your email blasts to them. We'll talk more about laws related to marketing and publicity in chapter 11.

It is worth being aware that if you publish, on your website, information about another person—say, someone you might be writing about in a nonfiction piece—and that person is an EU resident, it's possible you may run afoul of EU privacy laws. An early case decided under the 1995 Data Protection Directive surprisingly held that a woman in Sweden who published information about fellow church volunteers on a website had breached the Directive. She had shared personally identifiable information about the other women on the website without their consent.

The requirement to obtain consent to share personal data about others is even stronger under the GDPR. It remains to be seen how aggressively those provisions will be enforced in the United States against, say, authors or journalists who write about EU residents. At the moment, the focus in Europe seems to be on making sure that larger-scale businesses that process massive volumes of consumer data are in compliance with the data-processing/privacy rules. However, it is possible that, in the future, authors who write about EU residents may have to think about the GDPR and seek consent from those they choose to write about. A 2019 decision by the Court of Justice of the European Union, relating to Google search results, held that Google only had to protect European residents from misleading search results in the European Union, and not in the United States. This decision may give authors and journalists in the United States some comfort.

As a matter of professional courtesy, it's always a good idea to try to obtain consent from people you want to write about. However, that's not always possible, particularly if the person is a very private individual or you want to write something critical and that person wouldn't be happy about it. Unfortunately, the laws on privacy in the European Union currently have us "watching this space" to see whether, and to what extent, they might become problematic for writers in the United States.

MOVING ON . . .

A single chapter can't possibly give anyone complete information on global privacy law. The laws are simply too complex and disharmonized. If you think you're likely to fall into a privacy trap, under either US or European law (or under the laws of any other country), it may be worth consulting a privacy expert in the relevant state or country. We'll talk more about how to find effective legal advice in chapter 13. For now, we'll turn to the law of defamation, which is better understood than privacy law but still very disharmonized between different states and countries.

Writing about Real People

CHAPTER TEN

Damaging Someone's Reputation

Defamation Law

In 1996, Joe Klein, a former *Newsweek* columnist, anonymously published *Primary Colors*, which was later made into a film starring John Travolta and Emma Thompson. The novel chronicled the presidential primary campaign of a charming and charismatic southern governor. Even though the book was billed as fiction, most readers—and subsequently moviegoers—realized that it was based on Bill Clinton's 1992 Democratic primary campaign. Many of the characters closely resembled real people in that campaign, and the movie's portrayal of the governor and his wife (played by Travolta and Thompson) were strikingly similar to Bill and Hillary Clinton.

Unsurprisingly, defamation litigation followed the publication of the book. Perhaps surprisingly, it was brought by Harlem librarian Daria Carter-Clark, who complained about the way she was portrayed in the novel and the movie. The librarian character played a fairly minor role in both works. Nevertheless, that minor character was memorably depicted in both the movie and the book as being sexually loose, with the implication that she had an affair with the fictional Governor Stanton. Carter-Clark lost the defamation action against Klein and the book's publisher, Random House, largely because the similarities between the fictional librarian and the real-life Carter-Clark were not sufficient to support her claim. The court noted that the fictional character had a different name, a different job, and a dissimilar physical description to the real Carter-Clark.

It may surprise you to learn that even authors of fiction (as opposed to nonfiction) can be sued for defamation. However, it will be of some comfort that, at least in the United States, it's very difficult to win a defamation suit against a fiction writer. Usually, a writer can avoid defamation liability, even when basing a fictional character on a real person, by changing names, personal details, and settings. For a defamation action to succeed, the character must be identifiable as a real person, and it's often relatively easy to "file off the serial numbers" and avoid these problems. It can be more difficult to avoid defamation claims if you're writing nonfiction works like memoir, history, and biography.

This chapter focuses on the American law of defamation—to the extent that there is an "American law" of defamation. As with privacy, defamation is a matter of state law, which is often disharmonized and raises all the jurisdictional problems that arise with privacy, including which state court can hear a given case and which state's law should apply. Also, again like privacy law, American defamation law is subject to the First Amendment guarantee of free speech. That doesn't mean that anything goes, but it does mean, particularly with respect to public figures and matters of public interest, that the law errs on the side of supporting, rather than preventing or punishing, publication.

It's important to bear in mind that defamation laws, like privacy laws, can vary greatly between countries. Some countries are much more deferential to the protection of individual reputations than to free speech. Australia is a good example: it has no specific constitutional guarantee of freedom of expression, so there is no automatic constitutional check on defamation as there is in the United States. As a result, public figures are much more likely to succeed in defamation actions in Australia than in the United States. If you're publishing in foreign markets and you're concerned that your book may be defamatory, you may want to seek the advice of an expert on the relevant countries' laws.

DEFAMATION: THE LEGAL LINGO

Before we survey the aspects of defamation law that writers may have to think about, it's worth unpacking some of the legal jargon used in this area. Often people are confused by the differences between defamation, libel, and slander. Really, there's no magic here. *Defamation* is an umbrella term for false publication of information that might harm an individual's reputation. Technically, *libel* refers to defamation in written form and *slander* to defamation in spoken form. If you stick with *defamation* as a general term, you likely won't go wrong.

Then there's the pesky distinction between *public figures* and *private individuals* as potential objects of defamation. Public figures get less protection than private individuals in the United States because of the public interest in hearing about what public figures are doing. Challenges can arise when defining who counts as a public figure. Of course, politicians and those holding high-level government offices are public figures, but then there's the question of celebrities: actors, musicians, athletes, and so on. Then there are people who are not, theoretically, public figures but may take a notable stance on a public issue—for example, the students of Marjory Stoneman Douglas High School in Florida who were at the center of the #NeverAgain movement after the school shooting there. What about social media influencers and reality TV performers? Your guess is as good as mine.

The line between a public figure and everyone else is blurry in the defamation context, and many of these situations need to be considered on a case-by-case basis. It's hard to set out any clear rules for whether a person (other than a high-level office holder) is a public figure or not. It's not even clear whether, say, professors like me are public figures. I might be

Damaging Someone's Reputation

DEFAMATION AND YOUR PUBLISHING CONTRACT

Because defamation law applies to both the writer and the publisher of a libelous publication, most publishers will include a clause in your publishing contract that you will indemnify them if they're sued for defamation over your book. This may be a separate clause or part of the general indemnification clause that basically holds you responsible for anything your publisher gets sued for (copyright infringement, trademark infringement, privacy, defamation, etc.). You won't typically be able to negotiate your way out of these clauses, but (as noted in chapter 6, where we talked about them in some detail) you may be able to get the publisher to agree to limit your responsibility. For example, they may be prepared to limit your responsibility to "nonfrivolous" legal claims (i.e., claims that have some merit and won't be immediately thrown out of court for wasting everyone's time). Alternatively, you might ask to have yourself included on your publisher's media liability insurance policy, which could help cover the costs of litigation. These are issues to think about when you're negotiating your contract.

Of course, if you're self-publishing, you take these risks on your own shoulders. You will also likely have to agree to indemnify the self-publishing platform you use in case they get sued over your work. Amazon's Kindle Direct publishing contract, for example, includes a clause requiring their authors to indemnify them for any liability they incur in relation to defamation, among other legal issues (including copyright and trademark infringement).

considered a public figure if I'm involved in writing a high-profile brief for a case of public interest, but in my private life, I'm probably not a public figure. I wish I could provide clearer guidance on who is and who isn't a public figure, but the important lesson for authors is that anyone who truly is a public figure will have significantly lower chances of bringing a successful defamation claim against you than a person who is not a public figure.

Other terms that come up in the defamation context are related to defenses to defamation actions, like *parody, satire, opinion,* and, of course, our old friend *truth!* We'll talk about those in more detail below.

HOW DEFAMATION WORKS

Defamation, like privacy, is a tort. Therefore, depending on the state law in question, the way to prove a claim may be found in a (legislated) state statute, in (judge-made) common law, or in a combination of both. The basic defamation action typically requires the person complaining to prove *publication* of a *false statement* about her that causes *damage* to her reputation. Defamation involving public figures also requires the person complaining to establish that the statement was published *with malice,* which is a legal way of saying that the author knew the information was false or acted with "reckless disregard" of whether it might be false. Again, the legal test is explained differently in different states, but this is the basic structure of the tort. *Defamation* applies to living people. This is different from, say, the celebrity right of publicity tort, which extends, in some states, to the estates of deceased celebrities (see chapter 9 for a refresher).

Most state laws also allow corporations and other organizations to bring defamation actions for damage to the organization—for example, loss of customers as a result of false statements. The rules are very similar for corporate and personal defamation, so this chapter focuses on defaming individual people. If you are concerned about defaming a corporation or other organization, it's a good idea to seek legal advice because the rules on damages can be different in different states, and sometimes corporations can claim very large damage awards for defamation, depending on the circumstances or the state.

THE BASIC DEFAMATION ACTION

The keys to a successful defamation action are (a) publication of (b) a false statement; (c) identification of the person in question—who must be a living

DEFAMATION ON THE INTERNET

The laws in different countries often differ substantially on how defamation works—in particular, whether the law is more deferential to protecting a complainant's reputation or the right to publish/right to free speech. These differences didn't matter so much in practice in the days before the Internet, when most publications were confined to a single country, state, or province. It wasn't usually the case that an Australian magazine would find its way to the United States or vice versa. However, in the early days of the Internet, it soon became clear that the ready availability of so much information across national borders could easily cause problems for publishers (whether media outlets or private individuals) who uploaded content in one country and then potentially faced defamation liability in other countries with very different laws. This problem isn't limited to defamation. It holds true of all laws related to publication of information online, including copyright, trademark, and privacy laws.

An early defamation case that raised this problem was the Australian case of *Gutnick v. Dow Jones,* in which a well-known Australian businessman sued a New York newspaper for an allegedly defamatory comment it had posted about him on its subscriber website. The content was available to subscribers in many countries, including the United States and Australia. Because the American laws on defamation are much less deferential to public figures than those in Australia, Gutnick brought his case in the Australian courts. Years of litigation followed to determine whether Australian courts were the appropriate courts to hear the matter and, if so, whether they should apply Australian or New York defamation law. In the end, the Australian High Court, the equivalent of the US Supreme Court, held that both Australian courts and Australian law were appropriate. This and other early cases made it clear that even though the Internet itself is theoretically borderless, different countries and courts may still apply their own laws, even to wide-reaching online conduct.

person or, in most states, a corporation or other organization—as the subject of the statement; and (d) reputational harm to that person. Because defamation requires a *false* statement, truth is always a defense to defamation. However, if the statement is true but paints the person in a false light, a *false light publicity* action under privacy law could be successful (see chapter 9). False light publicity claims don't often succeed in court, but it's the obvious step for a person who is upset about what you wrote and the harm it might cause to their reputation, even if the statement is technically true.

An example of the difference might be if you published, say, a photograph of a person passed out on a sofa with a drink in her hand, giving the impression she's an alcoholic, without providing the context that the photo portrayed a performance in a local theater production and didn't accurately depict the individual. The photograph is technically "true" in the sense that it hasn't been doctored or photoshopped, but it does provide a false impression of the person if taken out of context.

Publication

Publication in the defamation context means publishing or sharing the information in question with a third party, not with the subject of the information. If I write a letter to you privately stating that I think you have a drinking problem, that may or may not be true, but it's not a "publication" for defamation purposes because I'm not sharing the letter with anyone else. However, if I were to write on my blog that I think you have a drinking problem, that would be defamatory (if untrue) because it is published to other people.

Another important point about the idea of publication in the defamation context is that you can be liable for defamation even if you publish someone else's comments. You don't have to be the person who originally made the statement in question. If you republish the information, you can be held responsible. That's why publishers are often sued for defamation alongside authors. If I write a book that defames you, and I publish it with Simon & Schuster, both the publisher and I can be sued for defamation. The same goes for quoting other people's defamatory words in your book. If I write in my book that I heard John say that Mary is a drunk, I could still be liable for defamation even though I'm repeating something originally said by John. By writing those words in my book, I've published them.

Words Identifying a Particular Person

It's also important that the statement you publish actually identifies the person in question in order for it to be defamatory. You don't have to name the person, but if you provide enough detail that it's obvious who you're talking about, that will usually be sufficient to support a defamation action. This was the argument Carter-Clark made (unsuccessfully) in the *Primary Colors* case. She felt that she was sufficiently identifiable, even though Klein used a different name and physical description for her. The court disagreed and said that Klein's portrayal didn't sufficiently identify her to support her defamation claim.

On the other hand, when former Minnesota governor Jesse Ventura sued author Chris Kyle for a portrayal of Ventura in Kyle's book *American Sniper: The Autobiography of the Most Lethal Sniper in U.S. Military History,* the court accepted that Ventura was identifiable even though Kyle hadn't used Ventura's name. The lengthy and contentious litigation between Ventura and Kyle (and, ultimately, Kyle's estate after his death) was settled in 2017. However, the original decision was an interesting example of a public figure convincing a court that there was at least a possibility he had been defamed by the publication.

DEFENSES TO DEFAMATION

You've probably heard people say things like "truth is a defense" or "parody is a defense" to defamation. For the most part, these statements are, indeed,

COMPOSITE CHARACTERS IN FICTION

An issue that sometimes comes up in fictional retellings of real situations is that of composite characters, when an author creates a character that is an amalgam of more than one real person for narrative or artistic reasons. If one or more real people think the character is too close to portraying them personally, and potentially harms their reputation, they may sue for defamation. This occurred in relation to the 2013 film *The Wolf of Wall Street*. Former Stratton Oakmont general counsel Andrew Greene sued the film's producers under both privacy and defamation law for what he claimed was a portrayal that depicted him in a poor light, particularly in relation to engaging with prostitutes and using illegal drugs.

Paramount Pictures won the case, largely because the character in question was a composite of three different people and had a different name, nickname, employment and personal history, and criminal history than Greene. Additionally, the movie included a disclaimer saying that the characters portrayed were not based on real people. Because the character in question was a composite, it was not possible, according to the court, for the movie studio to have acted with malice in presenting false information about Greene, who wasn't readily identifiable as the character in the film. This case highlights another important feature of defamation law in relation to a person's identity: the person must be reasonably identifiable *to the relevant public,* not just to himself or herself. It's not typically enough that I recognize myself as the subject of your writing. Other people must be able to identify me as the person you wrote about for my defamation action to succeed.

true. Defamation only covers false statements that harm a person's reputation. If you say something that's true, it's not defamatory by definition. The trick here is to *ensure* that it is true and not just something you believe is true. If possible, it's always a good idea to have sources you can cite to establish that a statement is true. For example, if you say that someone is a convicted

JOURNALISTS' SOURCES AND THE FIRST AMENDMENT

When we talk about "sources" of information republished by writers, often journalists, there is a common misconception that journalists have a special First Amendment privilege (often called the "reporter's privilege") to keep their sources secret and don't have to answer questions raised, say, in defamation claims, about information they've published. In fact, there is no special First Amendment rule for journalists. While freedom of the press is an important aspect of a democratic society and is expressly mentioned in the First Amendment, journalists do not have any special protection against disclosing information about sources and other information when required to do so by a court. Journalists will often offer confidentiality to sources for the sake of a story, but they do so at their own risk. Writers of works such as novels, memoirs, and biographies equally have no special protections if they want to keep sources confidential, if a court requires them to disclose their sources. And, of course, you can't avoid liability for defamation by saying you were only repeating something someone else told you.

felon, and you have evidence (say, from a newspaper or other media outlet or from court records) that the person was convicted of a felony, then you likely won't be found guilty of defaming the person. However, if you say that someone is a "thief" or a "crook" or a "felon" without any evidence, that could be a problem for you.

Generally speaking, expressing an *opinion*, rather than stating something as fact, is usually a defense to defamation. If it's clear from what you wrote that you're not factually stating that a person is a drunk or a crook—but only stating your opinion that they are—you might be okay. It will largely depend on how a reasonable reader would interpret your words. If it's clear from the context that you're only expressing an opinion, it's less likely that what you wrote will be ruled defamatory.

This may be one reason why fiction is arguably less problematic than nonfiction in the defamation area: when you have written a fictional account and created a fictional character based on a real person, readers are more likely to read your work as opinion than fact. However, as we have seen from some of the examples discussed in this chapter, you can't count on writing fiction as a cure-all for being accused of defamation.

A useful rule of thumb when trying to distinguish between opinion and a statement of fact is that, technically speaking, opinions aren't capable of being objectively proven. For example, statements calling me "high-maintenance" or saying that I have a "Type A personality" (which I admit I probably do) can't be proven objectively one way or the other. These are colloquial terms that no one can really prove or disprove. On the other hand, stating that I have a particular mental illness or a specific learning disability is something that likely could be objectively proven.

Another defense to defamation is *parody* or *satire*. We've already looked at how these forms of writing can raise defenses to copyright and trademark infringement (see chapters 5 and 8 on copyright and trademark, respectively). Generally, because of First Amendment concerns about protecting freedom of expression, the parody and satire defenses are pretty well respected in the United States. If you're clearly lampooning someone, rather than making a factual statement about them, you're probably going to be in the clear. Again, it's usually a question of context.

For example, in 2004, the Supreme Court of Texas held that a newspaper (the *Dallas Observer*) and its staff were not liable for defamation in relation to a satirical article they had published. The article made fun of a real-life incident in which a juvenile court judge—Judge Darlene Whitten—had detained a seventh-grade student in a juvenile detention facility pending potential

DEFAMATION AND CONTRACT LAW

We already know that you can't defame the dead, but occasionally there are other legal options for the estates of deceased people to pursue if you write something damaging about them. For example, as I mentioned in chapter 9, some states protect the right of publicity for celebrities after their deaths, so if you make an unauthorized commercial use of their name or likeness after they die, their estates may still sue you. Additionally, particularly in relation to famous people, or people who have been the subject of public concern or criticism, certain publishers or media outlets may have signed contracts agreeing not to disparage the person during their life and/or after their death.

In 2019, HBO was sued by the estate of Michael Jackson for breaching a contract clause not to disparage Jackson, when the network decided to air a documentary entitled *Leaving Neverland* that chronicles Jackson's alleged sexual abuse of two young boys. Because Jackson was deceased, HBO could not be sued for defamation. However, HBO had signed a contract many years earlier, in 1992, when it obtained rights to air the live special *Michael Jackson in Bucharest: The Dangerous Tour.* Because of Jackson's concern about negative publicity at the time, the 1992 contract prohibited HBO from airing anything derogatory about Jackson's character. Jackson's estate claimed that the same contract should have prevented HBO from airing *Leaving Neverland,* not on the grounds that the documentary was defamatory, but because it breached the earlier contract.

It won't often be the case in practice that you or your publisher have previously signed a contract not to publish anything damaging or deroga-tory about a particular individual, but it could come up. For example, a past employee of a famous person who wants to write a tell-all book about working with that person may have agreed, under a term of the employ-ment contract, not to publish anything derogatory about the person. Non-disclosure agreements can have a similar effect. This issue was raised when Omarosa Manigault Newman was threatened with legal action, on behalf of

(Continued)

(Continued)

the president, over the publication of her book *Unhinged: An Insider's Account of the Trump White House*. Contracts are usually easier to enforce than defamation and privacy laws when trying to protect a famous person's privacy and reputation. However, even contracts can have limitations when the person attempting to publish the information is a public servant like Manigault Newman.

These situations raise complex First Amendment concerns that are outside the scope of this book. In most cases, if important government information is the subject of your writing, it's wise to seek the advice of an attorney—and if you approach a publisher with the information, they will likely do the same before offering you a contract.

---

prosecution for writing a school essay that included "terroristic threats." The student was ultimately not prosecuted and was released early from the facility by the judge. The essay in question was written in response to a teacher's assignment to write a scary story for Halloween.

A staff writer for the *Observer* wrote a parodic article about Judge Whitten detaining a six-year-old student for writing about violent and cannibalistic practices in a book report on Maurice Sendak's *Where the Wild Things Are*. The article made fun of comments that the judge and public prosecutor had made in the real case, but portrayed them in a fictional and humorous light. Thus, the plaintiffs were readily identifiable as the real people in question—the judge and prosecutor—but the statements attributed to them were false and were made in the spirit of satire.

The court emphasized the importance of protecting humorous speech as a form of opinion or criticism, particularly where public figures are concerned. The court noted the long-held tradition of lampooning political figures and other public figures as a means of spurring political debate. While acknowledging that some readers might have believed the fictitious and humorous article to be true, the court said that most readers would understand that it was satire. The newspaper actually reworked the format of the online version of the article so that it was headed "satire" rather than "news." The original paper-based publication had included the piece under the "news" heading, as an aspect of the satire, but this heading apparently confused some readers about the truth of the story.

Because the plaintiffs in this case were public figures (a judge and prosecutor), they also had to establish that the newspaper and its staff had acted with "actual malice." As we noted earlier, this means that the plaintiffs had to prove that the newspaper either knew the statements were false or acted with reckless disregard as to whether they were true or false. While the newspaper and its staff knew the story was false, the falsity was part of the satire. The story was funny precisely because it was so obviously untrue, but made fun of what had really happened. In this case, the court said that a finding of "actual malice" really boils down to a need to examine the publisher's *intention* in writing/publishing the piece. If the intention was clearly to make fun of something, and there was little or no awareness that anyone would take the piece seriously, then there was no actual malice.

DEFAMATION OUTSIDE THE UNITED STATES

As we've already noted, different countries have quite different defamation laws. One notable difference is the amount of protection given to public figures. In the United States, public figures have a much harder time establishing that they've been defamed than they would in some other countries. In Australia, for example, it's relatively easy for public figures, including politicians, to bring successful defamation actions when harmful or embarrassing information is published about them. Of course, if the information is true, the publisher will generally have a good defense, but it's often difficult to

DEFAMATION AND FANFICTION

While most defamation cases come up in the memoir and general nonfiction areas, some have to do with fictional works based on real-life characters and situations. The recent explosion of online fanfiction communities has led to situations where people write fanfic stories based on imaginary exploits of real people. One notable example is Anna Todd's best-selling *After* series, originally published on Wattpad free of charge and later picked up by Simon & Schuster. It has also been adapted into a movie. The series focuses on a romance between the heroine, Tessa, and leather-clad British musician Hardin Scott, a character based on real-life singer Harry Styles from the band One Direction. While there has been a lot of fanfiction based on popular figures, including Harry Styles, the issue with *After* (both the book and the movie) that has upset One Direction fans is that the "Harry" character is portrayed as an abusive boyfriend, in a way that romanticizes his behavior.

Harry Styles has not sued (or threatened to sue) Todd or her publishers for defamation, although fans have suggested that he should. If he did, it would be an interesting case. The book is clearly fiction, which might initially count against a defamation suit, but the fact that so many people so clearly identify Harry Styles with Hardin Scott, and the fact that the portrayal of Hardin Scott is of a kind that could damage Styles's reputation, suggests that a defamation action might be successful. The book is clearly not opinion or satire: it's a fictional portrayal of an identifiable real person in a damaging light. Styles may well be regarded as a public figure because of his celebrity, and so, if he were to bring a defamation action, he might have to establish "actual malice" on the part of Todd and her publishers. It seems pretty clear that Todd and her publishers know that Styles isn't an abusive boyfriend or, at the very least, that they have acted recklessly in portraying his character that way. This could be an interesting case if a court ever had to deal with it.

prove whether information is true or not, particularly when it's one person's word against another's. Australian courts typically put the onus on the publisher to prove truth, rather than on the public figure to prove falsity.

Other countries' laws may also make it a little easier for public figures to win defamation actions. A 2014 decision by a French court, in relation to the publication of a novel in France that depicted actress Scarlett Johansson in what she saw as an unflattering light, is a good example. French author Grégoire Delacourt's novel includes what was intended by the author to be an amusing scene in which a mechanic, who has little success dating women, finds himself attracted to a Scarlett Johansson lookalike who complains that men regard her as a sex object. While it is clear that the character in the novel is not actually Johansson, the similarities to Johansson are striking and intentional: the point of the scene is that the character is a model who looks like the famous actress but has a looser approach to sex. The model has two affairs, which Johansson argued was a smear on her own character—even though, again, the model is a Johansson lookalike, not the real actress.

Johansson sued Delacourt for defamation under French law, among a series of other claims, including fraudulent exploitation of her name, image, and celebrity. She wanted 50,000 euros in damages, as well as an order to prevent the book's translation into English or adaptaion into a film. The court awarded her only 2,500 euros for the defamation claim and declined to make an order preventing translations or film adaptations of the book.

In some ways this was a victory for the author and publisher, because Johansson didn't win anything close to what she was asking for. However, it's still an example of a public figure successfully suing an author for defamation outside the United States. If the claim had been brought in the United States, Johansson may not have succeeded in the defamation claim because she's a public figure and would have had to prove that the author and publisher had acted "with actual malice"—that they knowingly presented false information about her or acted recklessly in relation to whether it was true

EVEN AUTHORS CAN BE DEFAMED

With the rise of the #MeToo movement and the growing sense of a need for accountability in many industries, including arts and entertainment, more and more creative personnel have been accused of immoral and unethical conduct, including movie producers (like Harvey Weinstein), television personalities (like Matt Lauer), and even authors (like James Dashner). While these moves to expose bad behavior are laudable in many ways, they also raise the specter of *wrongful* accusations of immoral conduct and, in turn, the possibility that the accused will bring defamation actions against the media and others who accuse them.

One recent example has come up in the children's writing industry, where best-selling author Jay Asher *(Thirteen Reasons Why)* was accused of improper sexual conduct at functions and workshops run by the Society for Children's Book Writers and Illustrators (SCBWI). He was ultimately dropped by his agent and gave up his SCBWI membership under a cloud of negative publicity. He has subsequently sued the organization and its executive director for defamation and intentional infliction of emotional distress, saying that the public statements to the SCBWI community and the media by the organization and its executive director have harmed his reputation. It's likely that Asher is a sufficiently public figure that he'll have to prove actual malice to support his defamation claim. The claim he lodged in a California state court alleges that SCBWI and its executive director either published the statements knowing that they were false or were reckless as to their truth or falsity. This case may well be settled before it can be decided by the court, but it's clear that writers themselves aren't immune to defamation.

or false. This would have been a high hurdle for Johansson to clear in an American court, because it seemed reasonably clear from the evidence that the author's intention was to pay homage to Johansson as a woman whom other women wanted to look like, and to whom many men were attracted. Delacourt described the book as a "love story and a homage to feminine beauty," rather than an attempt to smear Johansson's character.[1]

MOVING ON . . .

Now that we've covered the torts involving harming an individual's reputation or private life, we're going to move on to a handful of other important issues that you may come across as a writer. Chapter 11 focuses on the legal issues that can come up when authors engage in social media marketing and publicity. The Internet and other digital technologies allow, and in fact now effectively impose, a significant onus on authors to do a lot of this work themselves, so of course you have to be careful you don't infringe other people's copyrights, trademarks, and privacy in these online forums. We'll also talk about the kinds of contracts you may find yourself facing if you seek the professional help of marketing and publicity experts, website designers, and others on a freelance basis. Chapter 12 turns to thorny issues related to the use of photographs in your books, on websites, and in other media and marketing materials, and chapter 13 sets out some advice for finding any additional legal or other help you may need with law-related problems going forward.

CHAPTER ELEVEN

Marketing and Social Media

Websites, Blogs, Book Trailers,
Social Networking, and More

Digital technology, including social media, presents many traps for the unwary, some of them legal, some more social or reputational, as Tomi Adeyemi learned in the anecdote I shared in chapter 8. While her online faux pas in accusing veteran author Nora Roberts of plagiarizing her book title probably did little to decrease her own sales, the episode demonstrates that even the most successful authors and social media participants can make mistakes.

In the digital publishing world, authors are increasingly expected to engage in their own marketing and publicity, often on their own dime. The technology makes it easier than ever for authors to engage directly with their readers, although the amount of information online can be overwhelming and can make it difficult for any particular author to stand out. Authors increasingly engage in online marketing campaigns involving things like cover reveals, swag, contests, giveaways, and book trailers. Many authors have their own YouTube channels, maintain email lists for online followers, and participate in blog hops and other cross-promotional efforts.

Authors often find themselves spending almost as much time marketing and publicizing their work as they do actually writing it. If you're someone who likes digital technology and social networks, the lure of these online platforms can be irresistible, and fun. If you're more hesitant about going online, these marketing efforts can feel like a chore. However you feel about interacting online, it's part of the modern publishing game for better or worse.

When you interact online, you should be conscious of the legal issues that can arise in this context. The good news is that most of them are the same kinds of issues we've already covered earlier in this book—things like making sure you don't infringe other people's copyrights or trademarks in your online posts, and that you don't defame other people or invade their privacy. You should also try to comply with the terms of service of the online platforms you use—the contract terms imposed on you as a condition of using a service like Facebook, Twitter, or Instagram. We'll talk about common terms of service below.

This chapter surveys the kinds of legal issues authors should think about online. Not much of this information is necessarily specific to authors. Everyone engaging online is supposed to follow the law, just like you're supposed to follow the law in your regular interactions in the real world. However, there are some issues that may be particularly relevant to authors. For example, if you maintain a digital mailing list for fans, and if any of those fans reside in the European Union, you likely need to make sure you have consent from them to be on your mailing list in order to comply with EU law.

It's important to emphasize that this chapter isn't about how to be a successful online marketer. There are plenty of other resources for that, including a number of helpful websites—from simple how-to guides for novice website creators,[1] to examples of authors with effective approaches to online marketing,[2] to checklists of what really can work well on an author website.[3] The best way to figure out what works for you is to check out various web hosting companies and social media platforms, and to talk to peers about what works for them. Google may be your best friend here!

TO INSTA OR NOT TO INSTA?

In many ways, Instagram is the new kid on the block in terms of social networking, although it's risky to make this kind of statement in such a quickly evolving online world, where platforms and trends change so rapidly. Instagram is owned by Facebook and is similar to other social networking platforms except that its focus is on photo and video content. While Twitter is more about words, Instagram is more about pictures. Many authors use it to promote their work, posting things like book jackets, photographs of author events, and book trailers. But as with posting anything, you need to be careful about your rights and responsibilities here.

If you're posting other people's artwork, make sure you have permission. If you're posting photos of other people, try to obtain a photo release if you need it. The laws related to copyright, trademarks, and privacy will apply to Instagram just as they apply to content posted on other social networks. While Instagram hasn't yet raised any major legal concerns, there's no reason that won't happen in the future. (Who knows? By the time you read this paragraph it may already have happened.) The bottom line is not to stress out about what you post on Instagram or any other social network, but to simply be respectful and cautious when you post images or videos in which other people may have rights.

AUTHOR BRANDING AND YOUR OWN ORIGINAL CONTENT

Most authors today are advised to establish an online platform—you can think of this as your virtual "home base"—where readers can easily find you. Many authors choose simple websites, although some rely on a Facebook page or other social media. Websites can be advantageous because generally they allow you to control all the content and usually there aren't too many complicated terms of service involved.

In comparison, services like Facebook may change their terms of service periodically, notably in relation to things like privacy and how many "friends" you can have for a personal page. Of course, you don't have to choose between a basic website and a Facebook page. Many authors maintain both, as well as often keeping up profiles on other services like Twitter, Tumblr, or Instagram.

If you set up an author website, you'll have many options about how you design and organize it and what content you choose to include. You can stick to simple pages with basic information for your readers (e.g., information about your books and your writing career), or you can get more fancy and include things like a blog, an interactive contact form, book trailers, and other multimedia content.

As with the books you write, you also own copyright in the original material you post on your website. Recall from chapter 1 that copyright applies to any original work of authorship fixed in a tangible medium of expression. This is basically legalese for "You own the stuff you write down either on paper or on a computer." If your web design is your own original work (i.e., you've written the text and created the imagery, video, music, etc.), you own copyright in it. Even if you hire a website designer, you can contract to own the copyright by hiring the designer on that basis. I'll come back to hiring website designers in a bit.

Many people actually put the copyright symbol, the © notice, on their website. It's not a bad idea just to let people know that you're claiming copyright in your own original work. You don't have to register your website to put the © notice on it (for a reminder on why, see chapter 1). You can just put "©, your name, date" in your website footer. That will let people know of your ownership of the copyright in the website's contents. You may also choose to register your website design for the additional benefits registration gives you, like presumptions of valid copyright ownership, ability to sue for statutory damages, and so on (for a refresher on the advantages of registration, see

DEVELOPING YOUR AUTHOR BRAND

A lot of people in the publishing business talk about "developing an author brand." In fact, many actually specialize in helping authors develop brands—for example, by helping design a website or a marketing campaign. We'll talk about the pros and cons of engaging these services in a bit.

While *author brand* has become something of a buzz word (or words), my advice to new writers is not to be too stressed out about it. Many authors try to create an enticing brand before they even publish—sometimes before they even finish writing—their first book. Some marketing experts will tell you this is essential, but many others will reassure you that marketing is no substitute for a focus on getting a good-quality book into the marketplace and trying to develop your readership from there. Of course, lots of authors engage in prepublication contests, giveaways, and other promotions, but that's usually after the book is written and while it's being prepared for pub-lication (whether through self-publishing or a more traditional channel). Doing a lot of promotion before you even finish writing the book can be quite a waste of time.

Not many legal issues arise in relation to author branding. While authors, artists, and other creative people often come up with similar designs for their websites and other properties, their fans are usually sophisticated enough to find the person they're actually looking for in the virtual world. Other than concerns about, say, confusingly similar domain names (see chapter 8) or plagiarism (see chapter 2), author branding is less about the law and more about creating an online persona and having fun with it.

chapter 1). Again, registration is something you can do easily and cheaply on your own without legal assistance (chapter 1 explains the basics of that, too).

YOUR WEBSITE AND OTHER PEOPLE'S RIGHTS

Whatever you choose to include on your website, take care that anything you post complies with the law. Theoretically at least, you shouldn't post copyrighted text, music, video, or images without the copyright owner's permission—unless you're reasonably sure you're making a fair use (for a refresher on fair use, see chapters 4 and 5). Of course, the fact that you post something that is copyrighted *without* the owner's permission doesn't necessarily mean you're going to be sued or even threatened with a lawsuit. In many cases, a copyright holder won't know or care that you used their material. But be aware that some copyright holders do care, including big movie studios and music companies, which typically use technology to search the Internet for unauthorized copies of their work. So don't assume you won't be found, but know that if you are, the copyright holder may only ask you to remove the material and may not do anything worse than that. Technically, though, they could also sue you for significant damages.

If you want to include photographs on your website or other social media, make sure they're free to use and check whether the photographer wants to be credited (we'll talk more about using photography on your website and in your books in chapter 12). If you want to quote lines from poems or songs, check the copyrights there too (for a refresher on copyright infringement and copyright permissions, see chapter 2).

When you post more complex multimedia content—for example, a book trailer incorporating, say, someone else's music or video—make sure you obtain any necessary permissions. One of the big copyright faux pas we looked at back in chapter 1 is people assuming that just because they found something on the Internet, it's free for them to use without permission or payment. Another common mistake many people make is assuming that if

COVER DESIGNS AND OTHER ART IN YOUR BOOK

When you promote your work online, you'll likely want to reproduce the cover design of your book and, if your book is illustrated or contains photographs, you may want to include some of those images on your website. Be aware that you likely won't hold any copyrights in that artwork unless you have commissioned or created it yourself. Generally, your publisher won't have a problem with you reproducing book jacket designs and other art on your website. Often, a specific provision for you to do so will be included in the publishing contract. The contract may also require you to give credit to any artists who have been involved in cover design and artwork.

If you're self-publishing and have obtained the artwork through a contract with an independent artist/illustrator or from a stock photography or art website, check the terms of your contract with the artist or website to ensure that you're allowed to make those marketing uses of the art without paying additional fees. A lot of stock photo art can be reused in this way without a problem. Sometimes the artist/photographer will want to be credited. In chapter 7, we noted that a downside of such artwork in practice is that everyone is free to use it. This means that your book jacket and your website may not end up looking all that distinctive in the marketplace—remember the story of Tammara Webber's original cover design for *Easy* in chapter 7? This is a commercial/marketing decision for you to make: risk versus reward of cheap or free artwork. The legal point is to make sure you have permission to use any art you want to post on your website and that you're not infringing anyone's copyrights in doing so. Remember, too, that giving credit to the artist is always nice and is often required by contract.

you include a notice on your book trailer or other content saying "No copy-right infringement intended" or "This is fair use," that will excuse you from a claim of copyright infringement.

Remember that copyright infringement is a strict liability issue: copying without permission can amount to a copyright infringement regardless of whether you meant well or not (see chapter 4). It may be that some of your uses of other people's work online are fair uses, but that's often difficult to know with any certainty.

Remember, too, that giving credit for work you use on your website doesn't automatically excuse you from copyright infringement. Copyright is about copying without permission. While some authors, artists, musicians, and other creators will give you permission to use their work if you credit them, that's not a matter of copyright law, but a contractual issue: they're giving you a license to use their work in return for crediting them. Again, if any of this is confusing, revisit chapters 1 and 2.

DEFAMATION AND PRIVACY ONLINE

Similar points can be made about defamation and privacy online as for copy-right infringement. Try to avoid posting information on your website that would libel another person or infringe their legal privacy rights. If you're confused, refer to chapters 9 and 10, and remember that under American law, it's actually pretty difficult to infringe these rights. These laws typically work in your favor as an author. If you refer to real people on your website— say, because they appear in your books or because they've endorsed your book—the chances are that you haven't infringed their privacy or defamed them in most cases. However, if you share private information about residents of the European Union, you may face some challenges under European privacy law. More about that later in this chapter.

Trademarks, too, should be reproduced with care, at least if they're not your own trademarks. If you use someone else's trademark on your website

HIRING MARKETING PROFESSIONALS

There's nothing wrong with paying people to help you market your work, but make sure you know what you're getting into before you sign the contract. Many marketing experts charge a lot of money, and none can really guarantee success. Make sure they're not charging you for work you could just as easily do yourself at a fraction of the cost—for example, sending emails out to book bloggers in the hope of securing an author interview.

Marketing professionals may be particularly useful in certain situations, usually where the author's time is best used working on other things. For example, hiring publicists and a marketing team can be useful for authors with large *backlists* (books already in print) who don't have time to maintain marketing and publicity efforts for those books while ensuring they have enough time to produce new work. Celebrity authors are another group who can benefit from marketing and publicity professionals. They have the money to hire this kind of help, and their time is best spent doing what they do best: engaging in the activities that made them famous (which, in turn, helps sell their books anyway).

For a debut author, on the other hand, the expense of hiring a marketing team versus the likely rewards can be an unattractive proposition. You may find yourself paying hundreds or thousands of dollars for very little in terms of concrete results. Marketing professionals generally won't guarantee success in terms of increased sales. This is reasonable—even the best marketer can't promise that her efforts will result in increased, or indeed any, book sales.

Marketing professionals may guarantee to send a certain number of press releases or requests for interviews to media outlets or bloggers. However, many of those requests will likely be ignored, particularly for new authors competing in a crowded publishing space. There's nothing wrong or illegal about working with marketing and publicity professionals. Just make sure you understand what you're signing on for, and especially what promises are, and are not, being made.

in a way that suggests a commercial connection with the trademark owner, they may object to your use and threaten you with trademark infringement (for a refresher, see chapter 8).

HIRING A WEBSITE DESIGNER

Authors who are uncomfortable or unfamiliar with designing websites, or who simply don't have the time, may hire professional web designers to help them. Usually a web designer will ask you to provide content for your website and they'll incorporate that content into their design, which means that you still need to be careful that the content you use doesn't infringe anyone else's copyrights, trademarks, or other legal rights.

If you decide to hire a website designer, keep in mind that she will probably do the work for you as an independent contractor, and will likely provide you with a contract setting out the terms of service. As with all contracts, make sure you understand what you're being offered, notably what the designer is promising to do and how much she's going to charge for it. Also be on the lookout for clauses about indemnifying her (reimbursing her) for any complaints about her work. For example, if someone argues that her web design infringes the copyright in their own web page, will you be liable for that? Check what the contract says.

It's actually pretty difficult to successfully argue that a web design infringes copyright in someone else's design, largely because most website design templates are pretty standard in terms of the layout, colors, and fonts used. However, if a designer creates a particularly distinctive look for your website, you might consider trying to protect it through copyright law, and/ or trademark law, to avoid other people capitalizing on your, and your designer's, work.

Of course, if you're hiring an independent web designer, you will likely want the contract to clarify who owns copyright in the website design. Some independent designers will want to keep the copyright in their work and

TO TWEET OR NOT TO TWEET?
(AND WHAT NOT TO TWEET . . .)

The good news is that you don't have to be on Twitter to be a successful author. In fact, if you don't like Twitter, or if you fear you can't control yourself on it (e.g., can't help getting into fights and political debacles), maybe stay away. Twitter can be a blessing and a curse. Some authors quickly develop large platforms of followers and use their following to bolster their careers. Those who do this most successfully are often writers who have something fun or intrinsically interesting to say. Illustrators often use Twitter to share their artwork and develop a following that way.

However, as most of us know, Twitter conversations can easily escalate into flame wars and online shouting matches. Remember that what you say on Twitter can haunt you for a long time. Even if you close your account, others may have kept copies of what you tweeted, taken screen shots, reposted, and so on. If you are unpleasant on Twitter, it can damage your reputation significantly.

While most of these concerns don't escalate into legal issues, the same laws apply to tweets as to other forms of communication. If you defame someone or infringe a privacy right on Twitter, you might face threats of legal action. Again, those laws in the United States are pretty weak, so you should probably be more concerned about the reputational hit you'll take for being unpleasant than about the threat of legal action. If you post other people's copyrighted work, you could face a claim for copyright infringement. Again, it's not clear that many people would actually sue over copying on Twitter, but it's possible. The bottom line is to treat Twitter as you would any other form of communication and make sure you're not infringing others' rights or conducting yourself in a way that may embarrass you in the future.

give you a nonexclusive license to use the design. This will enable them to use similar designs for other clients. If you're worried about that possibility, you should discuss it with the designer and make sure you understand the scope of the contract and who owns what with respect to the design.

SOCIAL MEDIA MARKETING

You'll probably get a lot of advice, during the course of your career, about social media marketing. People will tell you which service you ABSOLUTELY have to be on for people to notice you, and that advice will change from time to time. Who even remembers MySpace today? Everyone's on Facebook now.

While this isn't a legal issue, I suggest that you find a platform that works for you and stick with it unless there's a reason to change. There's no need to feel obligated to use every social networking platform known to humanity to get yourself, and your message, out there. Find what works for you and enjoy it. If you like Twitter, tweet away. If you like Facebook, go for it. If you like posting photos on Instagram, have at it. Your message will come across louder and clearer if you're comfortable with the platform and enjoy what you're doing.

As with websites, be aware that any borrowed content you use could be subject to copyright or trademark. Again, be careful when you use other people's work that you either have or don't need permission before using it. If someone asks you to stop, or to remove something you've posted because they think you've infringed their rights, take the request seriously, and seek a lawyer's advice if you think they're wrong.

Also be aware, on social media, that the laws related to privacy and defamation apply to all online communications. As noted earlier in this chapter (and in chapters 9 and 10), these laws aren't particularly robust in the United States, but to the extent that you share information about people in countries with stronger privacy and defamation laws, you may want to think more carefully about what you're posting.

When you use social networking platforms like Facebook and Twitter, you are subject to the terms of use provided by the company. Most of these terms (the contract between you and the social network provider) will require you to agree that you won't infringe other people's legal rights and that you'll indemnify the service provider for any legal liability they incur for anything you do on their service. Of course, you likely won't have actually *read* the terms of service. Who does? But they're there and you are bound by them regardless of whether you read them.

EU LAW AND AUTHOR MAILING LISTS

One recommendation you may hear from a lot of authors is to keep mailing lists of fans/readers. It's a good idea to maintain a mailing list, especially if you're the type of person who likes sending newsletters with updates, writing advice, and giveaways. You can also use your mailing list to tell your readers when your new books are coming out and notify them of readings and other author events. There are easy services you can use to set up and manage mailing lists. One of the most popular is Mailchimp, which offers mailing-list services at various price points, from a basic free service to a professional service that costs up to $200 a month.[4] It's very user-friendly and many authors swear by it.

Obviously, if you use a service like Mailchimp, you are bound by their terms of service. These terms include the standard requirements that you will abide by all relevant laws, especially in relation to other people's rights.[5] This includes the provisions of the European Union's General Data Protection Regulation (GDPR; for a refresher on this law, see chapter 9). Basically, the GDPR will apply to anyone on your mailing list who is a resident of an EU country. You are not allowed to process personal information about EU residents without their permission, which includes sending emails to them as members of your mailing list. The good news is that it's fairly easy to get the permission you need by simply requiring the users to click a consent box on your website when they sign up for the mailing list. Here's an example from

AMERICAN LAWS ON HEALTH, FINANCIAL, AND CHILDREN'S PRIVACY

While the United States does not have strong privacy laws in general, it does have some special laws dealing with particular kinds of personal information, notably health and financial information. Additionally, there's a federal law that protects the privacy of children's information: the Children's Online Privacy Protection Act (or COPPA). If you happen to collect health or financial information from your readers, or if you allow children to sign up for your mailing list—for COPPA purposes, children are defined as being under the age of thirteen—then you may want to consult a lawyer about what you can and cannot do with this information and what kinds of notice you have to give readers, and/or what permissions you have to obtain from them to collect and use this information.

Most email services (e.g., Mailchimp) require you to assure them that you will comply with these laws, under their general terms of service. If you, say, sell merchandise on your website and collect credit card or other payment information, you might be running risks. However, as long as you use a secure payment service such as PayPal or Venmo when selling items online, you won't likely face these kinds of problems.

If you deal with children in some way on your website, or through your email list, you may want to learn a little more about COPPA. Technically, the easiest way around COPPA is to require anyone signing up for any interactive activities on your website to be over the age of thirteen. Facebook has actually done this, although many parents help their children set up Facebook accounts in breach of Facebook's terms of service.

the website of Alexandra Bracken, an author of young adult fiction (it appears below the online form for fans to sign up for her newsletter):[6]

Marketing Permissions

I will use the information you provide on this form to be in touch with you and to provide updates and information about new releases. Please confirm that you would like to receive emails from me by ticking the below box:

☐ Email

You can change your mind at any time by clicking the unsubscribe link in the footer of any email you receive from me, or by contacting me at alex(at) alexandrabracken.com. I will treat your information with respect. By clicking below, you agree that I may process your information in accordance with these terms.

We use MailChimp *[sic]* as our marketing platform. By clicking below to subscribe, you acknowledge that your information will be transferred to MailChimp for processing. Learn more about MailChimp's privacy practices here.

Bracken explains clearly at the beginning of the page exactly what she will and won't do with a subscriber's personal information (their name and email address). That's required under the GDPR. It's also important to mention whether a subscriber's information will be shared with your email service (in this case, Mailchimp) because the GDPR requires the subscriber's consent to sharing their information, including their name and email address, with other people and companies. Because Bracken is sharing that information with Mailchimp, she has to tell her readers that's what she's doing, and they have to click on the "subscribe" button at the bottom of her page to give their consent, as well as checking the "email" box.

MOVING ON . . .

Now that we've looked at the basics of marketing and publicity, we'll turn in chapter 12 to specific issues about using other people's photography and artwork in your books, on your website, and on social media. Photography is challenging because it's often hard to work out who, if anyone, holds copyright in a particular image. It's also important to understand that the question of ownership of rights in the photograph itself is separate from the question about rights in relation to what's *in* the picture—for example, trademark rights in a McDonald's restaurant that appears in a photograph. The question of who owns the trademark rights (McDonald's) is a separate legal issue from who owns the photograph (usually, the photographer).

CHAPTER TWELVE

Photographs, Illustrations, and Other Artwork

We're all authors here. Words are our stock-in-trade, but sometimes our words need a little help, or illustration. That's where photographs, artwork, and other imagery come into play. Writers in many genres find themselves, at some point or other, in need of graphics to illustrate a book, a website, or promotional material. Writers of nonfiction, including notably history and biography, will often want to use images of the subjects they write about. Children's writers often need illustrators for their work (the publisher usually hires the illustrator in children's literature, and that's a whole other conversation). Who hasn't heard the saying "A picture is worth a thousand words"? The problem is that sometimes a picture can be worth about a thousand legal permissions as well. This chapter talks about the different situations in which an author might need to use photographs, illustrations, graphs, charts, or other artwork. These situations can be legally tricky, depending on the artwork.

If you use, say, your own original drawings, you'll hold copyright in those images and can do pretty much what you want with them, as you can with your own copyrighted text. However, if you use someone else's drawings or photographs or other imagery, you'll likely have to contract with that person to use their work (we talked a little about this in chapter 1). Then there's the question of what happens if a photograph or illustration depicts, say, a trademark or a copyrighted work? Or a famous person? Do you need the permission of the trademark or copyright holder, or the person depicted, to use the image in your book or on your website? If I write a book about a famous artist and want to include photographs of her paintings, or even photographs of her, do I need her permission? Do I have to pay for it?

This chapter focuses on these issues. If you're unlikely to ever use imagery in your work, feel free to skip this one. However, at some point, any author who sets up a website is likely to use some form of design or imagery created by someone else. A lot of the things covered in this chapter reinforce issues we've talked about in previous chapters, like how to secure copyright permissions and when the fair use defense might apply to your use of someone else's artwork.

COPYRIGHT IN PHOTOGRAPHS AND OTHER IMAGES

As we know from chapter 1, copyright exists in all original creative works set down in a tangible medium of expression—or, with less legalese, if a person takes a photograph or creates any artwork or imagery (including graphs and charts), that person generally holds copyright in that work. Of course, in the case of a work for hire, or other forms of commissioned work, the person commissioning the work will hold the copyright. See chapter 3 for a refresher on those kinds of arrangements.

Don't assume that the person who created a work is always the owner of the copyright in the work. If you want to use someone else's artwork or imagery, you have to figure out who holds the copyright and then find out whether they'll give you permission, provided that the copyright hasn't expired. If the copyright has expired, the work will be in the public domain and free for you to use without the need for permission or payment.

WHO CAN OWN COPYRIGHT IN A PHOTOGRAPH?

Under American copyright law, only individual creators can claim initial ownership in a copyrighted work (though they can then transfer the copyright to a publisher or other company). Because copyright is about human creation, it's generally been understood in the United States that other animals can't own copyright in artwork. This issue received a lot of attention, and litigation, in 2011 when freelance photographer David Slater was on assignment in Indonesia photographing macaque monkeys. One of the macaques took his camera and, famously, took a monkey selfie. The shot was pretty amazing (see below) and became quite famous. Slater claimed copyright ownership so that he could charge license fees to people who wanted to use the photograph in books, magazines, and so on. However, after several court cases it became clear that Slater didn't own the copyright at all, because the picture was taken by a monkey, and animals can't own copyrights in the United States.

Monkey selfie. Public domain.

(Continued)

(Continued)

An associated question is whether computer-generated art can be copyrighted, because technically humans program computers to create the art. If a human using a camera to take a photograph can own the copyright in the photograph, why can't a human who programs a computer to make art own the copyright in the art? This is a question that law professors love to argue about. The answer isn't 100 percent clear, although many computer programmers, notably those who code art-generating artificial intelligence, argue that they do own copyright in the works their programs produce.

If this is possible, why can't a photographer own a copyright in a photograph taken by a monkey, when the photographer gave the monkey the camera and showed it how to use the device? If I can teach a computer how to create art and claim the copyright myself, why can't I teach a monkey how to take a photograph and claim the copyright myself? These are areas where, unfortunately, our laws just aren't all that clear and where legal advice may be helpful or necessary if you find yourself dealing with computer-generated artwork.

How do you know if a copyright has expired in the artwork you want to use? That's actually a tough question, because the copyright laws in relation to the duration of copyright in artwork and photographs have changed so much over time in the United States. There are few clear guidelines to figure out whether, and when, a picture might have fallen into the public domain. Even really old photographs can still be copyrighted, depending on factors like whether the photographer is still alive, whether the photo was taken in the United States, and whether it has been published. If you're not sure about whether a photograph is in the public domain, it might be worth getting the advice of a copyright permissions expert (I'll talk more about how to do that in chapter 13).

For photographs and other artwork created after 1978, the duration of the copyright, like that for a written work's copyright, is the author's life plus seventy years. See chapter 1 for a refresher; that chapter also talks about the duration of copyrights in anonymous and pseudonymous works, which typically dates from the year of publication if you can't find or identify the author.

If you're self-publishing—or using imagery on your website—you may decide to simply take the risk of using the photograph or artwork in question and see if anyone complains. If you can't find out who owns the copyright, there's a good chance that person isn't carefully monitoring the use of the image and wouldn't object to your using it anyway. However, if you deal with a traditional publisher, they'll probably ask you to obtain a permission or to omit the image from your work. It is worth noting, for those who use copyrighted imagery on their blogs, that the costs of infringing copyright can be very high despite the low risk of being caught. Several bloggers who used images they had found in a Google search have learned this the hard way.[1]

PICTURES OF COPYRIGHTED WORKS

What if you want to use a picture or photograph that depicts someone else's copyrighted work—for example, a photograph of a famous painting, or a painting of a copyrighted sculpture? You end up with two levels of copyright permissions to worry about. You have to know who owns copyright in the picture or photo itself, and then who owns copyright in the work depicted in the picture or photo.

If you took the photograph yourself, or painted the picture, at least you know you own copyright in the image. The question remaining is whether you need permission from the person who owns copyright in the work depicted. For many older artworks, like classical paintings and sculptures, the work will be in the public domain, so your use will be fine. However, for more recent artwork, you may have to get permission to print your photograph of the art.

PICTURES OF BUILDINGS

One interesting area of intellectual property law involves buildings and architectural works. Technically, the Copyright Act allows copyrights in architectural designs, as well as in models or drawings of buildings, as well as in the actual buildings themselves. Architectural designs were

Photographs, Illustrations, and Other Artwork

included as protected works in the Copyright Act in December 1990, so any designs, plans, drawings, models, or buildings created after that time can be copyrighted.

What does this mean for authors? Well, if we want to include a photograph of a copyrighted building in our work, it would seem that we need permission from the copyright holder. However, when the 1990 law was enacted, Congress made it clear that taking, distributing, or displaying a photograph, painting, or other picture of a copyrighted building is not an infringement of the architectural copyright, *provided that the building itself is located in a public space or ordinarily visible from a public space.* So as long as you don't break into private property to photograph a building, you're not likely to be in trouble for copyright infringement. The building's interior architecture, though, may be another story. Given that interior architectural features of a building are generally not open to the public, taking and distributing pictures of those aspects of a copyrighted building may be a problem, and you should probably obtain permission.

In the past, buildings have also raised trademark concerns. For example, the owners of the Rock and Roll Hall of Fame in Cleveland have sued photographers for trademark infringement in relation to unauthorized photoposters of the Hall of Fame building. While it's theoretically possible for owners of distinctive buildings to claim trademark infringement if you take or use an unauthorized photograph of the building, it's a pretty difficult hurdle for them to cross in practice. Your use would have to be one that actually infringed or diluted the trademark (for a refresher, see chapter 8). Most photographs of trademarked buildings used in books and on author websites would not suggest sponsorship or affiliation with the building/business in question, so trademark infringement is not an issue.

Most buildings, even those whose features are protected by "trade dress" (effectively a form of trademark in design features of an object or building), probably also aren't sufficiently "famous" in the legal sense to support a trademark dilution action. Remember, to succeed in a dilution case, the trademark holder has to establish that the trademark is "widely recognized by the general consuming public of the United States as a designation of source of the goods or services of the mark's owner." It might be possible to argue that, say, the Rock and Roll Hall of Fame is recognized by the public as the source of historical rock-and-roll memorabilia, and this might support a trademark dilution argument. However, most famous buildings are famous as landmarks in and of themselves, rather than as indicators of where particular products or services come from. For example, the Statue of Liberty is famous as a symbol of American history and for its placement on Ellis Island. It doesn't identify any particular goods or services.

REPURPOSING OTHER PEOPLE'S ARTWORK: FAIR USE?

What if you don't want to simply reproduce someone's photograph or artwork in your book, or on your website, but instead you want to alter it in some way to make a particular point? Do you still need permission from the copyright owner, assuming that the image isn't yet in the public domain? Many readers will remember the iconic "Hope" poster that became emblematic of then candidate Barack Obama's initial run for president in 2008. The poster was created by artist Shepard Fairey and was based on a 2006 photograph of the president taken by Associated Press photographer Mannie Garcia. Ultimately, Fairey made a lot of money from the poster, which was reproduced on coffee mugs, campaign pins, and t-shirts both during and after the 2008 presidential election cycle. The Associated Press sued Fairey for copyright infringement, and Fairey claimed he had made a fair use of the photograph. Actually, the facts were a little more complex because it wasn't clear which of two separate Associated Press photographs the poster was based on. However, in either case, the AP owned the original work and was entitled to sue for infringement.

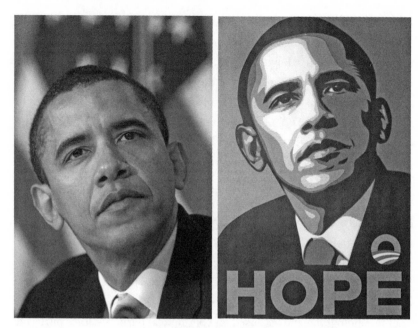

Obama Hope. Permission granted by Associated Press and Shepard Fairey.

Unfortunately, we didn't get any useful legal rules out of the Hope case because the parties settled privately, but it was a good test case for fair use arguments. Remember what I said in chapter 4 about the first fair use factor, involving the concept of *transformative use?* If you don't remember, have a look back there for a refresher. The idea is that the more transformative your use of someone else's work is, the more likely your use is to be a fair use. In this context, *transformative* refers to changing the work to create new insights and meanings, which is arguably precisely what Fairey was trying to do.

Of course, if a court had decided the case, Fairey may have lost even if his use was transformative, because it was also ultimately commercial (for a refresher on those issues, see the discussion of fair use factors 1 and 4 in chapter 4). Remember that there are four fair use factors: (a) the purpose and character of the use, including whether the use is commercial; (b) the nature of the original work—highly artistic or more functional; (c) how much of the original work was used by the defendant; and (d) the likely impact of the defendant's use on the value of, or market for, the original work.

The issue of transformative use (fair use factor 1) doesn't come up often in the publishing industry in relation to photography or art. Most publishing cases involve text (written words) while most image-based cases arise in other industries—for example, the entertainment and gaming industry. A famous example of transformative use under factor 1 involved a movie poster promoting the film *Naked Gun 33 ⅓: The Final Insult*. To create the poster, Paramount Pictures used a nude photograph of heavily pregnant actress Demi Moore, originally taken by photographer Annie Leibovitz for the cover of *Vanity Fair* magazine, superimposing the face of the leading actor (Leslie Nielsen) over Moore's. The company's transformative use argument succeeded, even though the poster had repurposed a significant amount of the original photograph and was used for commercial purposes. The court said that, all things considered, the parodic nature of the advertisement "tips the first [fair use] factor significantly toward fair use" but noted that not all parodies are necessarily fair use. It's always a case-by-case exercise.[2]

One recent case of a copyright claim involving artwork arose in the publishing industry. It's not often that authors, other than author/illustrators, confront these types of questions in practice, but it's worth knowing that occasionally they do crop up, even in the publishing industry. In March 2019, a California court held that a Dr. Seuss/*Star Trek* mashup parody did not infringe the copyright in the Dr. Seuss book *Oh, the Places You'll Go!* The authors and publishers of the mashup created a book, intended largely as a college graduation gift, called *Oh, the Places You'll Boldly Go!* The book mixed the distinctive structure and illustrative style of Dr. Seuss with the characters and plotlines from the original *Star Trek* television series. The creators of the mashup were ultimately not liable for copyright infringement because

Side-by-side comparison of covers of *Oh, the Places You'll Go!* and *Oh, the Places You'll Boldly Go!* Public domain.

the court held that the mashup was a fair use.[3] In particular, under the first fair use factor, the judge felt that the work was highly transformative, creating very different meanings and messages from the original Dr. Seuss work, despite the similarities in artistic style.

One interesting feature of the case was the way the court compared the parody with the original Dr. Seuss book under the third fair use factor, the one that deals with how much of the original work the defendant copied. The court's decision here looked at both how similar the parody's text was to Dr. Seuss's original text and, importantly, how similar the artwork was to the original *Oh, the Places You'll Go!* The court decided that, under fair use factor 3, the parody had used no more of the original Dr. Seuss art than was necessary to convey the message intended by the parody. In making this decision, the court engaged in a point-by-point comparison of elements of the original artwork with the parody art. Just for fun, and to give you an idea of how courts make these decisions, here's a sample of what Judge Sammartino said about the similarity between the cover artwork on the original book jacket and the parody:

> Plaintiff may claim copyright protection in the unique rainbow-colored rings and tower on the cover of *Go!* [the original Dr. Seuss book]. Plaintiff, however, cannot claim copyright over *any* disc-shaped item tilted at a

particular angle. . . . But that is essentially what Plaintiff attempts to do here. Instead of replicating Plaintiff's rainbow-ringed disc, Defendants drew a similarly-shaped but decidedly non-Seussian spacecraft—the USS Enterprise—at the same angle and placed a red-and-pink striped planet where the larger of two background discs appears on the original cover. . . . *Boldly*'s [the parody book] cover also features a figure whose arms and hands are posed similarly to those of Plaintiff's narrator and who sports a similar nose and eyes, but *Boldly*'s narrator has clearly been replaced by Captain Kirk, with his light, combed-over hair and gold shirt with black trim, dark trousers, and boots. . . . Captain Kirk stands on a small moon or asteroid above the Enterprise and, although the movement of the moon evokes the tower or tube pictured on *Go!*'s cover, the resemblance is purely geometric. . . . Finally, instead of a Seussian landscape, *Boldly*'s cover is appropriately set in space, prominently featuring stars and planets.[4]

The judge's comparison of all the prominent elements of the original work and the parody work demonstrate that portions of the original work were incorporated into the new work but were used in a new context. While this discussion is about the third fair use factor (how much of the original work was used in the parody), you can see the overlap with the first factor (how much the parodists transformed elements of the original work to create something new). Interestingly, Paramount Pictures, the owners of copyright in the *Star Trek* series, apparently did not sue the parodists over the book.

While there are no clear answers as to how a court might decide any particular case, if you use other people's artwork but change it in some way, you may be able to argue fair use and avoid a claim of copyright infringement. That said, remember what we talked about in chapters 4 and 5: one of the problems with the American fair use doctrine is that you never know for sure if your use is a fair use unless, and until, a court says so. We don't have clear rules to decide fair use, only the four fair use factors, which are intended to be applied flexibly on a case-by-case basis by courts. Because of the uncertainties surrounding the application of the fair use doctrine, traditional publish-

Photographs, Illustrations, and Other Artwork

PICTURES ON YOUR WEBSITE

We've all done it, haven't we? Copied and pasted images we find online onto our own websites? It's fair use, right? It's okay if I found the picture online? No, no, no. Have we learned nothing from chapters 1 through 5? But seriously, we all do it. It's very difficult, in many cases, to work out who owns a picture we want to use on our own blog, website, or social media feed. Often, the person who owns the image won't even care if we use it, or they'll never notice if we use it.

However, legally speaking, pictures aren't free to use just because they're on the Internet. They may be copyrighted, and the copyright owner may not want you to use them without permission and/or attribution. You also can't claim fair use simply because you're using the work on your website, rather than, say, on the cover of your book. A lot of folks think that using someone else's artwork on a website is okay because it's not a commercial use and it's not likely to interfere with the market for the original work (think factors 1 and 4 of the fair use test). However, many courts won't see it that way. If you're using the art on your website to promote yourself and your writing career, that may well be seen as a commercial use under fair use factor 1, and it's probably not a transformative use if you simply cut and paste the image. Copyright holders could also argue that you're interfering with their market for the image by not paying when they could have asked for a license fee.

The upshot is that, in practice, it's often safe to simply cut and paste stuff you find on the Internet because many copyright owners won't care about this kind of use. However, it's not automatically a fair use in the legal sense, and you could be running a risk of a copyright holder complaining and maybe threatening an infringement action. I'm not saying this to make everyone paranoid about what they do and don't do on their websites, just to emphasize that you shouldn't assume you'll never get in trouble in today's digital copy-and-paste culture, even if your intentions weren't to harm another copyright owner.

ers are likely to ask you to seek permission to use another person's artwork, even if you're adapting the artwork or transforming it significantly. If you're self-publishing or working for a smaller publisher, you may have more leeway here, but then you may risk a claim of copyright infringement later on.

PICTURES OF TRADEMARKS

What about a picture (photograph, painting, sketch) that incorporates someone else's trademark? What if you're writing a book about the fast food industry and you want to include the McDonald's or Burger King logo on your cover? What if you're writing an exposé on the casting practices of a particular Hollywood movie studio and you want to include photographs that include the studio's trademarks? Again, it's worth taking a look back at chapter 8 for a reminder of the basics of trademark law. As with images of other people's copyrighted works, you can also run into trouble with images that incorporate other people's trademarks.

However, trademark law is a little more flexible than copyright law in a number of ways. For one thing, in a basic trademark infringement action, the question is whether your use of the trademark is likely to confuse consumers about the source of your products and services. In other words, would the typical consumer think your book was in any way sponsored by, or affiliated with, McDonald's or Burger King or the movie studio? Probably not, particularly if your book or article is a commentary or criticism or parody of the trademark holder, and especially if you include a disclaimer stating that the book is not authorized by the trademark holder. The question will be whether you're using the trademark unfairly to garner attention for your work by tricking consumers into thinking you have some association with the trademark holder, or whether you're simply commenting on the trademark holder. Trademark law also has pretty flexible defenses, which include things like parody, commentary, and criticism (again, go back to chapter 8 for a reminder of how they work). If you include, say, a photograph in your book that incorporates a trademark somewhere in the background of, say, a cityscape, you're probably not going to be in any particular legal trouble. For one thing, if you're writing about the history of New York City and you include an old photograph of Times Square that contains trademarks of the businesses that operated there at the time of the photograph, you're not using the trademark in a way that would be likely to infringe any of the trademark holder's rights. You're simply using the photograph to illustrate a cityscape.

Of course, that's not to say that a trademark holder would *never* complain about this kind of use. It happens frequently that trademark holders complain about unauthorized uses of their marks in the backgrounds of movies and other visual media. But at least you'll have a good argument that an incidental use of a trademark in a photograph in your book or website is unlikely to be a trademark problem. If the trademark appears in an image on the book's cover, that might be more problematic because there might be a stronger argument that the use could attract and confuse consumers about the affiliation of the book. As with pretty much everything else in this chapter, if you can avoid using trademarks in this way, that's terrific. If not, and if you're concerned about legal liability, it may be best to seek legal advice.

Another tip for using trademarks in imagery is to include a disclaimer saying that your work is in no way related to the trademark holder. While disclaimers typically aren't all that effective in the copyright context, they are often effective in trademark law. This is because trademark law is largely about avoiding consumer confusion. Where a disclaimer makes it clear to your readers that there's no connection between your book and the trademark holder, this can go a long way toward convincing a judge or jury that there's no trademark infringement.

PHOTOGRAPHS OF PEOPLE
If you're considering including photographs of recognizable people in your book, either on your cover or within the book itself, you might come up

against some of the privacy and defamation issues we talked about in chapters 9 and 10. In the United States, this often isn't as much of a problem as it might be in other countries. As we noted in chapter 9, American privacy laws are fairly weak. Defamation law doesn't often impact photographs because it focuses on untrue and damaging comments likely to damage an individual's reputation. While theoretically some photographs could damage a person's reputation—for example, a photograph of a person drinking to excess, maybe suggesting the person is an alcoholic—most photographs don't carry particular commentary. A photograph of me in my garden planting petunias doesn't really connote anything particularly damaging about me.

Famous people may have more ability to bring privacy actions in the United States in relation to unauthorized uses of photographs under the right of publicity tort (see chapter 9 for a reminder on how that one works). Remember, the tort allows a famous person to sue you if you make an unauthorized commercial use of their name or likeness. The exact reach of the tort differs from state to state in the United States and typically doesn't apply in other countries. However, there might be situations where a celebrity could sue you for using their picture without permission under the right of publicity tort.

This is a different question than the issue of copyright in the photograph, so don't get the two confused. The photographer will typically own copyright in a photograph she has taken of a famous person, while the celebrity may have the right to bring a right of publicity claim with respect to the content of the image. These two different laws can apply in relation to the same photograph at the same time. Even if you have a copyright permission to use a photograph of a famous person, that doesn't necessarily mean that the person in question can't sue you under the right of publicity tort.

If you're working with a traditional publisher and writing, say, a biography of a famous person, the publisher may ask you to secure clearances for all photographs you want to use, including copyrights and photographic releases from the people depicted in the photographs. This can be a major headache in practice and may require the help of a permissions expert. Remember that in some states the right of publicity tort survives the death of a famous person, so you may have to get permission from that person's estate to use the photograph. This is different from defamation. As we know from chapter 10, you can't defame the dead, so if you're writing about a famous person after their death, you won't be facing defamation claims in relation to your text or any images you use.

If you do need permissions from photographic subjects to use their images in your book, and if the person is happy to provide permission, there's no magic about how to draft a release to use the photograph. You've probably signed them yourself if you've attended events at local recreation centers, libraries, art shows, and so on. It's usually just a piece of paper that says something like "[Person's name] grants permission to use my name and photographs of me [or describe particular photographs] in [title of your book] and associated marketing and publicity materials while the book remains in publication [or some other length of time you agree]." Then, simply have the person sign and date it.

Hopefully this chapter hasn't been too scary. Permissions to use images are one of the more difficult areas of publishing law. They can be difficult to secure, and they can be expensive, depending on the images you want to use. Publishers often shy away from using particular images for fear of claims of copyright, trademark, privacy, or even defamation liability. This is one reason we often see the same pictures used again and again in the media or in books; those are the pictures for which permissions have been cleared, even if other images would illustrate the text more effectively. Unfortunately, this is a challenging area of the law and, if you're dealing with a traditional publisher, chances are that your publisher will err on the side of caution rather than take the risk of publishing a picture in which the rights haven't been cleared.

MOVING ON . . .

We're almost there! We've covered pretty much all the legal stuff I wanted to share with you, and now I'm going to talk briefly about some avenues for finding legal and other assistance. There are lots of ways to find effective help, some more useful and affordable than others. The next chapter will hopefully give you some ideas.

Finding Additional Help

One of my main reasons for writing this book is to guide authors toward effective, affordable, and accurate legal information and assistance. That can be difficult to find—and this was probably the hardest chapter to write. Nevertheless, there are some good places you can go to find help (and some places that are better avoided). Throughout the book, I've highlighted the kinds of situations in which you may want to seek—and even pay for—formal legal advice, as well as situations where you can easily deal with an issue yourself. For example, you can easily register your own copyrights, but you may want to use an attorney to register a trademark. If someone sues you for copyright infringement, or if you want to sue someone for copyright infringement, you may want to retain an attorney. However, if you want to use a stock photograph from a website like Shutterstock.com under a standard license, you can likely handle that easily enough yourself. The point of this chapter is to give you some guidance for approaching those situations in which you need formal advice beyond the scope of the basic information contained in this book.

BEFORE YOU LAWYER UP

Not all problems need a lawyer. Some you can deal with on your own, and others you may be able to resolve without a lawyer, either by talking through the issue with the other people involved or by seeking informal help (short of formal legal advice). For example, if you're a member of a writing organization, you may be able to use their legal services.

For example, the Society of Children's Book Writers and Illustrators (SCBWI) maintains a discussion board where a lawyer answers questions posted by members: the SCBWI Blueboard headed "Legal Discussions." You have to be an SCBWI member to access it, and nothing discussed online is formal legal advice, but this discussion board is monitored by an attorney who can at least point you in the right direction, give you some general information about your problem, and suggest whether you need further formal legal assistance.

If you're an Authors Guild member, you can avail yourself of the various legal services the organization provides, including contract reviews, copyright advice, First Amendment advice (including trademark and privacy issues), and dispute resolution advice. Information about the guild's legal services is available on its website.[1] The Authors Guild also publishes, and regularly updates, a legal guide for authors that deals with a number of these issues, including contract negotiation, self-publishing advice, and dispute resolution issues, as well as general business and tax issues for authors.[2]

Some writers' organizations provide services and information dealing with particular issues that come up often for authors. For example, the Authors Alliance provides a set of rights reversion resources for authors seeking to recover their rights from publishers, usually after the work is out of print. These resources include a template to use for a letter to a publisher, videos, and free guides on rights reversion issues.[3]

Other writers' organizations provide different levels of legal information and services for members, so check out what might be offered by other groups you may want to join. Possibilities include the Romance Writers of America, the Science Fiction and Fantasy Writers of America, and the American Society of Journalists and Authors. While not all of these organizations will provide individualized legal services or advice for members, a number of them do take action when a group of members is affected by a particular problem. For example, the Romance Writers of America became involved in the litigation about the "Cocky" trademark (outlined in chapter 8) because it impacted so many of their members. The Authors Guild became involved in the Google Books litigation (outlined in chapter 4) for the same reason.

In addition to writers' organizations, some of the government departments that deal with particular areas of law have very useful information on their websites. For example, the US Copyright Office maintains an extremely useful FAQ page.[4] The Copyright Office also releases, and includes on its website, a number of "Circulars" explaining particular issues in copyright law.[5] Additionally, it engages in periodic studies of various areas of copyright law, often considering whether changes to the law might be desirable. While most of these studies will be beyond the scope of what authors need to think about on a daily basis, a list of the studies with links to the full PDF versions is available on the Copyright Office website.[6]

Like the Copyright Office, the US Patent and Trademark Office (USPTO) also includes lots of helpful information on its website.[7] On trademarks, in particular, the USPTO has a very useful web page with basic information, including instructional videos about aspects of American trademark law.[8] While authors don't often have to deal with trademark issues (see chapter 8 for a refresher on why), answers to many basic trademark questions can be found on the USPTO website.

For authors interested in registering their names or other aspects of their writing as Internet domain names, ICANN (or the Internet Corporation for Assigned Names and Numbers) maintains some useful information on its website.[9] Some of the organizations that deal with domain-name disputes also release useful information on how to deal with disputes over who should own a particular domain name. The World Intellectual Property Organization (WIPO) provides on its website a free and easy-to-read guide about domain names and related disputes: "Guide to WIPO Domain Name Dispute Resolution."[10]

Another source of legal information that can be useful for authors is blog posts by lawyers and publishing industry professionals, such as Rights of Writers, a blog maintained by New York attorney Mark Fowler.[11] Bear in mind that the Internet can be a challenging place to find accurate legal information, so if you're searching online for blogs like this, do your best to ensure that the person writing the blog is an expert in the area. There's a lot of inaccurate and misleading, sometimes outdated, information online. When you do find a blog or website with reliable information, bear in mind that the person providing the information isn't intending it as formal legal advice, but rather as guidance for those dealing with a particular issue. If you need more personalized and directed legal help, you may have to find yourself an attorney.

So how do you do that?

LAWYERS ARE NOT ALL THE SAME

Let me reiterate a point I made in the introduction. Like medical professionals, lawyers specialize in different areas of the law. You wouldn't go to an OB/GYN to deal with strep throat, and you wouldn't hire a criminal lawyer to help you register a trademark. Actually, most law firms can probably help you with a trademark—a reasonably large firm will likely have someone with experience in trademark registrations. However, if you have a copyright issue, you need to find a lawyer who knows specifically about copyright law. If you need a copyright permissions expert, that's an extra level of specialization, so make sure you ask whether the person you're consulting is qualified to handle your problem.

More importantly—and this is an area where a lot of folks get tripped up—most general contract lawyers aren't necessarily experts in publishing contracts. While a lawyer in a general practice will be able to work out, say, whether your publishing contract is valid and enforceable, if the contract deals with copyright issues, you'll want a copyright lawyer or a publishing—or entertainment—specialist to look at it. If you have a general practice lawyer who handles personal or business matters for you, you can start out by asking if she knows anything about copyrights or the publishing industry. If not, she may know someone who does specialize in these areas. If I had a dime for every time someone said they used their general practice lawyer to scan their publishing contract and missed important issues, I'd have more than a dime!

HOW DO YOU FIND THE RIGHT LAWYER?

If you do need to hire a lawyer, the Internet can be your friend. Services like AVVO.com are becoming very popular—they're like any other online review service, but for lawyers. You can see what others have said about lawyers working in the areas where you need help.

While some lawyers who are reviewed on services like AVVO.com will offer pro bono (i.e., free) legal advice or services, others will charge fees. Sometimes lawyers will charge *contingency fees*, which means that you don't pay them unless they win your case or otherwise obtain money for you from another party. Then, if they are successful, they take a percentage of that amount. Contingency fees are legal in the United States for most publishing issues. However, lawyers typically are required to explain up front both that they are taking a contingency fee and the basis on which the fee will be calculated, such as the percentage they will take. Usually, these arrangements have to be in writing and signed by the client.

Most good lawyers will talk to you about your situation before offering formal legal representation. They will also explain their fees and should give you something in writing about the terms of their representation and the fees they'll charge. If a lawyer won't talk to you about your case without charging you money first, or if the lawyer won't explain the basis on which they charge fees (e.g., flat fees, hourly fees, contingency fees), that might be a red flag.

Some lawyers or law firms will try their best to make their fee structure work for you or will offer to represent you pro bono. However, there are also legal services that are *always* free if your case fits within their practice areas, and if they have the capacity (resources, people, etc.) to help. Obvious examples are legal clinics at law schools and volunteer lawyers' organizations. Most law schools have pro bono legal clinics where students handle cases under the supervision of licensed attorneys. The problem with authors relying on these kinds of services is that not many law school clinics have attorneys on hand who are experts in publishing law. The closest you may find is a small-business law clinic or a general-practice law clinic. Some law clinics specialize in intellectual property, but this typically means patents and/or trademarks, rather than copyrights. The USPTO, in fact, provides funding and certification for law schools that want to operate clinics focused on patents and trademarks. As far as I'm aware, nothing similar currently exists for copyrights. In other words, even if a law school clinic will take your case, they may not have the expertise you need, depending on what your problem is.

Another shortcoming of relying on law school clinics is that a number of them are means-tested, in the sense that only people who can't otherwise afford legal help are permitted to use their services. Many authors won't meet these criteria. Of course, clinics vary on this issue, so it's still worth checking out your local law schools to see if they can help you, but many law school clinics won't be much help to authors.

Volunteer lawyers' organizations may be more useful to authors, because many are focused on authors and artists. Most major cities have some form of a "Volunteer Lawyers for the Arts" organization. The oldest Volunteer Lawyers for the Arts organization was founded in New York City in 1969 and still operates there. You can Google the term along with the name of your city to find out whether such an organization exists in your neck of the woods. These organizations typically retain attorneys who have some expertise in the arts, and who practice independently at their own firms, while devoting a certain number of hours to the volunteer organization. If you deal with a volunteer arts lawyers' group, you are likely dealing with a legal expert in your area. The problem is that many of these organizations have long waiting lists and can't always deal with a matter as quickly as you would like. The good news in publishing is that not many things move all that quickly, so if you do have to wait for a volunteer lawyer, that may not be a major problem.

Bear in mind that there is no central international or national volunteer lawyers' coordinating or organizing authority. Each volunteer lawyers' organization is a separate entity that provides whatever services it can offer its community. If you want to find the closest organization to you, do a little research. Google them to find out what services they provide and what you have to do to use their services. Some of them may also be means-tested.

WHAT ABOUT MY AGENT OR PUBLISHER? CAN'T THEY HELP ME?

Many authors assume that their agent or publisher will take care of any legal problems they face in relation to their work. Unfortunately, this is usually not the case. For one thing, most agents do not have in-house lawyers, and most agents will try to avoid legal situations rather than defending legal problems on their clients' behalf. For example, if you write a book that may be defamatory or that may include material that infringes someone's copyrights, your agent might suggest that you remove the problematic material, or that you write something else, rather than trying to sell a book that involves a potential legal problem. Even if the agent is prepared to go ahead, the publisher will likely steer clear of the book or, at least, seek an indemnity from you for any legal problem your book might cause them if they publish it. Look back at chapter 6 for a reminder on publishers' indemnification clauses.

If someone infringes the copyright in your book, it may be that your publisher is prepared to bring an action on your behalf, or to join you in a legal action. In these cases, it's likely in their and your interests to stop the infringement. However, it's important that you don't rely on a publisher to defend all your rights in your work. For one thing, not all potential legal problems are related to what you write in your books. Someone may sue you for something you say on your website or social media, which won't be the publisher's problem or responsibility.

Also, a publisher may well be prepared to sue someone who infringes, say, a best seller they have published. However, they may be less inclined to spend the time and resources in relation to backlist books from midlist authors. It's usually up to the publisher when, or whether, to sue other people to protect your interests in your work. In some situations, your publisher may help you with legal problems, but in many situations they won't. Additionally, as noted above, if your book *causes* legal problems for your publisher, the publisher will likely seek an indemnity from you.

FINAL THOUGHTS

Again, the law can be difficult and challenging, particularly in the absence of many cost-effective and accurate legal resources for authors. *However*— and this is a big "however"—the law should never be an impediment to you in writing what you want or need to write. As this book has hopefully demonstrated, there are usually ways to deal with legal problems that arise in the course of your publishing career. In fact, though, most authors don't face a lot of serious legal problems. The most common problems can be dealt with quite easily—things like copyright registrations and rights reversions.

Many issues can be resolved through respectful discussions with agents, publishers, and other rights holders. Sometimes a person complaining about your use of their work will be happy if you just give them attribution, without giving them money. It's always worth being professional and respectful: respecting other people's rights and respectfully objecting if other people infringe your own rights. A lot of good, free legal information can be found out there, as this chapter has outlined. Hopefully, you can resolve many problems before you even get to the stage of needing a lawyer.

If you do need a lawyer, there are ways to find cost-effective and appropriate representation. The biggest issue is to make sure anyone you pay for their services is sufficiently expert in the area you need help with. You'll often be better off without a lawyer, or at least waiting for a volunteer lawyer, than paying a lawyer who doesn't understand the kinds of issues you're dealing with.

Well, we've finally reached the end—whew! I've given you a lot of information, which I hope is useful to you on your onward publishing journey, whether you're a newbie or an established author, whether you're self-publishing or freelancing or traditionally publishing or a combination of these approaches. If you read the book straight through and you feel like you have information overload, I don't blame you. It is a lot to take in. But you can always go back and dive into relevant chapters when you need them. Thank you for joining me on this journey into the wonderful world of the law for authors. I wish you all the best in your publishing careers.

Write on!

INTRODUCTION

1. A pen name.

2. White describes this situation in more detail in Meredith Maran (ed.), *Why We Write About Ourselves: Twenty Memoirists on Why They Expose Themselves (and Others) in the Name of Literature* (New York: Penguin Random House, 2016), 253.

CHAPTER ONE. COPYRIGHT BASICS

1. Intellectual property law is the law related to human creation and innovation and includes copyright law, patent law, trademark law, and trade secrets law. The most relevant of these to the publishing industry are copyright and trademark law.

2. Tess Gerritsen, "The Difference between 'Breach of Contract' and 'Copyright Infringement,'" February 1, 2015, www.tessgerritsen.com/difference-breach-contract-copyright-infringement/.

CHAPTER TWO. KNOW YOUR (COPY)RIGHTS

1. See Daniel Burke, "Publisher Pulls Book by Hillary Clinton's Pastor, Citing Plagiarism," CNN, September 5, 2017, www.cnn.com/2017/09/05/politics/clinton-pastor-book-pulled-plagiarism/index.html.

2. Alison Flood, "Philip Pullman Leads Call for UK Government Action on Ebook Piracy," *Guardian*, April 8, 2019, www.theguardian.com/books/2019/apr/08/philip-pullman-uk-government-ebook-piracy-kazuo-ishiguro.

CHAPTER THREE. WRITING FOR SOMEONE ELSE

1. See www.jobiehughes.com/AboutJobie/BriefBio.aspx.

2. See Ben East, "Author James Frey Stirs Up Controversy Again," *National*, November 29, 2010, www.thenational.ae/arts-culture/books/author-james-frey-stirs-up-controversy-again-1.503259.

3. Suzanne Moses, "James Frey's Fiction Factory," *New York Magazine*, November 12, 2010, http://nymag.com/arts/books/features/69474/.

CHAPTER FOUR. FAIR USE BASICS

1. This litigation is ongoing at the time of this writing.

2. See Del Vecchio & Stadler LLP, "The Fair Use Doctrine and Weird Al Yankovic," March 7, 2017, www.dvands.com/fair-use-doctrine-weird-al-yankovic/.

CHAPTER FIVE. SPECIFIC FAIR USES

1. See www.youtube.com/watch?v=RZwM3GvaTRM.

2. Anne Rice, "Anne's Messages to Fans," Anne Rice: The Official Site, September 14, 2009, retrieved from www.webcitation.org/6YzlkUmK6.

3. Alison Genet, "Stephenie Meyer Talks 'Twilight' Fanfiction and 'Breaking Down' (Her Own Private FF)," Twifans (blog post), July 7, 2010, retrieved from https://web.archive.org/web/20160306185914/http://www.twifans.com/profiles/blogs/stephenie-meyer-talks-twilight.

4. Hugh Howey, "A New Wool Book! (And It Isn't Mine)," January 19, 2013, www.hughhowey.com/a-new-wool-book-and-it-isnt-mine/.

5. Neil Gaiman, untitled blog post, April 8, 2002, http://journal.neilgaiman.com/2002/04/in-relation-to-current-burning-topic.asp.

6. Hugh Howey, "Writing in Vonnegut's World: On Training Wheels, Fanfiction, and Stories in the Cave," *Slate*, January 14, 2014, www.slate.com/articles/arts/books/2014/01/wool_author_hugh_howey_on_fan_fiction_and_kurt_vonnegut.html.

CHAPTER SIX. CONTRACTS WITH AGENTS AND PUBLISHING HOUSES

1. Brianna Schofield and Robert K. Walker (Eds.), *Understanding and Negotiating Book Publication Contracts* (Authors Alliance, 2018), www.authorsalliance.org /wp-content/uploads/2018/10/20181003_AuthorsAllianceGuidePublication-Contracts.pdf. See, in particular, ch. 13, which explains calculation of royalties and provides sample contract clauses.

2. Ibid., 199.

3. Ibid.

4. See, for example, clause 13 in this sample publishing contract: www.maine.edu/pdf/PublishingAgreementStandard.pdf.

5. Schofield and Walker, 184.

6. Ibid., 190.

7. Ibid., 102–110.

CHAPTER SEVEN. SELF-PUBLISHING CONTRACTS

1. J. A. Cipriano, "You Can't Find Me on Amazon and Here's Why," July 18, 2018, www.jacipriano.com/wordpress/2018/07/18/you-cant-find-me-on-amazon-and-heres-why/.

2. Ibid.

3. J. P. Mangalindan, "Amazon Self-Published Authors: Our Books Were Banned for No Reason," Yahoo! Finance, August 10, 2018, www.yahoo.com /amphtml/finance/news/amazon-self-published-authors-books-banned-no-reason-134606120.html.

4. The "Big Five" publishers are the largest traditional publishing houses in North America: Penguin Random House, HarperCollins, Simon & Schuster, Hachette, and Macmillan.

5. Jessica Park, "How Amazon Saved My Life," *Huffington Post,* June 7, 2012, www.huffingtonpost.com/2012/06/06/how-amazon-saved-my-life_n_1575777 .html.

6. Mangalindan, "Amazon Self-Published Authors."

7. Derek Haines, "Draft2Digital, Smashwords or KDP Select?," Just Publishing Advice, March 15, 2018, https://justpublishingadvice.com/draft2digital-smashwords-or-amazon-kdp-select/.

8. See, for example, clause 5.8(c), Kindle Direct Publishing Terms and Conditions, August 27, 2018: "You [the author] represent and warrant that . . . neither the exercise of the rights authorized under this Agreement nor any materials embodied in the content nor its sale or distribution as authorized in this Agreement will violate or infringe upon the intellectual property, proprietary or other rights of any person or entity, including, without limitation, contractual rights, copyrights, trademarks, common law rights, rights of publicity, or privacy, or moral rights, or contain defamatory material or violate any laws or regulations of any jurisdiction . . .").

9. See "Low-Cost e-Book Formatting and Cover Design," www.smashwords.com/list.

10. For example, Smashwords contains detailed guidelines for those seeking to publish erotica using its platform. See clause 9f, Smashwords Terms of Service, updated May 23, 2018.

11. See clause 10, ACX Audiobook Production Standard Terms, www.acx.com/help/production-standard-terms/201481920.

12. See clause 3, ACX Audiobook Production Standard Terms, www.acx.com/help/production-standard-terms/201481920.

13. For a useful summary (from early 2018) of pricing and royalty options for Audible and other audiobook production and distribution services, see Ricci Wolman, "How to Publish an Audiobook: Your Guide to Audiobook Production and Distribution," Written Word Media, February 21, 2018, www.writtenwordmedia.com/2018/02/21/self-publish-audiobook-production-and-distribution/.

CHAPTER EIGHT. PROTECTING YOUR AUTHOR BRAND

1. The tweet was later removed, but it is quoted in Tina Jordan, "Seeing Double on the Shelves," New York Times, December 14, 2018, https://www.nytimes.com/2018/12/14/books/review/nora-roberts-tomi-adeyemi-of-blood-and-bone-best-seller.html.

2. Ibid.

CHAPTER NINE. WRITING ABOUT REAL PEOPLE

1. Kim Willsher, "Court Awards Duchess of Cambridge Damages over Topless Photos," Guardian, September 5, 2017, www.theguardian.com/uk-

news/2017/sep/05/topless-photos-of-duchess-of-cambridge-were-invasion-of-privacy.

CHAPTER TEN. DAMAGING SOMEONE'S REPUTATION

1. Kim Willsher, "Scarlett Johansson Wins Defamation Case against French Novelist," *Guardian*, July 4, 2014, www.theguardian.com/film/2014/jul/04/scarlett-johansson-wins-french-defamation-case.

CHAPTER ELEVEN. MARKETING AND SOCIAL MEDIA

1. See, for example, Jane Friedman, "The Basic Components of an Author Website," www.janefriedman.com/author-website-components/.

2. See, for example, Diana Urban, "29 Author Websites with Stellar Designs," https://insights.bookbub.com/author-websites-with-stellar-designs/.

3. See, for example, Reedsy Blog, "12 Author Websites That Get It Right," https://blog.reedsy.com/author-websites/.

4. See https://mailchimp.com/pricing/.

5. See https://mailchimp.com/legal/terms/. Note in particular clause 20, which talks about complying with privacy laws, including the GDPR.

6. See www.alexandrabracken.com/newsletter.

CHAPTER TWELVE. PHOTOGRAPHS, ILLUSTRATIONS, AND OTHER ARTWORK

1. See Living for Naptime, "The $7,500 Blogging Mistake That Every Blogger Needs to Avoid," January 7, 2016, www.livingfornaptime.com/starting-a-blog/blogging-mistakes-to-avoid/; and Roni Loren, "Bloggers Beware: You CAN Get Sued for Using Pics on Your Blog—My Story," July 20, 2012, https://roniloren.com/blog/2012/7/20/bloggers-beware-you-can-get-sued-for-using-pics-on-your-blog.html.

2. The *Vanity Fair* cover and the Paramount movie poster can be viewed and compared on the Wikipedia page discussing the litigation: https://en.wikipedia.org/wiki/Leibovitz_v._Paramount_Pictures_Corp.

3. *Dr. Seuss Enterprises v. ComicMix LLC*, US District Court, Southern District of California, Case No. 16-CV-2779-JLS (BGS), December 7, 2017. Full text available

at www.courthousenews.com/wp-content/uploads/2017/12/Suess-ComicMix-MTD-ORDER.pdf.

4. *Dr. Seuss Enterprises v. ComicMix*, US District Court, Southern District of California, Case No. 16-CV-2779-JLS (BGS), March 12, 2019. Full text available at http://business.cch.com/ipld/DrSeussEnterprisesComicMix20190338.pdf.

CHAPTER THIRTEEN. FINDING ADDITIONAL HELP

1. See www.authorsguild.org/member-services/legal-services/.

2. See www.authorsguild.org/member-services/legal-services/writers-legal-guide/.

3. See www.authorsalliance.org/resources/rights-reversion-portal/.

4. See www.copyright.gov/help/faq/index.html.

5. See www.copyright.gov/circs/.

6. See www.copyright.gov/policy/.

7. See www.uspto.gov/.

8. See www.uspto.gov/trademarks-getting-started/trademark-basics.

9. See www.icann.org/resources/pages/about-domain-names-2018-08-30-en.

10. See www.wipo.int/export/sites/www/amc/en/docs/guide-en-web.pdf.

11. See www.rightsofwriters.com/.

registration-based trademark system, 146, 148. *See also* trademarks

registration of copyright, 15, 23–26. *See also* copyright

registration of trademarks, 147–52. *See also* trademarks

remedies, defined, 36. *See also* copyright

reproduction rights, 29–30, 34. *See also* copyright

reputation damage. *See* defamation law

reversion of rights, 119–20

Rhett Butler's People (McCaig), 16–17

Rhiannon's Law (Saare), 1

Rice, Anne, 33, 92

right of publicity tort, 154, 158, 174–76, 179, 234–35

rights, defined, 36. See also *specific types of rights*

Rights of Writers blog, 240

rights reversion, 119–20. *See also* copyright

right to be forgotten, 182

Roberts, Nora, 156–58, 203

Rock and Roll Hall of Fame, 225, 226

Romance Writers of America, 51, 238, 239

Romeo and Juliet (Shakespeare), 33

Romeo + Juliet (film), 33

Rough Guide series, 84

Rowling, J. K., 153

royalties: clause in work-for-hire agreements, 50; negotiation of, 113–15; in self-published works, 134, 141, 144. *See also* advances

®symbol, 151. *See also* trademarks

Saare, J. A., 1, 8, 35

satire *vs.* parody, 84–86. *See also* parody

Schwartz, Tony, 56

Science Fiction and Fantasy Writers of America, 51, 238

sculptural works, 16

secondary liability, 40. *See also* copyright

section 106 rights. *See* US Copyright Act (1976)

section 107 rights. *See* US Copyright Act (1976)

Seinfeld *Trivia Book Case*, 77–78

self-publishing: artwork and, 223–24; of audiobooks, 125, 139–44; benefits and challenges of, 125, 130–32; contracts in, 121, 123–27; copyright notice in, 15; copyright registration and, 25; defined, 128; of e-books, 125, 132–37; hybrid author, defined, 129; *vs.* independent author designation, 128–30; print-on-demand, 125, 137–39

sequels and contracts, 108

series titles, 148, 150, 155

Shabazz, Ilyasah, 56

Shaffer, Andrew, 80–81

Shakespeare, William, 33

Sherlock Holmes series (Doyle), 20–21

Silo series (Howey), 92

Simon & Schuster, 53, 118, 127, 192, 199, 249n4 (ch. 7)

slander, defined, 187. *See also* defamation law

Slater, David, 221

Smashwords, 125, 132, 135

Smith, Danielle, 106

social media: copyright issues on, 208; defamation and, 156–58, 177; marketing on, 204, 205, 214–15; privacy on, 206, 210, 214. *See also* Internet; websites, author

Society for Children's Book Writers and Illustrators (SCBWI), 51, 201, 238

song lyrics, 78–79, 208

soundalikes, 176

verbal contracts, 98. *See also* contracts

video reproduction, 69–70

Volunteer Lawyers for the Arts, 242–43

Waits, Tom, 176

Warner Bros., 9, 49

Warrior Cats (Hunter), 53

Wayne, John, 154, 175

Webb, Darin, 104

Webber, Tammara, 36, 121, 122, 136, 209

websites, author, 205–14, 231. *See also* branding; marketing; social media

West Side Story (drama), 33

WGA Registry, 20

White, Edmund, 7

Whitten, Darlene, 195–98

Why We Write About Ourselves (Maran), 16

Wikipedia, 16, 182

Wind Done Gone, The (Randall), 17, 34, 37, 38, 69, 83, 88

Wizard of Oz (Baum), 20

Wolf of Wall Street, The (film), 193

words, copyright of, 17–19

work-for-hire agreements: benefits of, 57–59; book packaging, 44–45, 49, 52–53; clauses in, 49–51; copyright ownership in, 22, 30, 44–46; defined, 47; employee *vs.* independent contractor in, 48; ghostwriting, 44–45, 52, 55–57; IP projects, 46, 53–55; joint ownership and, 49, 56. *See also* contracts

World Intellectual Property Organization (WIPO), 239–40

world rights. *See* foreign rights

Writers Guild of America West Registry, 20

Writer's Market, 52

writers' organizations, 51, 201, 238–39

Yankovic, Weird Al, 74, 83

Yiannopoulos, Milo, 118

Yoon, Nicola, 45, 49, 59

Zeta-Jones, Catherine, 181